D0379818

DISSENT FROM WAR

Robert L. Ivie

Kumarian
Press, Inc.

Dissent from War

Published 2007 in the United States of America by Kumarian Press, Inc.
1294 Blue Hills Avenue, Bloomfield, CT 06002 USA

Copyright © 2007 Kumarian Press. All rights reserved.

No part of this book may be reproduced or transmitted in any form or by any means, electronic or mechanical, including photocopy, recording, or information storage and retrieval system, without prior permission of the publisher.

For permission to photocopy or use material electronically from *Dissent from War*, please access www.copyright.com or contact Copyright Clearance Center, Inc. (CCC), 222 Rosewood Drive, Danvers, MA 01923, 978-750-8400. CCC is a not-for-profit organization that provides licenses and registration for a variety of users.

Copyedit by Claire Slagle
Proofread by Beth Richards
Design and production by UB Communications, Parsippany, NJ.
The text of this book is set in 11/13 Adobe Sabon.

Printed in the USA on acid-free paper by Thomson-Shore, Inc.

∞ The paper used in this publication meets the minimum requirements of the American National Standard for Information Sciences—Permanence of Paper for Printed Library Materials, ANSI Z39.48-1984.

Library of Congress Cataloging-in-Publication Data

Ivie, Robert L.
   Dissent from War / by Robert L. Ivie
      p. cm.
   Includes bibliographical references and index.
   ISBN-13: 978-1-56549-240-0 (pbk. : alk. paper)
1. Pacifism—United States. 2. Pacifism—Religious aspects—Christianity.
3. Rhetoric—Political aspects—United States. I. Title.
   JZ5584.U6185 2007
   303.6'6—dc22
                           2007019757

DISSENT FROM WAR

For Natalie Jane

May the children of our children
inherit from their parents
a more generous and forgiving world.

Contents

Acknowledgments

A number of the ideas developed in this book were advanced initially in presentations at the University of Massachusetts in Amherst, DePauw University in Greencastle, Indiana, the annual convention of the National Communication Association, the Figures of Democracy conference at Concordia University in Montreal, Canada, and two international colloquiums sponsored by the European Institute for Communication and Culture in Slovenia.

Articles that I have previously published and subsequently woven into various chapters of this book include: "Fighting Terror by Rite of Redemption and Reconciliation," *Rhetoric & Public Affairs* 10.2 (Summer 2007): 221–48; "Academic Freedom and Antiwar Dissent in a Democratic Idiom," *College Literature* 33.4 (Fall 2006): 76–92; "Web-Watching for Peace-Building in the New Communication Order," *Javnost—The Public* 12 (October 2005): 61–78; "Democratic Dissent and the Trick of Rhetorical Critique," *Cultural Studies—Critical Methodologies,* 5 (August 2005): 276–93; "A Presumption of Academic Freedom," *Review of Education, Pedagogy, and Cultural Studies* 27: 1 (2005): 53–85; "Savagery in Democracy's Empire," *Third World Quarterly* 26.1 (2005): 55–65; "Prologue to Democratic Dissent in America," *Javnost—The Public* 11 (June 2004): 19–35; and "The Rhetoric of Bush's 'War' on Evil," *KB Journal* 1 (Fall 2004) available online.

I have benefited throughout the writing of this book from the close reading and helpful comments of friends and colleagues. I am especially grateful to Oscar Giner and Scott Welsh for their detailed and insightful commentary on each chapter, to Jeff Motter for his helpful reactions to the manuscript as a whole, and to John Lucaites and Robert Terrill for their encouraging responses to chapter two. Eric Erickson's reading of portions of the manuscript and engaging conversation about the project were spiritually enriching.

I am indebted to Warren and Ruby Poling for making available to me a copy of Frank Strain's Civil War memoir and related materials on the Strain family history and to Carol Miller for giving me access to the box containing Jack Haley's World War II letters.

I draw strength each day from Nancy's love. She gives purpose to my life and reason for writing.

DISSENT FROM WAR

1

War Is Easy

War is easy. Peace is difficult. That's the hard reality of human history. War occurs with such frequency that it seems inevitable, even natural. By one count, approximately a hundred international or civil wars occurred in the decade of the 1990s alone.[1]

Yet, to say war is inevitable and that it is inherent to the human condition is to profess a dictum so abstract and general that it tells us nothing about when or where or why any particular war will occur, who will fight whom, how intensely they will struggle, or anything else specific to the case at hand. Such a universal pronouncement of war's inevitability also says nothing about wars that never occur, wars that are averted, wars that are attenuated, or wars that end sooner rather than later. It simply means war happens, often—indeed, too often—so often, in fact, that resisting war seems unrealistic, even risky. Aspiring to peace except by means of military victory appears quixotic—a fantasy at best, a diversion at least, a threat to national security at worst.

We know war is inevitable when it happens, because it happened. It is the reality delivered at our doorstep with the morning paper, the necessity proclaimed by the political establishment and reiterated by the mainstream press. Supporting each war that comes our way is the realistic and right thing to do as citizens in good standing. It is a matter merely of submitting to war's gravitational pull. One cannot swim upstream against a raging current for long before being pulled under. It's better just to conform, to float downstream in the reassuring flow of public opinion and conventional wisdom.

The rhetorical presumption of war's necessity makes the violence regrettable but sane, rational, right, proper, and easier than bearing the heavy burden of dissenting from war. Curiously, placing one's self or loved ones in harm's way seems less difficult and more reassuring than questioning the necessity, legitimacy, or sanity of war in any given case. Indeed, many—perhaps most—Americans believe that dissent in times of war and crisis is improper and unpatriotic, that fighting wars in the name of democracy is more virtuous than, and actually incompatible with, exercising freedom of speech. Thus, when the President, Vice President, Secretary of State, and Secretary of Defense

1

all come to town to rally the people behind a stalled war effort in Iraq, one is not surprised to read on the front page of the local newspaper that 45 percent of those polled believe war protesters are aiding the country's enemies, while 28 percent are not sure whether protest is good or bad, and only 27 percent affirm dissent's role in debating national policy.[2] The "moral and intellectual confusion" of war's critics appeases the nation's enemies, threatens national security, and weakens a free society's ability to persevere, asserts a combative Secretary of Defense.[3]

Of course, war is terrible, too. That goes without saying, usually. Surely we wouldn't resort to deadly, destructive warfare without good cause, and there are so many causes of war. Nations fight for land, vital resources, markets, independence, security, a way of life, a political system, an alliance, human rights, prestige, and power. People make the blood sacrifice for "God, country, nation, race, class, justice, honor, freedom, equality, fraternity," and more.[4] Truth be told, war is less a matter of strict rationality and cold calculation of strategic interests than it is an exercise in ritual, a sacrament of symbolism, and an enactment of tragic theater. Indeed, Chris Hedges contends that "war is a force that gives us meaning"—a god that "makes the world understandable, a black and white tableau of them and us" that suspends "self-critical thought."[5] Issues of good and evil are the ethical core of war's motivation. The "supposed rationality" of political objectives is a "thin veneer" covering deeper symbolic motives of a just cause.[6] Death is war's awful sacrifice to life's relentless struggle for meaning, identity, purpose, and exoneration.[7] Such is the human project that makes language and rhetoric crucial to understanding and coping with the ready desire to wage war and the gnawing guilt of a nation's arrogance.

This terrible attraction to the flame of war is America's red badge of courage, a time of testing the people's mettle and true virtue. Like Stephen Crane, America's exceptional war novelist and the volatile son of a Methodist missionary, the nation found a lifelong companion in war. Crane never experienced battle but lived life violently, imagining brilliantly the soldier's fearful quest for glory and redemption on the battlefield.[8] The guilty pleasure of war—and deep yearning to prove one's nobility under fire—is a powerful narcotic for recurring fits of a better conscience.

The nagging conscience of the nation, though, is never fully assuaged by the narcotic of war's false calling to redemptive violence. Succumbing to war's seduction is easier than dissenting from war and less complicated than making peace with one's adversaries, but the guilt of killing even a sacrificial scapegoat to atone for the nation's transgressions is a chronic aggravation to the soul of a self-proclaimed Christian people. Choosing peaceful reconciliation over redemptive violence is the Savior's command in the Sermon on the Mount addressed to all who would be his disciples. "Blessed are the peacemakers, for

they will be called children of God".... "Love your enemies".... "If you forgive others their trespasses, your heavenly Father will also forgive
you".... "In everything do to others as you would have them do to you."[9]
The Teacher's "new commandment" delivered to his followers in anticipation
of his crucifixion and their salvation was to "love one another" just as He
loved them.[10] His blood sacrifice, not the blood of an enemy, was to be the
way of reconciliation and the way to salvation. Redemptive violence, thus, is
an inconvenient violation of the Christian conscience no less than it is a politically convenient salvation device of vicarious sacrifice.

The residual dissonance of engaging in redemptive violence goads Americans to make new enemies each time they vanquish or otherwise finish with
the last enemy. Enemy-making is the seemingly perpetual vocation of an
"exceptional" people and their guilty conscience. The perception of threat—a
chronic sense of national insecurity—is hopelessly conflated with the ritual of
enemy-making as an addictive but not-so-satisfactory salvation device. At a
minimum, conjuring images of an enemy's diabolical savagery raises the calculation of danger.

When enemies are represented as evil, something more happens to com-
pound the incentive to fight. The very rhetoric that demonizes enemies also
dehumanizes those who would vanquish evil, which is the work of gods, not
humans. Just as enemies are reduced to villainous devils, our side is elevated to
divine warriors. Heroic nations are thus prone to hubris, to overreaching the
limits of humanity. America is inclined to think of itself in messianic terms as
if it has inherited the election of biblical Israel and is itself a chosen nation.
"In Christian theology," though—as Jim Wallis underscores—"it is not nations
that rid the world of evil—they are too often caught up in complicated webs
of political power, economic interests, cultural clashes, and nationalist dreams.
The confrontation with evil is a role reserved for God." To think otherwise "is
a serious theological error that some might say borders on idolatry and blas-
phemy."[11] When a president uses "coded Christian language," which Stephen
Chapman warns happened "unmistakably" to justify an imperial war on Iraq,
it is done "to use the authority of Christ as a talisman."[12] In the process, messianic America becomes less human and more godlike in its own rhetorical
image, quite contrary to the Christian ethic of humility. War rhetoric caricatures everyone, dehumanizing us no less than our enemies.

In this way, the rite of dehumanizing rhetoric that deifies the US by demonizing its enemies contributes to war's self-sustaining momentum. War is no
exception to the dominant motif of American political rhetoric. Indeed, the
proliferation of demonizing rhetoric in the US is indicative of a basic and dangerously divisive moral paradox. This moral paradox, according to Tom De Luca
and John Buell, is deeply rooted in the dilemma of Puritanical hedonism—a

tension of two fundamentalisms, one social and the other material, that produces hidden fears and forbidden desires so easily projected onto "despised others" to undermine the democratic values of respectful inclusion and egalitarian participation.[13]

The polarizing rhetoric of political demonization, which reduces difference to deviance and evil, is as common to culture wars at home as fighting terrorism abroad. An undifferentiated war on evildoers criminalizes dissent, threatens civil liberties, and undermines healthy debate and dialogue among citizens, between citizens and their government, and between the US and foreign nations. Manichaean logic dominates political culture at the expense of democratic practice and effective problem solving. Americans fall prey to caricaturing and scapegoating at the very moment they need most to understand an adversary's perspective and motivation in order to respond appropriately to the current challenge of terrorism and the recurring condition of war.

If the dehumanizing rhetoric of enemy-making—both the demonizing of others and the corresponding deification of self—makes war easier to condone, even at the expense of a nagging conscience and dreadfully polarized political relations at home and abroad, it also designates a key task of peacebuilding dissent. The hard work of reconciliation between enemies—of building bridges of constructive communication across the abyss of sheer antagonism—is never-ending and always cuts against the grain of politics as usual. Peacebuilding is necessarily therefore an exercise in dissent from war, and a difficult one at that. There is no easy way to resist the call to arms, but there is nothing more vital to democratic citizenship than to try.

Constructive dissent from war is difficult but not infeasible for ordinary citizens doing what they can to promote peace as a consideration of conscience. Accordingly, this book speaks to the matter of feasibility, of what can be done with effort by conscientious citizens, that is, what common people can do in common to inhibit war by adopting a humanizing strategy of political communication. The give and take of politics—the vibrant clash of opinion and the contestation of perspectives—is agonistic but not necessarily antagonistic. Indeed, political theorists such as Chantal Mouffe consider the basic challenge of pluralistic politics to be one of converting antagonistic into agonistic relations. In her words, "The aim of democratic politics should be to provide the framework through which conflicts can take the form of an agonistic confrontation among adversaries instead of manifesting themselves as an antagonistic struggle between enemies."[14] Even as conflict and division define the human condition, Kenneth Burke stresses, we can develop strategies of identification along various dimensions of communication to bridge differences and increase tolerance. "Identification is compensatory to division," he maintains, in a world where communication is never absolute or perfect. Sustained effort backed by "richly humane" imagery can help us to understand better and value more highly "people in circumstances greatly different from our own."[15]

The importance of cultivating a humanizing discourse of dissent would be difficult to overstate, especially since enemy-making war propaganda is designed to desensitize the public to the human attributes of adversaries by demonizing one side and deifying the other. Yet, anti-war dissent tends toward an idiom of negative criticism chiefly, if not exclusively, and a dehumanizing exercise in reverse recrimination that demonizes the nation at war and its leadership. This, too, is a polarizing discourse, which readily reverts to the alienating language of good and evil.

To transcend the dilemma of recrimination is perhaps the greatest challenge of peacebuilding dissent. A public forced to choose between an absolute claim to national virtue and a bleak charge of collective malevolence is disinclined to the latter and thus disposed by default, if for no other reason, to stay the course of belligerence. The sharp criticism of an impending or present war, and of a warring regime, is an indispensable demonstration of nonconformity to the call to arms, but it is not the only gesture in a peacebuilding idiom of counter-persuasion. A second gesture, an expression of humanizing solidarity, is required to escape the downward pull of reciprocal recrimination. The double gesture of peacebuilding dissent from war—of nonconforming solidarity—transcends competing attributions of evil by redirecting our attention to the human realm of error, imperfection, limited perspective, and the greater need for tolerance and reconciliation. Thus, at its best, dissent is a nonconforming expression of humanizing solidarity. That, at least, is the argument of the book.

My aim is to focus attention on dissent from war as a viable and healthy practice of democratic citizenship. We are "democracy's children," in John McGowan's words, "called into existence in plural societies in which freedom of speech and the press combines with wide-open debate among competing visions of the good life [and] the good polity."[16] To champion democracy is to remain vigilant against the suppression of dissent but also to promote the best practices of dissent. Thus, it is especially important during periods of crisis and an ongoing global war on terrorism to examine—even interrogate—the cultural status, political role, and rhetorical characteristics of dissent as a vital democratic practice in the US.

Dissent is critical to holding ambitious governments and misguided policies accountable to public scrutiny and democratic standards. Without open debate, government defaults to secrecy, repression, and extremism in the name of national security. As Cass Sunstein argues, freedom of speech is a safeguard against senseless conformity; a culture of free speech is the foundation of democratic self-government; and dissent within the polity is a protection against ideological extremism, political polarization, and unchecked power. Thus, "well-functioning societies take steps to . . . promote dissent."[17]

A healthy democracy encourages wide criticism and robust debate. It fosters a culture of constructive contestation that respects diversity of opinion and variations in perspective on matters of political judgment. It values dissent for questioning and contesting the views that most people hold at any given point in time. Consistent with the nation's commitment to the democratic principle of collective self-government, dissent is opposed to political orthodoxy. As Steven Shiffrin observes, "The commitment to sponsor dissent assumes that societal pressures to conform are strong and that incentives to keep quiet are often great."[18] The democratic value of dissent, then, consists largely of honoring, protecting, and practicing "speech that criticizes customs, habits, traditions, institutions, or authorities."[19] This is especially the case, Nancy Chang insists, when the nation's security is threatened and the temptation is greatest to curtail freedom of speech.[20] Thus, it is particularly important for a democratic people to understand what is at stake when dissent from war is curbed, to recognize such dissent as an everyday practice of responsible citizenship and productive deliberation—not as something to be despised and marked as strange, disloyal, or threatening—and to explore how dissent can help to address a crisis of terror in today's volatile world.

Toward this end, and for the purpose of making war appropriately difficult rather than nearly automatic, we should seek to orient dissent to a robust conception of democracy so that it might resist war propaganda's reduction of the image of a rival to the figure of pure enmity, so that it might convert hostilities into relations of constructive rivalry where possible, so that it might articulate more complex characterizations of adversaries that consist of shades of difference intermixed with degrees of similarity between the parties in conflict, so that it might bridge divisive distinctions well enough to sustain nonviolent political relations short of effacing separate and even opposed identities. Dissent, in this sense, is a mainstay of democratic citizenship, not a luxury, a nuisance, or a malfunction. Without such a mode of healthy contestation, there would be no play of differences or means of accommodating to a pluralism of opinions, interests, identities, and diverging orientations, or of exercising judgment and acting on decisions while remaining responsive to changing circumstances, unresolved disagreements, and continuing uncertainties. Without dissent there can be no truly democratic polity, only submissive quiescence, or violent resistance. Indeed, dissent should be understood as a practical, if underappreciated, necessity in a complex and volatile world, a medium of collective self-rule and a resource for managing the human divide. It is a lively affair and a sign of political health.[21]

Yet, an exigency of war and terror presses hard against polemics of any kind when patriotism is measured by a standard of political conformity instead of democratic contestation. Dissent is more difficult to carry out at the point of greatest tension in human affairs and when it could especially benefit the political process. Periods of war and crisis reveal, usually in retrospect and by way of negative examples, how deeply democracy is invested in dissent to maintain its own vitality and viability. By challenging reified discourses of good and evil and the violence such rigidity engenders, dissent from war returns human struggle to the realm of political contestation, renders politics less heroic, and opens democracy to greater participation by ordinary citizens. Dissent, that is, can be an impetus to peacebuilding consistent with a people's conscience and commonsense notions of democratic citizenship, a vehicle of communication for everyday citizens to speak up and speak out against a chronic state of warfare.

How do ordinary citizens find their voice to express humanizing themes? In part, I argue, the motive to speak stems from listening to conscience, confronting the question of war's hypocrisy, contemplating the consequences of dehumanizing people, and coming to the realization that we should always resist dehumanizing others. To make that general point more tangible and personal, I tell an ancestral story of a Civil War footsoldier who fought to end slavery but never resolved the tensions of conscience or the ambiguities of friendship and enmity. Victory in war, with all its devastation, did little to change the plight of emancipated but still dehumanized Blacks living under the thumb of Jim Crow. Frank Strain's war story, it turns out, is a record of the nation's troubled Christian conscience—a haunting disenchantment with the Manichaean divide between righteous comrades and evil enemies. What lurks in the shadow of Frank's unsettled account of lethal estrangement is a citizen-soldier's profoundly human sentiment, a residual impulse to reconnect the broken circle of humanity. Thus, a locus of peacebuilding is found in the realization that war is fundamentally and wrongfully dehumanizing.

Yet, the dehumanizing trope of evil savagery is indigenous to US war culture and forms the baseline image of war propaganda's recurring ritual of national redemption. The problem is largely a matter of public memory. Even fallen warriors are depersonalized by cold stone monuments to war's past, official remembrances that stifle the voice of dissent. Telling a familial story of Private Jack Haley, killed in action during World War II (which is now remembered as the good war, the model war to vanquish pure evil) recovers a young soldier's down-to-earth humanity to make his sacrifice more real and regrettable, less easily forgotten and rationalized. The stories we tell about the protagonists of war can either suppress or inspire the voice of peacebuilding dissent and reconciliation, and when we see that it is our nation's own dark shadow cast onto the image of an enemy whom we have made into a sacrificial vessel for the hubris of a chosen people, we begin to understand the role of enemy-making narratives—the projection of self-doubt and self-loathing, the desire for an unburdening of the collective guilt of national arrogance, for redemption by vicarious sacrifice—in the production of fear and the perception of national insecurity. We begin to appreciate the importance of dissent that rehumanizes the parties in conflict if we hope to address the problems at hand more realistically and less violently.

Communicating a bond of humanity, which is the personal and collective responsibility of everyday citizens, is more than a matter of conveying information or transmitting knowledge. It is instead a strategic persistence and tactical exercise in democratic persuasion that involves outmaneuvering the reigning discourse of ruling authorities to dispose public opinion gradually toward a peacebuilding attitude. Resisting the dehumanizing strategy of war propaganda is no simple or straightforward matter of direct rebuttal and immediate rejection. It requires a certain rhetorical sensibility to break free of—to avoid reversing and thus being recaptured by—the governing framework of disdain and damnation. It involves an artful circumvention from a position of political weakness rather than a command or proclamation of authority from a position of power. It is an oblique critique, not a head-on confrontation, which aims to produce a new order of meaning, or revised perspective, by weaving a web of reconciliation that would supplant the ruling paradigm of victimization and redemptive violence. Positive and negative lessons of such rhetorical maneuvering can be drawn from considering both more and less artful examples of a dissenting documentary about the declaration of war on Iraq, of a public intellectual exercising academic freedom to resist the war on terror by reversing the blame for 9/11, and of innovative media usage by citizens engaged in creative web-watching on the internet to locate incipient metaphors with humanizing potential.

These are important lessons to learn because the peacebuilding rhetorical work of dissenting citizens is to produce persuasive redescriptions and symbolic transformations of enemy images, to engage in a constructive critique of reified metaphors and denigrating myths that resists the demonizing language of war. Differentiating the undifferentiated, totalizing language of anti-terrorism and tyrannizing image of Islamists is a case in point. Terrorism, especially holy terror, under close scrutiny turns out to be a dangerously misleading term to guide policymaking and a problematic metaphor for justifying wars of empire. Developing a language of political friendship is a necessary corollary to resisting demonizing war propaganda if we are to talk ourselves down from fear and anger to establish a modicum of goodwill between adversaries. Thus, it is useful to consider options for cultivating a sense of common humanity with adversaries on what has been called the axis of evil. Moreover, peacebuilding citizens must be mindful of transcending the very viewpoint of war by articulating a positive image of peace. They must be able to see above and beyond conventional wisdom, much as an artist transcends orthodoxy, to articulate a positive, for-peace perspective. Ultimately, they must apprehend the adversary's perspective, the worldview of an adversary understood as a complex protagonist rather than simplistically as an evil enemy.

None of this kind of constructive language critique can be done well in strict isolation from the rites and initiatives of a larger peacebuilding community. Making war difficult is never easy. Resisting the prevailing habit of war propaganda is a collective effort, not just an individual lament, which must be undertaken in common to achieve its full potential. By democratizing a peacebuilding practice of dissent from war, we might hope to develop over time a collective attitude of reconciliation more conducive to the nation's conscience and less accommodating to wars of empire. We might hope to progress cautiously but resolutely toward a culture of peace, coming together along the way even though each of us begins earnestly alone—breaking the quiet solitude by telling one another stories of human strife, stories on which we may reflect charitably, stories that stir us to act ever more generously toward prospective foes.

NOTES

1. John L. Allen, *Student Atlas of World Politics*, 3rd ed. (Guilford, Conn.: Dushkin/McGraw-Hill, 1998), 43–45; cited in Francis A. Beer, *Meanings of War and Peace* (College Station: Texas A&M University Press, 2001), 3.

2. Heather May, "Utahns: Dissent Aids Enemies," *The Salt Lake Tribune*, August 28, 2006.

3. Ann Scott Tyson, "Rumsfeld Assails Critics of War Policy," *Washington Post*, 30 (August 30, 2006).

4. Martin van Creveld, *The Transformation of War* (New York: The Free Press, 1991), 166.

5. Chris Hedges, *War Is a Force That Gives Us Meaning* (New York: Anchor Books, 2003), 10.

6. Creveld, *Transformation*, 187; see also 157, 166, 170–71, 176, 178, 190.

7. Beer, *Meanings*, 21–22.

8. A recent trade edition of this classic novel, first published in 1895 and since read by many generations of high school students, is Stephen Crane, *The Red Badge of Courage* and *Selected Short Fiction* (New York: Barnes and Noble, 2004).

9. *The Holy Bible*, New Revised Standard Version, Matthew 5.9, 5.44, 6.14, 7.12.

10. John 13.34.

11. Jim Wallis, "Dangerous Religion: George W. Bush's Theology of Empire," *Sojourners* (September-October 2003): 20–26, cited in Stephen B. Chapman, "Imperial Exegesis: When Caesar Interprets Scripture," in *Anxious About Empire: Theological Essays on the New Global Realities*, ed. Wes Avram (Grand Rapids, Michigan: Brazos Press, 2004), 100. See also Jim Wallis, *God's Politics: Why the Right Gets It Wrong*

and the Left Doesn't Get It (New York: HarperSanFrancisco, 2005) and Gregory A. Boyd, *The Myth of a Christian Nation: How the Quest for Political Power is Destroying the Church* (Grand Rapids, Michigan: Zondervan, 2005).

12. Chapman, "Imperial Exegesis," 95, 96.

13. Tom De Luca and John Buell, *Liars! Cheaters! Evildoers! Demonization and the End of Civil Debate in American Politics* (New York: New York University Press, 2005), 48–49.

14. Chantal Mouffe, *The Democratic Paradox* (London: Verso, 2000), 117.

15. Kenneth Burke, *A Rhetoric of Motives* (1950; Berkeley: University of California Press, 1969), 22, 34; see also xv.

16. John McGowan, *Democracy's Children: Intellectuals and the Rise of Cultural Politics* (Ithaca, NY: Cornell University Press, 2002), xi.

17. Cass Sunstein, *Why Societies Need Dissent* (Cambridge: Harvard University Press, 2003), 82, 213.

18. Steven Shiffrin, *The First Amendment, Democracy, and Romance* (Cambridge: Harvard University Press, 1990), 95.

19. Steven Shiffrin, *Dissent, Injustice, and the Meanings of America* (Princeton: Princeton University Press, 1999), xi.

20. Nancy Chang, *Silencing Political Dissent* (New York: Seven Stories Press, 2002), 92.

21. Robert L. Ivie, "Rhetorical Deliberation and Democratic Politics in the Here and Now," *Rhetoric & Public Affairs* 5 (2002): 277–85.

2

A Question of Conscience

A colleague called me a pacifist one day in 1991, and I bristled. He called me a pacifist because he considered himself a patriot, and I had criticized the way George H. W. Bush talked us into the first war with Iraq. We did not know then that a decade later there would be a second President Bush and a second war with Saddam Hussein's Iraq, but my colleague did know that I had dedicated my academic career to the study and criticism of war rhetoric. I had analyzed the recurring pattern of America's call to arms against our many enemies over the course of two centuries of warfare, not counting our own bloody civil war. My colleague knew, too, that my scholarship was motivated by the trauma of the Vietnam War, in which both he and I had served active-duty stints stateside. Neither of us faced the foreign enemy directly, but both of us contributed to the war effort, he as a commissioned officer and I as a petty officer.

My military duties were to help train sailors and marines fresh out of boot camp for their impending service in the war zone. The marines were agitated and anxious to fight, resentful of the eight-week delay for technical training in aviation maintenance administration. The sailors were more settled and seemed in no hurry to join the fleet at sea. Some of the sailors even showed signs of doubt about the legitimacy of the war effort. Perhaps I was projecting my own misgivings onto them, my deeply conflicted guilty feelings. Perhaps some of them were similarly conflicted about the war and their role in it. At any rate, except for a quirk of fate, I would have been one of those sailors on my way to deadly duty on an aircraft carrier.

My fate was determined when I entered active duty just after earning a Master of Arts degree. The Navy had granted me a deferral from active duty after my graduation from college to allow me to attend graduate school. My request for this deferment was initially denied but then granted on appeal to everyone's surprise. It had been difficult enough to determine how to make such an unusual request in the first place. After the request was at first denied, no one at Alameda Naval Air Station, where I had enlisted in the US Naval Air Reserves four years earlier, thought an appeal would succeed. Thus our great surprise when an apparent exercise in futility yielded positive results. Upon completing the M.A. degree and reporting for active duty at Treasure Island in the San Francisco Bay Area, I expected to receive the usual orders of an airman, pay grade E3, to serve as a plane pusher on an aircraft carrier deck. Instead, because I held a graduate degree, my orders were to report to Millington Naval Air Station in Tennessee where I served as an "A" school instructor for the two-year duration of my active-duty obligation. Only when I was assigned to this instructor's billet did I learn that the Navy had such a policy to utilize the advanced degrees of its enlisted personnel.

I believed at the time that Vietnam was a wrongful war, a war to which I was contributing against my conscience and out of harm's way. I could not duck that awful reality or assuage my doubled sense of guilt. My younger brother believed in the war, or so it seemed to me, and had come under enemy fire in Vietnam while flying low-level reconnaissance missions during his four-year enlistment in the Navy. He, like my father before him in World War II and the Korean Conflict and my ancestor, Frank Strain, in the Civil War, experienced fear and a patriotic sense of purpose as military men at the front. I was safe, profoundly compromised, and deeply troubled by conscience.

I returned to graduate school afterward, driven by the question of how we talk ourselves into war. Although that question was expressed objectively and had the ring of universal significance, it was driven by an underlying attitude of criticism directed particularly at the Vietnam War. It was the question that became the focus of my doctoral studies in rhetoric and then guided my academic work for nearly three decades. Only after 9/11 and the subsequent declaration of an open-ended global war on terrorism did my focus shift to asking how we might talk ourselves out of a persistent state of warfare. Only then did I begin to address the question of war as a matter of articulated conscience rather than primarily as a consideration of objective academic analysis, and about then I encountered Frank Strain's haunting memoir of four long years of fighting on the frontlines of civil war. It revealed a conscience that would not yield even in the midst of killing.

I have never thought of myself as a pacifist, but my reply to my colleague's temerity in 1991 troubled me then just as it intrigues me now. It wasn't so much what he said but how I reacted that proved unsettling and illuminating. I replied as though he were an enemy. I spoke in the backwash of war, becoming too much like the very thing I was fighting against.[1] I did not know what to say except to deny that I was a pacifist and to resist with raised voice and in menacing overtones the implication that I was soft, cowardly, naïve, or unpatriotic. When I recounted this episode a few years ago to a friend and colleague where I now teach, he said that he did not consider me a pacifist either. In his view, I just had never met a war I liked.

THE HYPOCRISY OF WAR?

My friend's astute observation brings to mind the question of hypocrisy and specifically Leo Tolstoy's commentary on hypocrisy as the cause of war. How can we tolerate and even serve in, begrudgingly or otherwise, armed hostilities that we cannot bring ourselves to like and that we so commonly despise? Are we feigning such a dislike or, instead, acting against our conscience in a manner that perpetuates belligerence and denies us the peace we desire?

In the final decade of the nineteenth century, Tolstoy confronted his own equivocation on the issue of war and peace in order to call the rest of us to account as a matter of conscience. Born of Russian nobility, he was inspired by American Quakers and the nonresistance doctrine advanced by two specific Americans, William Lloyd Garrison and Adin Ballouto, to pursue a vision of nonviolence with the fervor of a prophet. His argument was aimed at all Christians, whom he called upon to recognize and profess the revealed truth of the faith, the very truth that we feign not to recognize and that we disguise from ourselves and others in our secular lives, such as when I bristled at being called a pacifist. "However confused we may be by hypocrisy and by the hypnotic suggestion which results from it," Tolstoy wrote, "nothing can destroy the certainty of this simple and clearly defined truth."[2] Peacemaking must be the sole and certain guide of our rational conscience if we are to serve the kingdom of God that is within and among us. The one duty and essential meaning of a Christian life is to acknowledge this basic truth and to refuse to lie about it or to rationalize state violence as necessary or just.

Christians are commanded to serve humanity and to achieve a union of human beings in all their diversity by acknowledging and acting on the principle of love and humility. Even if circumstances make it difficult to relinquish our privileges of position and wealth or dangerous to refuse the obligations imposed on us as citizens of a violent state, we should not mislead ourselves by maintaining that these tainted privileges and obligations serve the public good or the purpose of peace. Tolstoy insisted that any hope of improving the present dismal situation depended on making our actions consistent with these basic precepts of our faith.

If the essence of the religion is to love humanity, to forgive injuries, and to seek reconciliation over the use of force, its basic precepts are "the prohibition of evil speaking" and the commandment "of returning good for evil." Tolstoy insisted that we cannot adopt this far-reaching doctrine without conceding its impact on the way we lead our actual lives, for "one of the first conditions of Christian life is love, not in words but in deeds." People of faith only play at Christianity "so long as they ignore the question of war," observed C. D. Bartlett. Yet, a "flagrant antagonism" persists between our conscience and our actual way of life, an antagonism that leaves us embattled and complicit with war even as we profess a desire for peace.[3] Our Christian hypocrisy forestalls true progress toward ending violence between nations.

Indeed, humanity can advance toward the peace it desires only by developing a public opinion uncorrupted by habits of force and violence. We know from long and bitter experience that enemies cannot be suppressed by force— that violence breeds an attitude of violence—just as it is the case that "force can never suppress what is sanctioned by public opinion." Moreover, Tolstoy understood that "public opinion need only be in direct opposition to force to neutralize the whole effect of the use of force."[4]

Developing public opinion in opposition to violence comes about by a changing interpretation of life, not by instantly destroying prevailing forms of life. Such a transition of public opinion must occur over time, Tolstoy believed, but it eventually reaches a tipping point of rapid change. As more and more people act on the implications of spiritual truth—by following up on revealed truth in the actual conduct of their secular lives—the Christian principle of love and corresponding practice of reconciliation eventually will be diffused enough to be "suddenly assimilated by everyone." Just as humanity became habituated over time to social obligations and family values that did not always appear so natural or abide so deeply within our collective conscience, the time will come when the principles of equality, fraternity, and returning good for evil will seem normal, count as common sense, and even appear inherent to the human condition, if we acknowledge and act now on the precept of reconciliation rather than continue to rationalize our complicity with self-serving regimes of force and retribution.[5]

If I am honest with myself, then, I will acknowledge that I will never meet a war that I like. Indeed, by this logic, all Christians who consult their conscience and adhere to their basic beliefs will reject war in principle. They will never consider it to be a proper response to the provocations of their enemies or an appropriate means of protecting and advancing national interests. At a minimum, they will remain highly skeptical of any call to arms, and they will listen earnestly to those who dissent from war. They will be strongly inclined to the path of peace rather than the way of war, in deeds as well as words. They will not just claim to be a peace-loving people but will act in peace rather than fight so willingly and so often in the name of peace. They will acknowledge their own responsibility for the perpetuation of war rather than project their guilt so readily and conveniently onto a caricature of the enemy.

If, as Tolstoy affirmed, the kingdom of God is within us, then it is our obligation to overcome the temptation to resort to force against those whom we perceive to be evil, for that is Christ's message of reconciliation and nonviolence. We must seek to fulfill this doctrine of nonresistance to perceived evil,

Tolstoy believed, unless we would continue to succumb to fear and arrogance and thereby perpetuate the cycle of violence and death. As a doctrine that gives life a new meaning and that requires us to change the very life we lead, Christianity is a vehicle through which an evolving public opinion eventually will bring state violence to an end.

Yet, America has always perceived itself as a religious nation throughout its long history of warfare, and to this very day, the vast majority of Americans identify themselves as a people of Christian faith. I include myself among them. Christianity is my religious heritage, my moral outlook, and my point of departure.[6] Recent estimates place the number of Christians in the US at 77 percent to 88 percent of all adults, with as many as 92 percent of Americans professing a belief in God.[7] Moreover, as James Hillman observes, Americans are Christian psychologically and culturally, regardless of what faith we profess or church we attend, and even if we consider ourselves atheists. Christianity is central to awakening the nation's conscience on matters of war and peace.[8]

Thus, if Tolstoy was right, we should be closer to achieving the peace that is the kingdom of God than we were a century ago, unless we remain a nation of hypocrites. The troubling reality is that, since Tolstoy wrote his manifesto of Christian peace, America has been mired in the muck of war almost without interruption—from a war of empire against Spain and the lethal suppression of the subsequent Filipino resistance, to the first and second world wars, then four decades of cold war that erupted into sustained violence in Korea, Vietnam, and many lesser hot spots, followed by two wars against Iraq, another in Afghanistan, and a global war on terrorism.

I was born in 1945, just days before the US crossed yet another threshold of state violence by dropping an atomic bomb on the people of Hiroshima. I have never in my lifetime experienced a prolonged period of peace, even though I have witnessed my country's continuous calls to fight one war after another in defense of freedom, democracy, and civilization, always for the purpose of establishing a just and permanent peace. Thinking of ourselves as good citizens, we have heeded that call each time. Strangely, many Americans have even pressed their faith into the service of war. Conservative, evangelical Christians were the strongest supporters of America's impending war on Iraq, for example, 69 percent favoring military action early in the run up to that invasion.[9]

Are we a nation of hypocrites? If not, how do we square our beliefs with our behavior? Somewhere between the reading of scripture and the acts of citizenship we lose our new-testament bearings and disregard Christ's instruction, specifically when he said: "I give you a new commandment that you love one another. Just as I have loved you, you also should love one another. By this everyone will know that you are my disciples, if you have love for one another."[10] What could this mean other than, as Jesus said in the Sermon on the Mount, "Blessed are the peacemakers, for they will be called children of God"?[11]

This is a difficult question—a true conundrum—because hardly anyone professes a love of war, yet most of us feel duty-bound and even honored to serve our country in its time of great need. Americans have wrestled with the idea of nonviolence throughout their history, a struggle that persists into the present time without resolution. From the experience of that struggle we can learn a great deal about the challenge we face. Whether we turn to the Quakers or the Progressives, to Henry David Thoreau or Martin Luther King, Jr., or to a number of other key influences that comprise the American tradition of nonviolence, there are important lessons to be garnered for our time. The history of the American idea of nonviolence, which is deeply rooted in Christianity, helps us to understand better why people commit themselves to peacemaking with more or less rigor as they negotiate a thicket of conflicted motives of war and peace.[12]

The best answer to the nagging question about our wavering devotion to nonviolence, I believe, is to be found in a consideration of rhetoric, that is, in a reflection on what can be said to resist the call to arms. War is not a simple issue of Christian hypocrisy. Matters of the heart and soul cannot be extracted from the public discourse that articulates our social concerns and shapes our political relations. The language of religious conviction and the rhetoric of political affairs are intertwined. It is impossible to transcend rhetoric in the affairs of state on issues of social justice. If we wish to negotiate as peacefully as possible the uncertainties of civic life, we must face the challenge of discovering and choosing among the available means of persuasion, and we must confront the task of reframing our violent ways of talking and thinking. Whether we appeal to the God of peace to reconcile our differences or call upon the God of war to settle our grievances depends on more than just our religious faith. It is a function also of how that faith is interpreted and aligned to prevailing circumstances through decidedly rhetorical transactions.

I should like to be as clear as I can about this relationship of rhetoric to the politics of war and the peacemaking-conscience of Christians. A Christian conscience requires us to dissent from war—to never meet a war that we like or like a war we fail to avoid and, if war does happen, to always consider it a failure of leadership, of citizenship, and of human relations in general. Anything short of that would amount to a violation of conscience. It would be hypocritical of a Christian people not to dissent from war as effectively as possible in order to make any final resort to arms extraordinary, regrettable, and otherwise fully accountable to the dictates of conscience. We must expect our leaders to deploy all their skill to avoid or minimize fighting rather than to promote or intensify military conflict. Taking our faith seriously means feeling spiritually damaged by any resort to arms, regardless of circumstances. The sympathy we feel for our soldiers and all the other victims of war should not translate into venerating leaders who failed them or congratulating ourselves on our militant patriotism. We should put rhetoric to work as a means of dissent and as a matter of conscience rather than as a justification for war, and we should never stop dissenting from, nor ever begin sanctifying, the killing that debases and dehumanizes everyone involved, no matter what the cause.

THE HIGHER PURPOSE OF CIVIL WAR?

The Civil War, as a case in point, is not a war to like, but it was a compelling struggle in its own time between people of faith, and it has remained deeply engaging to Americans ever since. A friend who is an historian once told me that the best-selling books in his field are about the Civil War. To this day, Civil War battles are reenacted in the North and South. I am among many with ancestors who soldiered in that war. One of my ancestors in particular, Frank Strain, left a memoir of his years of fighting in the Union Army. It conveys the absurdity of war along with his pride of serving a great cause. He was every man caught in the whirlwind of war. He fought on the frontlines in hand-to-hand combat in a number of intense battles, surviving to lead a productive life thereafter, but recording for posterity a haunting memory of combat that is neither heroic nor debunking, neither self-serving nor impersonal, neither maudlin nor unfeeling. It conveys instead a doubting sense of higher purpose that nearly reconciled him to the killing fields, but not quite. Frank Strain's story is worth telling for what it reveals about Americans trying to square their conscience when the great cause of abolition turned from nonviolence to internecine war.

The Strains immigrated to America from County Mayo, Ireland in 1794, landing first in the Shenandoah Valley of Virginia, where Frank's father was born in 1798. They settled in southern Indiana in 1810, after living on the other side of the Ohio River in Jefferson County, Kentucky for twelve years. Frank was born in Washington County on the tract of land that his immigrant grandfather, John Strain, homesteaded. Section 33, Range 4 East, in Pierce Township lay ten miles south of Salem, Indiana. According to Frank, his grandfather was a "non-Catholic," and his grandmother, Eleanor (Nellie) Strain, "whose maiden name was McGarvin, was an ardent Catholic," so ardent that Frank's father "was sent to Louisville, Kentucky for a Catholic priest to administer the rights of the church before her death."[13] John and Nellie may have been drawn initially to the Shenandoah Valley, where Scotch-Irish had previously settled, in search of religious tolerance and desiring to "live among their own people."[14]

Frank's father, Robert Strain, was the second of eight children born to John and Nellie. Robert took over the operation of the family farm after John's death in 1823 and ultimately inherited the homestead sometime in the 1830s. At age twelve, Robert had helped his father to clear the land and to plant their first crops in this hilly and rocky terrain. He assisted his father in building the family's first home, too, a cabin located on a good site near a branch of the Blue River and close to a clear spring that provided plenty of cold water.

Robert married Elouisa Burt in 1825. By 1832, he had constructed a new family home on the original homestead. It was built from bricks fired in his kiln and designed specifically to serve as a station on the Underground Railroad. The two-level, six-room house was nestled into the hillside. The partition separating the two rooms on the lower level consisted of two walls disguised to appear as a single partition. The space between the walls formed a concealed room that could not be accessed from the lower level of the house. A trap door under a carpet in the upstairs hallway opened to this secure hiding place for escaped slaves who could rest there during the day and then continue their journey northward under cover of darkness. In 1834, Robert was elected to a three-year term in the Indiana Legislature. Later he served as a Colonel in the Indiana Militia. Robert's children were raised by their father's example to despise slavery and to act in the cause of freedom. In 1863, when he became the enrolling officer for Jackson Township charged with registering able-bodied young men for military service, his son was already in the thick of battle.[15]

Elouisa died in 1860, Robert in 1873. They were buried next to one another near the north wall of the family cemetery, about 500 feet up the hill from their brick home where John Strain's tombstone marks the very center of the graveyard. Elouisa's gravestone bears the inscription, "Her nature was kind. Her religion to do good." Robert's gravestone says, "This world is my country and to do good is my religion." They were good people, with a broad perspective in their time and circumstances. Robert, despite his limited schooling, was known as "a friend of education" who "wrote well and read widely."[16] Clearly, he had been inspired by the spirit of the masthead on William Lloyd Garrison's *The Liberator*, which declared, "My country is the world. My countrymen are mankind."

Slavery was illegal in Indiana, but prejudice ran high, ignorance was rampant, and Southern sympathies were palpable. While relatively few Hoosiers defended the institution of slavery and most regarded it a violation of God's law, most also believed blacks were inferior to whites. Even though the anti-slavery movement gained strength over time, according to James H. Madison, strong race prejudice overshadowed "feeble anti-slavery activity," which "remained weaker in Indiana than perhaps in any other northern state."[17] Blacks in Indiana were prohibited by law from testifying in court, from marrying whites, and from voting. Mob violence against blacks sometimes broke out in towns around the state. "Indiana was something of a game preserve," reports Howard Peckham, "for honest and dishonest Southerners hunting their slaves." Indeed, as Peckham also notes, "most Hoosiers favored sending the slaves back to Africa rather than granting immediate freedom here."[18]

When black abolitionist Frederick Douglass came to Indiana in 1843 to speak of freeing the slaves, he encountered overt hostility and nearly lost his life to an angry mob. Indiana, as it turned out, was the state on Douglass's western speaking tour in which he was handled the roughest. He met opposition everywhere, in Cambridge on September 11 and Richmond the next day, then in Pendleton on the 15th, Noblesville on the 17th, and finally in Jonesboro where he attended the annual meeting of the Indiana Anti-Slavery Society, September 21–23. Even there he was badly received by skeptical anti-slavery Hoosiers at the meeting. When Douglass spoke in Indiana towns, hostile crowds would often gather to issue "murderous threats" and to throw eggs and stones at speaker and audience alike. Shouting "kill the nigger," one such mob in Pendleton took out after Douglass. Its leader struck the fleeing Douglass with a club and was about to administer a second, potentially fatal blow to his head when a member of Douglass's party arrived just in time to foil the ferocious assailant. An unconscious Douglass was then transported three miles by wagon to a friendly Quaker's home where he recovered from his wounds.[19]

Presbyterians and Quakers were the denominations most supportive of the anti-slavery movement in Indiana, and even the Quakers, who took the lead in actively promoting the Underground Railroad, were split over the issue of abolition. In particular, Levi Coffin, the so-called president of the Underground Railroad who operated out of Newport (now Fountain City), Indiana, was driven out of the main body of Indiana Quakers for a time over the issue of how best to oppose slavery.

Quakers had begun to dissent from slavery as early as the 1680s and eventually opposed it officially in 1754 because the institution could only be maintained by violence. As a Quaker youngster of fifteen living in North Carolina, Coffin acted early on the principles of his faith to help a slave escape to freedom. Six years later he opened a Sunday school for blacks that slave owners soon forced him to close, but his commitment to the anti-slavery movement never waned. Coffin explained in his memoir that he was willing to risk the dangers of aiding runaway slaves, when other Friends shied away from the hazard of breaking the Fugitive Slave law or were intimidated by the threats of slave hunters, because "the Bible, in bidding us to feed the hungry and clothe the naked, said nothing about color, and I should try to follow out the teachings of that good book." Moreover, he proclaimed, "if by doing my duty and endeavoring to fulfill the injunctions of the Bible, I injured my business, then let my business go. As to my safety, my life was in the hands of my Divine Master, and I felt that I had his approval."[20]

Coffin made this pronouncement after moving with his wife, Catherine, from North Carolina to Indiana in 1825. He became a successful businessman in Newport, expanding his country store into a pork-cutting and linseed oil operation, and served for twenty years as a leading figure in the Indiana anti-slavery movement before moving the base of his operations to Ohio. Three main lines of the Underground Railroad merged at his Newport home, which became widely known as "Grand Central Station." One of those lines ran near Salem through southern Indiana, moving north by way of secret stations spaced 10 or 15 miles apart from Jeffersonville on the Indiana side of the Ohio River to Newport. The Quaker Convention of 1846 met in Salem, not far from the Strain homestead, to fund a new free-labor enterprise that would move Coffin across the river to operate out of Cincinnati. There he opened what became a successful wholesale warehouse, handling cotton goods, sugar, and spice—all produced by free labor—and continuing his work with the Underground Railroad.

Many Hoosiers sympathetic to the fugitive slaves coursing through their state were willing to assist by providing clothing and other essentials, but few were willing to suffer the prejudices of disapproving neighbors or to hide run-aways in their homes with slave hunters lurking about. Coffin's description of the threats he often received is instructive of the pressures of the times. Even though he made light of such threats after the fact, they were intimidating enough to give most men pause. Consider, for instance, the following chilling account from Coffin's memoir:

> My business influence no doubt operated in some degree to shield me from the attacks of the slave hunters. These men often threatened to kill me, and at various times offered a reward for my head. I often received anonymous letters warning me that my store, pork-house, and dwelling would be burned to the ground, and one letter, mailed in Kentucky, informed me that a body of armed men were then on their way to Newport to destroy the town. The letter named the night in which the work would be accomplished, and warned me to flee from the place, for if I should be taken my life would pay for my crimes against Southern slaveholders.[21]

Fortunately, nothing came of this particular threat, but only those souls most deeply committed to principle could persist under the chronic condition of blatant intimidation and lingering fear of impending harm to one's person, reputation, and property. This was the troubled context in which Robert Strain acted for the sake of human dignity and freedom, thus setting the example that motivated his son, Frank, to risk his own life for that same cause.

Frank was the eighth child of nine born to Robert and Elouisa Strain. His body was strong and his arms powerful. At work in the timber, he wielded an axe with the best of men. He was a serious student, too, good in math and an avid reader with a well-developed vocabulary, even though his work on the family farm prevented him from attending school more than three months each year. When war came, he enlisted "in the service of his country" at age eighteen on June 27, 1861.[22]

Frank's company, designated company G and formed in Salem as part of the 18th regiment of the Indiana Volunteer Infantry, was mustered into service in Indianapolis on August 16, 1861. He was appointed Corporal, rose to Sergeant, and promoted to Second Lieutenant before mustering out of the service in September of 1865 with the final rank of Sergeant. "Of my military service," Frank wrote, "I feel that I may justly be proud. It was my good fortune to be of the right age to offer my services to my country in the hour of its supreme need. I am glad that I had a little part in carrying the flag to final victory, and forever freeing this great country from the blight of human slavery." He dedicated his personal story of fighting for freedom and against slavery to his "beloved children ... as well as to their children, and children's children." It was, he said, an event "in the life of an ordinary citizen."[23]

The nonviolent cause of abolition had turned irreconcilably violent, ultimately costing nearly a million casualties among soldiers on both sides of the divide, not to mention civilian deaths and other losses inherent to civil war. By one conservative count, a combined total of 184,594 soldiers were killed in action or died of wounds. Another 373,458, including prisoners of war, died from disease, privation, and accident. Those who did not die of their combat wounds numbered 412,175.[24] From Indiana alone, a state with a population of 1,350,000, nearly 200,000 men comprised 129 infantry regiments, 13 cavalry regiments, one heavy artillery regiment, and 26 light artillery batteries, not counting an additional 1,100 marines and sailors. Blacks in Indiana contributed more than 1,500 soldiers to the cause. Twelve percent of those Hoosiers who fought for the Union were killed—24,400 young men from Indiana alone.[25] What kind of sense did this devastation make? To William Lloyd Garrison, the great abolitionist leader and advocate of nonresistance, it made tragic sense.

Garrison declared his support of the war after the fighting had broken out because he now believed, as Ira Chernus reports, that "violence had become the only way to end slavery," and putting an end to slavery was his highest priority. Some who followed Garrison's earlier nonresistance lead were easily persuaded to shift their support to the war because they understood nonviolence as merely a means to the great moral end of abolition. Others believed this fight was an "apocalyptic battle of virtue against sin" and, accordingly, adopted "the language of holy war," seeing themselves as struggling on behalf of absolute good. The war was God's judgment of the nation's sins. It required, therefore, a complete and final victory over evil by any and all means to right a chosen people with their God. No compromise with Satan was conceivable. Notably, those opposed to the Union and on the side of the Confederacy also spoke of fighting a holy war and doing God's work.[26]

This consensus on the necessity of war had not always been the prevailing attitude among abolitionists. In the 1830s they had debated one another vigorously, some taking the position that emancipation should be achieved gradually, others that it should come about immediately. Some argued that women's rights should be given precedence over anti-slavery efforts. Differences existed even over interpretations of the Bible's position on slavery, whether or not it condemned slavery as a sin. Some took the nonresistance position of moral suasion; others pushed for political action.[27] Their attitude of nonviolence was marked by an escalating disagreement over how best to achieve the common goal of ending slavery. Those differences were finally smothered in 1861 under a blanket of war.

Rather than breaking the cycle of violence and seeking reconciliation as a first principle, a nation of Christians turned on one another ferociously and in righteous disregard of Christ's message of love and peace. Those fighting on the side of the Union thought of slavery in a religious context at least as much as in political terms, considering it an absolute wrong that must be abolished. Garrison understood slavery as a transgression of God's authority. Adin Ballou, however, was one abolitionist (and a Garrison associate) who maintained to the end that true Christians, who possessed within themselves the germ of the millennium, must "act as if the era of perfect peace and nonviolence were already here." The means chosen could not contradict the end sought; violence was therefore an inappropriate method of seeking a just peace.[28] Even the radical revolutionary, Emma Goldman, decades later, eventually embraced the premise of nonviolence, sans its religious grounds, saying that the "methods of revolution" to achieve human equality must change because "the gun decides nothing at all. Even if it accomplishes what it sets out to do—which it rarely does—it brings so many evils in its wake as to defeat its original aim."[29]

Abolitionist spokesman and Underground Railroad conductor, Frederick Douglass, was himself a fugitive from slavery. Recounting the horrors and brutality of a slave's life in his first autobiography, Douglass spoke eloquently and persuasively of a desire for liberty that might be achieved through political means. He broke with Garrison eventually because, unlike his abolitionist mentor, Douglass preferred political action to moral exhortation as the principal method of ending slavery. Politics was "a legitimate and powerful means for abolishing slavery," he wrote, and the US Constitution was "in its letter and spirit, an anti-slavery instrument, demanding the abolition of slavery as a condition of its own existence, as the supreme law of the land." It was a "dangerous error," he now believed, to withdraw from politics and to continue to take the rigid position of Garrison and the American Anti-Slavery Society that there could be "no union with slaveholders."[30] Like Garrison, Douglass earlier had spoken vehemently against union with slave states, stating in 1844, for example, that the Constitution was "*not* an Anti-Slavery document" but instead an instrument that fell "cold" and "dead" on his ear.[31] Unlike Garrison and the AASS, though, Douglass no longer believed in 1855 that "allegiance to God" and "the cause of human freedom" legitimized revolution against a government that pandered to the evil of slavery or made secession from "the existing national compact" a "religious and political duty."[32]

Douglass endorsed "Christianity proper" but not the "*slaveholding religion of this land*"; he professed his love for "the pure, peaceable, and impartial Christianity of Christ" but not "the corrupt, slaveholding, women-whipping, cradle-plundering, partial and hypocritical Christianity of this land."[33] Even as he depicted so vividly "the soul-killing effects" and "dehumanizing character of slavery," or in the words of Robert O'Meally, "how it feels to be a human locked in a struggle against tyrannical odds for freedom and culture," Douglass developed, as O'Meally observes, "a rhetorical strategy that train[ed] his mind for...turning the tables on the powerful," a trickster's sense of inversion and a corresponding image of freedom "through conscientious struggle" that grounded his political technique in his spiritual life.[34] He reported that after he had been awakened to religion at about age thirteen, he "saw the world in a new light": "I loved all mankind—slaveholders not excepted; though I abhorred slavery more than ever. My great concern was, now, to have the world converted."[35] He would hope to achieve this end by rhetorical means, by the way of public persuasion that negotiates the vagaries and complexities of political life for better or worse.

Douglass's account of his break with Garrison functioned as a kind of declaration of independence from serving as living testimony to, and Exhibit A of, the patronizing white abolitionist's uncompromising case against slavery. It was a break that had been in the making since 1847 when Douglass had returned from a two-year speaking tour in Europe to found and edit his own newspaper, the *North Star* (later renamed *Frederick Douglass's Paper*). By 1849, he had begun to question in public Garrison's extreme attitude toward the Constitution.[36] In 1855, *My Bondage and My Freedom*, Douglass's second autobiography, adopted a tone throughout that reflected the valuable childhood lesson he had learned about "the relativity of perspective," as Brent Hayes Edwards puts it.[37] "Early I learned," Douglass wrote, "that the point from which a thing is viewed is of some importance."[38] This prevailing tone of the "mature, reflective Douglass," Edwards observes, refused "to trade in stark oppositions and clear victories" but instead portrayed "a world of shadows" in which political objectives may be relatively clear "but one is less certain of the ground one stands on."[39]

As a case in point, the anti-slavery movement was "holy and beneficent" in its ends, he judged, "the very essence of justice, liberty, and love" and based on principles of enlightened conscience "easily rendered appreciable to the faculty of reason in man." The point of difference between abolitionists and their opponents was not those hallowed principles but instead "the manner of applying them." This observation made Douglass "sober, but not hopeless" over the prospects of the anti-slavery movement. Given the strength it had gained by the year 1855, he reasoned, the movement could falter only from inward decay, not outward opposition. The cause of anti-slavery would achieve its final triumph because of the affinities among men established by the Almighty and by expelling the demon of selfishness from human souls.[40] These were the sources of persuasion that would prevail in the arena of politics, he hoped, but in the end he was called to advise President Abraham Lincoln on matters of emancipation under conditions of Civil War instead of reconciliation. Lincoln himself had come into office as the voice of prudence and compromise to save the Union short of war, but ultimately to no avail. War would have its way with the rhetorically divided nation.

War, not peacemaking, had become rhetoric's principal vocation and deadly purpose. Its tragic calling was to rationalize the ritual of vilification and to perpetuate the cycle of violence rather than to persuade a badly conflicted people to change their troubled ways and to attend to their common interests. This tragic rhetoric lacked any considerable appreciation for irony, what Kenneth Burke has called "true irony, humble irony... based upon a sense of fundamental kinship with the enemy," that is, the kinship of an enemy contained within us.[41] There, within the body politic, the enemy resided—deeply embedded in a discourse of reciprocal hate and a self-perpetuating language of evil. This alienating dialectic turned moderates into extremists and rent a democratic people beyond repair.

As Stephen Hartnett observes, "Northern abolitionist radicals goaded Southern proslavery radicals to persuade democracy-loving moderates everywhere that slavery was destroying the Union."[42] The rhetoric of the day was littered with tropes of threat and with sweeping generalizations that articulated hyperbolic arguments and conveyed a tone of urgency and impending doom. Cultural fictions of freedom and national destiny were pitched at such high levels of abstraction and with such condensed emotion that they masked even the deep economic divide existing between ruling elites and the working poor in both North and South.[43]

Ernest Bormann notes that a "drifting sentiment" previously had existed throughout the nation that slavery was on the wane and eventually would die out, but aggressive agitation for immediate abolition moved Southerners to reassess and back away from that sentiment. A new and more recalcitrant consciousness began to emerge in the South. Slavery's positive value was advanced in a fantastical image of "an agrarian paradise of large houses, gracious landed gentry, and a well-mannered and polite society. . . . Cared for in sickness and in health and given security in their old age, the Southern black servant was, in the rhetorical vision of the defenders of the system, happier and better off than the white wage slaves of the Northern industrial system."[44] Just as abolitionists had characterized slavery as a sin, Southerners now found in scripture slavery's divine origin and Biblical sanction.[45] Southerners were radicalized to protect the very social and economic structures that Garrisonian abolitionists had set out to destroy nonviolently but in the alienating style of militant nonresistance. Radical abolitionists "asserted nonviolence," Bormann notes, but in a manner that "suggested attack and aggression."[46] Thus, the Garrisonian position offered Southerners no common ground on which to base a shared vision of emancipation.

The moral issue had become so divisive and compelling in the heated context of antebellum politics that it forced its will onto the debates between Abraham Lincoln and Stephen A. Douglas during the US Senate campaign of 1858. Both men attempted, without success, to approach the morality of slavery indirectly rather than head-on, as David Zarefsky explains. Douglas took the stand that democratic procedure and local decision making should prevail over any effort to impose a national mandate against slavery, whether or not slavery was immoral. "I care more for the great principle of self-government, the right of the people to rule, than I do for all the negros in Christendom," he proclaimed. Lincoln, on the other hand, while accusing Douglas of moral indifference, assumed the ambiguous position of ultimate emancipation, which was located somewhere between abolishing slavery and condoning it. Lincoln wanted to believe that slavery was on a course of ultimate extinction and that political moderation in the meantime would preserve the Union. Such moderation meant disavowing the equality of the races and opposing citizenship for blacks but, as Zarefsky observes, without offering a practical plan "that might hasten the demise of slavery."[47]

Neither Douglas nor Lincoln managed to duck the moral heat or political urgency of the issue, either by subordinating it to a higher value or deferring it to another time. Emancipation would be achieved by force in the crucible of war to save the Union—with all the evils that follow in war's wake to negate even its highest purpose—rather than by argument in public debate. Circumstances were difficult and times were challenging even without the added vexation of militant abolitionist agitation. An already divided people were driven beyond compromise or reconciliation, split asunder into warring factions by a radical rhetorical vision. On the brink of war, most Americans North and South wished for compromise and conciliation of some kind and felt no overwhelming desire for bloodshed. The final desperate recourse, though, was an appeal to God's judgment in the hope of making an otherwise awful war meaningful.[48] As James Darsey points out, God's judgment was to be rendered in the simplistic Manichaean dichotomy of a pure Us versus a sordid Them— even though the Civil War was fought for down-to-earth political and economic reasons, not to restore the kingdom of God.[49] Thus, the rhetoric of anti-slavery and disunion, in J. Jeffery Auer's words, was a "rhetoric that failed to maintain peace."[50] The peace movement's leadership now endorsed "a holy war against slavery."[51]

America's first organized anti-war movement was broken by the Civil War. It had been inspired at the turn of the nineteenth century, according to Charles DeBenedetti, by "war-weary Christians" who wished to convert the human heart against all forms of violence and coercion.[52] Indeed, the New York Peace Society was formed in 1815 by David Low Dodge to emphasize "the incompatibility of war and the Gospel."[53] Together with the Boston-based Massachusetts Peace Society, which was founded that same year by a Unitarian Minister, Noah Worcester, they undertook a sustained peace initiative designed to avert divine vengeance on a warrior nation that had lost its way. In his widely distributed essay, "A Solemn Review of the Custom of War," Worcester asked "every Christian seriously [to] consider the malignant nature of the spirit which war makers evidently wish to excite, and compare it with the temper of Jesus."[54] According to Merle Curti, these pioneers of peace inspired a movement that was religious and humanitarian in character: "War was condemned as contrary to the teachings of Christ, and as hostile to the interests of morality and religion...[and] denounced as a contradiction of the brotherhood of man."[55] Indeed, Garrison was one among the early Christian reformers who argued that nonresistant pacifists must abstain from violence in order to live with God. The nonresistant must return good for evil and, in Garrison's words, "*forgive* every injury and insult, without attempting by physical force...to punish the transgressor."[56] Yet, even a devoted nonresistant such as Charles Stearns could be persuaded to take up arms when he finally concluded that his enemies were "not men...made in God's image" but instead "demons from the bottomless pit and may be shot with impunity."[57]

AN ORDINARY CITIZEN'S ACCOUNT OF WAR

Frank Strain, who considered himself an ordinary citizen and who grew up in southern Indiana in a home on the Underground Railroad, marched off to war at age eighteen in 1861, not to shoot demon Southerners with impunity, but to free his country forever from the blight of human slavery. He survived four years of combat to tell a story of war in his later years that was written for posterity—for his beloved children, their children, and children's children. His memory was vivid but also tempered by experiences all too human. It was not written in a grandstanding style or even with the grand, heroic, and tragic vision of an uncompromising, moralistic, or arrogant Garrisonian abolition-ist. Its quotidian qualities, instead, cut to the quick of war's absurdity by blur-ring the distinction between friend and foe, comrade in arms and sworn enemy, valiant hero and inhuman villain. It was a profoundly conflicted story about a catastrophic conflict written from the vantage point of a tested vet-eran and tempered by the wisdom of a citizen.

Indeed, Frank's post-bellum life exemplified citizenship at its fullest. He returned to Indiana after the war to help his aging and arthritic father run the family farm. Soon thereafter he married a pretty neighbor girl, Susan Cather-ine (Kate) Ratts, who, while he was gone soldiering, had become an attractive and intelligent young pioneer woman of good judgment.[58] After a short while, it became apparent to Frank and Kate, who were living in the family home with Robert and Robert's second wife, "that the house big enough for two families has never been built." A few months after moving into a small house on the farm that he had built some distance away from his father's home, Frank determined that life was too short to endure the tensions with his step-mother that so persistently troubled the young couple to make them, as he put it, "uncomfortable most of the time." He sold out and bought a lumber busi-ness in Indiana with his brother, John, whom he then followed to Nebraska in 1872 before settling a year later in northwestern Kansas where he found "rich, level land" to farm.[59]

Frank and Kate, with their two sons, Robert Oscar and Elmer Franklin (their daughter, Minnie, had died at birth and was buried in the family ceme-tery in Indiana), traveled west by covered wagon to live in a dugout on the bank of a draw on their homestead in Phillips County, Kansas. There they started a church in their dugout home while farming 360 acres—coping with worrisome Indians and weathering grasshopper hordes, droughts, prairie fires, and blizzards—until Frank became engaged in politics in 1877, the year he was elected on the Republican Party ticket to the office of county treasurer. The growing family (Kate and Frank had two more sons and a daughter by then) moved to the county seat in Phillipsburg in 1878, where they joined the

Presbyterian Church in 1883. They were a religious family active in the church for generations to come.

Frank helped start the Citizens Bank of Phillipsburg in 1882, which in two years became the First National Bank of Phillipsburg. He was elected bank cashier in the beginning and served in that capacity until 1889. Kate was engaged in service activities as an officer in the Phillipsburg Eastern Star and as a delegate of the Woman's Relief Corps (WRC). The WRC, a national organization of patriotic women that became a powerful cultural force in memorializing the Civil War, worked in conjunction with the Grand Army of the Republic (GAR) in which Frank was active with other Union veterans.[60] Frank served as mayor of Phillipsburg in 1883–1884 and again in 1889–1890, as well as deputy sheriff in 1889, after which he returned to farming until 1896 when he was appointed probate judge and then re-elected to that same post for three full terms, acquiring a reputation as the fair and impartial Judge Strain. He was elected to a term in the Kansas Legislature (1912–1914) and served for three years on the Board of Managers of the State Soldiers' Home.

When Frank sat down to write his memoir of war, "by request of the family," which included Kate and their ten living adult children (a second daughter had died of diphtheria at age five in 1882), he had led an active postwar public life in Indiana and Kansas that consisted of running a lumber business followed by a decade of farming, long-term leadership in church and civic organizations, four years of service as county treasurer, two terms as mayor, six years as a banker, a stint as deputy sheriff, four terms as a probate judge, one term as a member of the Kansas Legislature, three years on the board of a state home for soldiers, and, together with Kate, four decades of raising ten children to adulthood in a surrounding of Christian values and fellowship.[61] His memory of war refracted through life's complexities made for a story that was anything but a simplistic Manichaean clash between the forces of good and evil—a pure Us on the side of freedom versus a sordid Them in the service of slavery. It was instead a narrative of nuanced relations among largely accidental adversaries caught in a deadly struggle that made little sense on the ground, certainly not the tragic and heroic sense that rationalized the rarified Garrisonian turn from nonresistance to warfare.

Frank remembered being recruited into military service by a veteran of the Mexican War living in Salem and a friend of the family who was a neighbor. His company of "one hundred and one men, or boys" assembled in Salem, the county seat, to elect their officers—one captain, a first lieutenant, and a second lieutenant, the first two being the same men who had recruited him into the army. They then traveled north to Indianapolis to join in the formation of an infantry regiment of 1,000 Hoosier volunteers. The formation of their regiment was delayed a few days by "the difficulties which arose over the election of field officers," causing "two or three companies [to] withdraw from the organization."[62] Disorder among these volunteer warriors became a recurring theme from that point forward in their long and twisting journey into combat, a constant presence in the daily routine of soldiering that taught them the hard lesson of war's vanity.

In mid-August, Frank's "Eighteenth" regiment of newly minted Indiana infantry boarded a troop train for St. Louis and, from there, was sent on to Jefferson City to defend Missouri's capital from a Confederate threat that ultimately did not materialize. Next, by train to Tipton, on foot across country to Boonville, and then aboard boats up the Missouri River, they and three other untested Indiana regiments advanced toward Lexington, Missouri, where General Mulligan was besieged, according to Frank's account, by a Confederate army of 20,000–25,000 men under the command of General Sterling Price. Harassed along the way by snipers firing from bluffs above the river's west bank, the untried Federal force decided to tie up their riverboats and reconnoiter the territory before attempting to pass the fortified town of Glasgow located on the river's east bank. In darkness, led by Major Gordon Tanner, four companies of men—one from each of the four regiments—were sent ashore to work their way at a considerable distance through dense timber and thick undergrowth on low ground, causing the companies to become separated from one another and to lose their sense of direction. The ensuing confusion was deadly ironic:

> It then happened that a company working its way up the river met a company with directions confused coming down the river. Each, in their inexperience, thinking the other an enemy, began firing. The other two companies, who were separated some distance, supposing the firing was coming from the enemy, began pouring fire in their direction. The upper boat, or the one lying nearest the firing, supposing the rebels were in force, gathered on the upper and lower decks and began firing into the timber also. This continued for several minutes, until by some means they recognized the fact that they were fighting each other and the firing ceased. Then began the gathering together of the dead and wounded and the carrying them back to the boats, which occupied most of the night. Among the severe losses sustained at that time was the death of Major Tanner, who was perhaps at that time the most brilliant young officer in that division of the army.[63]

Moreover, as they soon learned, their inadvertent sacrifice was made doubly pointless by Mulligan's surrender of Lexington before they could arrive to reinforce him, and they were too small a force to attempt to retake the heavily fortified city. Thus, four bloodied regiments of Indiana volunteers returned in their riverboats to Boonville after suffering severe but self-inflicted losses without ever engaging the enemy.

From Boonville, they marched back toward Sedalia to join a large force being organized by General John C. Fremont to pursue Confederate General Price, who had paroled his prisoners at Lexington and was now retreating toward Springfield, Missouri. Fremont, however, was relieved of his command just as the Union pursuers neared Springfield. Their new commander, General David Hunter, "about-faced the whole army and marched them back to Sedalia. Why General Fremont was superseded and why that foolish return march was made," Frank remarks, "is more than I ever understood, or have I ever heard an explanation of it."[64] In fact, as Frank may have suspected, political considerations and personal rivalries were a confounding variable.

Fremont had devised, at his headquarters in St. Louis, a grand but vague plan to strangle the Confederacy by controlling the Mississippi Valley, descending down the river from Missouri to take Memphis, then Vicksburg, and finally New Orleans. What he lacked in clarity and military savvy, he compensated for in dramatic gestures, pomp and circumstance, and the studied aura of a bold visionary. Missouri itself, though, was not firmly under Union control, as had been dramatically underscored recently by the bloody battle at Wilson's Creek in which 1,200 casualties were suffered by each side in the course of four hours of intense fighting (more than half the number that had fallen previously at Bull Run, which had involved three times as many troops and took three times as long to conclude). The Federal troops in Missouri were in disarray and retreat.

To stem the tide, Fremont, who had been the Republican Party's first candidate for the presidency, issued an unauthorized proclamation on August 30, 1861 that emancipated any slaves owned by disloyal Missourians, thus putting Lincoln, who had been the Republican Party's first winning candidate for the presidency, in a political bind between the demands of radical abolitionists who applauded Fremont's initiative and the anger of Union loyalists in the border states. In Kentucky, the legislature reacted against Fremont's proclamation by backing away from declaring for the Union, and a Unionist volunteer company quit their arms on the spot. Lincoln could neither endorse nor reject emancipation without worsening an already bad situation and, consequently, was attacked vigorously on all sides, including by members of the Senate, the press, and the pulpit.

After Mulligan's Irish Guard succumbed to Price in Lexington (before Frank and his bloodied comrades could arrive to fortify the Union defenders), Fremont notified Lincoln that he was taking the field with 38,000 men to chase down Price. Frank's "Eighteenth" regiment of Indiana volunteers joined the glorious chase, but Lincoln had determined by then that the extravagant and defiant Fremont was a political liability to be eliminated and therefore relieved of his command.[65] Thus, to Frank's befuddlement, their chase after Price was aborted before the impending battle, and the soldiers were marched back from where they had come to weather a severe Missouri winter and experience more of war's mundane absurdities.

After marching around and about—between and betwixt—Syracuse and Otterville most of the winter, Frank's regiment had just finished building huts beside the Lamine River to protect themselves from the harsh weather when they received orders one cold night early in February 1862 to march at daybreak a distance of "forty-five miles, over bad roads, through mud and slush, carrying full equipment of knapsack, haversack, canteen, gun, and ammunition, weighing perhaps thirty-five or forty pounds." When they reached Warrensburg, Missouri by nightfall they were exhausted and down to about ten men per company. The stragglers caught up by morning. A day later they surrounded and captured 1,300 Confederate recruits from northern Missouri after only a few shots had been fired and without anyone being killed, but soon thereafter a lot of Frank's comrades, weakened by little protection from the harsh winter weather, died of an outbreak of measles. Before the end of February, they were ordered to march toward Springfield, again in pursuit of Price even though "many of the boys were convalescing from the measles." They waded streams and wore wet clothing while marching in cold weather through territory where few bridges remained intact, which "brought a relapse to almost all of the boys, who had partially recovered, and at one point where we stopped to bridge a stream so large it could not be waded, we buried five men of my company, all of whom died after only a few hours' sickness."[66]

After six months of soldiering for the Union cause, these Indiana infantrymen had marched all over Missouri chasing after and even encountering Confederate forces willy-nilly, suffering self-inflicted casualties along the way and dying from exposure and disease but not from enemy fire. However, they soon confronted the next absurdity of war that same winter of 1862, when they crossed the Osage River to continue the pursuit of General Price into Arkansas where they engaged the enemy in three continuous days of vicious hand-to-hand combat, culminating in a victorious slaughter at Pea Ridge.

By Frank's account, brisk fighting began on March 6 in the extreme northwest corner of Arkansas at Sugar Creek, ten miles north of Bentonville, between a Union army of 10,000 and a Confederate force of 30,000 (the number probably was more like 10,500 to 17,000). That night the Confederates moved their forces through snow and wind around the Union army's flank and attacked the next morning from the rear. After several hours of "rather desultory fighting," the rebel infantry advanced in full force. Under the division command of Indiana-born and combat-experienced Colonel Jefferson Davis, Frank's regiment formed its line of battle near Leetown behind "a thick growth of black-jack with a dense undergrowth of hazelbrush." It was impossible to see more than about 100 feet ahead. Under pressure from an aggressive attack by Price's men, who came crashing through the brush, the Union line that was 100 yards in front of the Indiana Eighteenth broke and retreated in disorder through Frank's line. "Confusion prevailed" until the fleeing soldiers had passed through and the Eighteenth was free to commence firing: "How long the firing continued I cannot tell, but, in any event, it lasted until the hazelbrush between the lines was mown down almost as if done by a scythe." Even as the Confederate line in front of them gave way after their commander, General Ben McCulloch, was killed, a second line of rebels attacked the embattled Eighteenth from the rear, "so that we were compelled to about-face and fight for our lives against an enemy on either side of us."[67]

The fighting continued "strenuously" until dark. The surviving members of the Eighteenth spent a "dreary, lonesome night" among the fallen and the dead—without the comforts of food, drink, or fire—listening to the "pitiful" moans of the wounded. At midnight, they moved out through the underbrush slowly and as quietly as possible to form a new line three miles away.

At sunrise the great artillery duel of the Pea Ridge battle opened with every piece of artillery in both armies in use. The noise was terrific and, for an hour or more, nothing was heard but the roar of cannon, the screaming of shells, and the crash of falling timber. When the artillery firing ceased, the infantry on both sides were ordered to advance. The crisis had come. The death struggle was on.

In the frenzy of battle, Frank lost track of time until a final determined Union charge, through "a shower of grape and canister...and a hail of minieballs," forced the Confederate infantry to retreat: "The battle of Pea Ridge was over, and our flag waved in victory," but the excitement of that glorious moment quickly faded when Frank looked around to "see the upturned faces of the dead, and hear the piteous moans of the dying" and thus to realize "for the first time the real horrors of war."[68]

It was a bloody affair. Missouri had been secured for the Union at the estimated cost of 1,000 Confederate soldiers killed or wounded and the precise count of 203 Federal soldiers killed, with another 980 wounded. An additional 201 were captured or missing from the Federal ranks, and an estimated 300 Confederates had been taken prisoner. The combined total was nearly 2,700 casualties and losses—ten percent of the clashing armies but under average for the war as a whole. In the somber words of a victorious General Samuel R. Curtis, as the burial squads worked through the taint of human decay, "The vulture and the wolf have now communion, and the dead, friends and foes, sleep in the same lonely grave."[69]

The victors of Pea Ridge spent the next year in rugged marches along the White River into southern Arkansas and across to the Mississippi River without meeting much resistance. They took boats back to southeastern Missouri, where they marched "desperately hard" through hills along the Current River in severe weather on snow-covered ground "without having accomplished anything."[70] So ended the winter of 1863, Frank and his now battle-tested comrades encamped once again in Missouri after a long and sobering campaign.

In April, Frank's regiment joined Ulysses S. Grant's army for an assault on Vicksburg, a key Confederate stronghold on the Mississippi that, after weeks of continuous fighting, finally surrendered on July 4, 1863. Grant's assault on Vicksburg was a remarkable campaign, his greatest achievement, according to historians J. G. Randall and David Donald, and the main event of the war on the western front in 1863. It, along with a simultaneous Union victory at Gettysburg, reversed the prospects of the war that until that moment had favored the Confederacy. Taking Vicksburg—which commanded the Mississippi and provided a vital railway to Texas—was like severing an artery to drain the South of its remaining vitality.[71]

Contrary to military theory, Grant chanced a long march over difficult terrain to approach Vicksburg from the south, which required him to operate in enemy territory while cut off from his own supplies. In one of many sharp battles fought along the way, Frank's company sustained its heaviest losses of the war, seventeen of their thirty-seven men killed or wounded, "most of them within five minutes' time." On the morning of May 22, General Grant—"urged on by the clamor of the Northern press and by General Halleck, Secretary of War"—ordered a full-scale assault on the heavily fortified river city.[72] Grant, himself, was optimistic that the momentum of his previous victories in the field would carry over to a quick and final triumph. The first failed assault had been attempted on May 19, with heavy casualties, but Grant remained optimistic. The second failed attempt cost the Union army even more dearly in killed and wounded. The 4,141 Federal casualties in those two grand exercises in futility almost equaled the previous Union losses suffered in three weeks of intense battles on the way to Vicksburg.[73]

When Frank's regiment charged ahead through blistering Confederate fire, they discovered that ditches had been dug in front of the fort 8 feet deep, into which about half of the onrushing regiment tumbled. Most of the remainder of the day was spent shooting at the enemy to keep them from firing down on Frank's exposed and entrapped comrades while digging escape trenches with picks and shovels "to get the men out of the deep ditches." They next discovered that even concentrated cannon fire could not breach the city's strong defensive walls, which were "composed of tightly pressed cotton bales of great thickness covered with earth." So, the Union army "settled down to besiege the place" until six weeks later "the Confederates came out, gave up their guns, and the work of paroling, which was one of the terms of the surrender, began." Their enemy, starved into submission, begged the Union soldiers for something to eat: "We gave them all we had and were ourselves without provisions about twenty-four hours."[74]

Before the surrender, there had been a good deal of friendly talk across the siege lines, often between brothers and cousins, which only intensified after the surrender to a level that, as Grant put it, "the men of the two armies fraternized as if they had been fighting for the same cause."[75] Indeed, a number of Confederates had deserted to the Union side during the long debacle. At the point of surrender, a total of 2,872 greybacks, as Grant called them, were killed, wounded, or missing; 28,687 were paroled; another 709 refused parole, requesting instead to be sent north to prison "rather than risk being exchanged and required to fight again."[76] Even as they fed, fraternized with, paroled, and otherwise harbored a defeated enemy, Grant's victorious army secured vast quantities of Confederate ammunition and a large stockpile of superior weapons to augment their killing capacity for the next round of fighting.

Frank headed north after Vicksburg up the river aboard a steamer to visit his old homestead in mid-July. He was one of two soldiers in his company chosen by lot for a brief furlough. After two years of hard fighting, he now returned to an unhappy scene in southern Indiana. His mother had died in the fall of 1860, and his father was remarried: "The old home hardly seemed home with a strange woman in my mother's place." The Union men and boys were nearly all off to war, leaving the "stay-at-home" Democrats in the ascendancy, at least in southern Indiana, most of whom were "Southern sympathizers, belonging to a treasonable secret order known as 'Knights of the Golden Circle.'" These "traitors" were busy planning a mass uprising to bring Indiana, along with Ohio and Illinois (or at least the southern halves of these three states), into the Confederacy.[77] On the home front, as in the battleground, it proved difficult to separate friend from foe by any definitive or permanent line of demarcation.

Morgan's raiders, coming up from Kentucky, had even turned southern Indiana into something of a battleground just prior to Frank's return from Vicksburg. Led by Confederate General John Hunt Morgan, this band of over 2,000 cavalrymen crossed the Ohio River into Harrison County on July 8. They soon met with resistance from the Indiana Home Guard in Corydon. After subduing the outnumbered defenders and robbing the people of Corydon, Morgan's raiders headed further north into Washington County to find food and fresh horses and then to attack the county seat of Salem on July 10. They passed right by, and even camped within a few miles of, the Strain homestead on their way to Salem. After looting the town, tearing up railroad tracks, burning the depot, and destroying two railroad bridges, they rode east toward Canton, Ohio drunk on stolen whiskey and ransacking farmers' homes along the way.

Terrorizing a number of other Indiana communities, but encountering continuing resistance from an aroused state militia, Morgan's harassing force crossed into Ohio on July 13 just ahead of pursuing Federal troops. Most of the raiders were captured in southern Ohio before the end of July. In November, Morgan managed to escape from a prison in Columbus, Ohio, only to be killed the following September in Greenville, Tennessee while fleeing from Northern troops.

The raid was a dashing failure. It stirred up as much resistance as fear among the people of Indiana and Ohio and caused too little damage to advance the Confederate cause. Yet, it also operated on a terrain of mixed sympathies and conflicted political relations among the citizenry. Neighbors opposed one another even as the collective citizenry—sans their most able-bodied men and boys who had gone soldiering for the Union—banded together to defend against an invading force. The line between friend and foe was often faint and fuzzy. The face of the enemy was too recognizable to be entirely alienating or rendered permanently subhuman. Fraternizing with the enemy at home and on the frontlines was the ever-present condition of a people at war with themselves—of civil war—where the conflicted relations among opposing people and parties that define a healthy order of political contestation had declined one fatal step into an unsteady state primarily, but not totally or always, of antagonistic relations.

After confronting the face of the enemy among his estranged neighbors at home, Frank was glad when his furlough expired: "My face was turned toward my regiment in the South," which he found encamped 1,500 combined river and rail miles away at Berwick Bay on the Gulf of Mexico. The emotion of his escape from the ambiguities of conflicted relations on the home front to the clarity and relative security of relations among his comrades in arms was overwhelming: "I am unable to find words to express my joy at again being with the boys, with whom my ties of friendship and affection had been welded in the fire of battle and who were dear to me as brothers could be."[78] These were bonds never to be broken and forever to be sustained, even post-bellum, in the Grand Army of the Republic. The purest and most satisfying form of friendship and engendered kinship existed under the most extreme condition of separation and alienation. The men of Frank's regiment (as dear to him as brothers could be) were identified so completely with one another in this familial way by risking their lives in combat, by contesting together the immediacy of death, and by their common estrangement from the most immediate instruments of death. They had escaped death conjointly and were welded as one in the heat of battle, or perhaps united by a common affliction into a bond of diseased cooperation. The enemy was neither a face nor an abstraction, but instead the concrete, immediate, and anticipated reality of hostile, deadly fire. Friendship was a function of surviving together.

After a brief and uneventful westerly march through beautiful country, "the finest I think I have ever seen," with "the object of the march, whatever it may have been, seeming to have been accomplished," Frank's regiment returned to base and traveled by rail to Algiers on the Mississippi, directly across from New Orleans. There they boarded one of four steamships at New Orleans that took a division of soldiers across the Gulf of Mexico for combat in Texas. As the ships approached Corpus Christi, they encountered "a terrific storm" on the open sea that lasted through the night and well into the next morning. It was a frightening experience: "I am sure that to me it was the most terrifying sight I ever saw." When the storm finally calmed enough for the army to disembark at the head of St. Joe's Island, they headed up the river by foot to capture Fort Esperanza at the mouth of Matogorda Bay. Before they could attack the fort, they had to endure a two-day-long blinding sandstorm. When the storm lifted, the Confederate defenders, who could now see they were outnumbered, abandoned the fort without a fight, all but thirty or thirty-five eluding capture. "No other fighting was done during our stay in Texas."[79]

They remained idle there a long while, encamped on Matogorda Bay until the following April. While stagnant, Frank's regiment reenlisted on January 1, 1864, entitling them to a thirty-day furlough. Their passage home stalled at Baton Rouge, though, because of a campaign in progress on the Red River, rendering Frank inactive again. He finally arrived home in late July. The third year of the war had been uneventful, except for the terrible fright at sea and a blinding sandstorm. Bonded in battle, the brotherhood of arms now also knew the tedium of war without combat. They could lose nearly half of their number in five minutes of intense fighting on the march to victory at Vicksburg but then spend a full year of doing little more than enduring the elements of nature.

In late August, Frank's regiment headed east from Indiana by way of Pittsburg and Washington to join Sherman's retreating army on September 1 in the Shenandoah Valley. Frank had returned to the site of his father's birth. On September 19, Sheridan advanced on the Confederate army of 45,000 to 50,000 men with a force of about equal size. At Opaquan Creek, a second Union charge routed the Confederates:

> Here I witnessed for the only time a great cavalry charge. When the infantry had broken the lines of the Confederates and thrown them into confusion and they were on the retreat, Wilson's division of cavalry, consisting of about eight thousand men, came around from the right and swung down on the retreating rebels with drawn sabers. The afternoon sun was some two hours up and just in the right position to make the swords and other arms of the cavalry glint in the light like a sea of silver. It was a most terrible sight to see them rushing on the confused and retreating rebels, riding them down in great numbers, and slashing them right and left with their sabers, and such a sight as I have no desire ever to see again.[80]

The engagement continued the next day and thereafter in pursuit of a retreating foe all the way to Lynchburg at the upper end of the valley. After some further maneuvering for several weeks, the two sides engaged one another again on October 19. Unable to check the Confederate advance in tough fighting at close range, Frank's outnumbered unit found itself hopelessly caught in a crossfire from three sides: "Many of our boys, unwilling to risk running the gauntlet between these fires, lay down and permitted themselves to be captured. Some of us, however, took the chance, ran away, and 'lived to fight another day.'" Escaping to the rear over a hill, Frank and his fleeing comrades quickly joined Sheridan's regrouping forces to form a line that attacked "with such vigor that the enemy was soon in full retreat."[81]

So went the battle of Cedar Creek from Frank's perspective. General Sheridan had saved the day, and Frank was of the opinion that Sheridan's men "would have followed him to purgatory had he given them the command to charge it." They were flush with victory, even though troubled by the hideous sight of fleeing enemy infantrymen being cut down from behind and above by the swords of pursuing cavalrymen. The remnants of Confederate General Jubal Early's demoralized army retreated to Richmond via Lynchburg to reinforce General Lee who was by then himself under pressure from Grant. Frank's regiment was ordered in November to join Grant's army below Richmond, where they took part in operations around Richmond and Petersburg until early February. Next, they were shipped to Savannah just in time to see Sherman's army off on its march of devastation from Atlanta to the sea. The fighting was over for Frank's regiment. On September 1, 1865, after being stationed at various points in Georgia, they were mustered out of service at Darien Bay in the southern region of the state and "put aboard ship for the trip home."[82]

The ship was an "old tub" that got stuck in shallow water and took a severe pounding by high waves and strong breakers. Frank was one of 250 men who chanced to jump from the stranded ship onto a rescue boat, leaving behind all of his possessions, including his gun and knapsack. Upon reaching shore at night, he and four others from his company decided it was too risky to try to reboard "that old vessel, fearing it would never be able to round Cape Hatteras, where the sea is always rough. We preferred taking our chances getting across country among strangers and Confederate soldiers just returned from the war, rather than finding a grave somewhere around on the Atlantic."[83]

They needed first to make 60 miles across country to Savannah, where they had previously served several months on police duty. Frank was broke, indeed penniless, because he had not been paid for six months, and thus had to rely on his fellow travelers to extend him credit. They marched through swampy country in the dark and rain, "getting as wet as water could make us," until daylight when they sighted "a cabin in which lived a Confederate soldier, his wife, and dog." They discovered they had traveled only three miles that night. "The confederate kindly took us in, divided what little he had to eat with us, and was kind enough to pilot us out two miles or more to the main road leading to Savannah." Their former enemy would not accept their offer of payment: "having been a soldier himself and knowing what hardship was," he refused the money and "told us to do likewise to the next unfortunate man we met."[84] The interdependence of these soldiers—bluecoats and greybacks—was striking despite years of shooting at one another.

To make his way home, Frank hitched a ride to Savannah on some teams loaded with cotton, got directions from citizens he knew there and headed off with his buddies for Augusta, a journey made partially by train and mostly on foot. Then they traveled from Augusta by train to Indianapolis (with the aid of General Steadman whom they encountered by chance along the way) via Atlanta, Nashville, and Louisville, reaching home two weeks ahead of the rest of their regiment. They received their wages and discharge from the Eighteenth Indiana on September 22: "Thereafter our battles were to be fought individually, with the world at large."[85] Frank had crossed back over the fuzzy line between civilian discord and military conflict.

He had learned in four years a hard-earned, but too easily ignored, lesson about the ambiguities of friendship and enmity, a lesson that did not match either the Christian vision of peace and reconciliation or the orator's rationalization of war and disaffection. Lincoln, who had worried during the height of the onslaught that the North would not persevere, tried to assign meaning to the foolhardy blood sacrifice at Gettysburg. The ugly reality of 50,000 men left dead, wounded, or missing on this single battlefield would be transformed, according to Garry Wills, "into something rich and strange" by Lincoln's 272 transcending words. A victorious General George G. Meade, in slow pursuit of an escaping General Robert E. Lee, had debased these same fallen men by declaring that he could not "delay to pick up the debris of the battlefield." This so-called debris referred to so dismissively by Meade was actually "rotting horseflesh and manflesh—thousands of fermenting bodies, with gas-distended bellies, deliquescing in the July heat."[86] Lincoln, unlike his tactless General, would not disrespect the dead, but he would disembody them.

As Wills explains, Lincoln understood the power of speech in human affairs. He was a student of words who "wrote as a way of ordering his thought." He knew that all speech, written or spoken, is unnatural and artificial, and that rhetoric does not stand in opposition to, or separate from, human reason and motivation. Lincoln turned to the eloquence of simple prose as a tactical marker of objective reality and thus as a medium for transcending the gruesome facts of war. He rose rhetorically above the carnage without a hint of artifice, justifying the gore by supplanting it with abstract ideals of union and equality and with organic and familial images of rebirth. His oratory ascended to such ideological heights that, as Wills tells us, "the stakes of three days' butchery are made intellectual.... He lifts the battle to a level of abstraction that purges it of grosser matter.... The nightmare realities have been etherealized in the crucible of his language."[87]

The promise of equality, which was the nation's revolutionary legacy that had since been compromised by the Constitution, might be reborn in this ordeal-by-death. In cadence and theme, Wills observes, Lincoln's war-justifying rhetoric echoed scripture so closely that the spirit of the Declaration of Independence "replaced the Gospel as an instrument of spiritual rebirth." Lincoln was not a man to condone violence or to vilify an enemy, but he would have the nation submit to Providence, repent its sins, and find its salvation in union based on the principles of liberty and equality. Slavery was a divisive particular that he did not even mention directly; the wasteful spilling of blood was a concrete reality that he surmounted in an abstract image of freedom reborn. Inadvertently or not, war was ennobled by Lincoln's cleansing abstractions and thus blessed by a transcendent Creator. New life would be extended to the nation through the sacrificial death of unseen soldiers.[88] Or would it?

Was freedom reborn? Was the promise of equality renewed, or did men like Frank Strain, who believed they had risked everything to rid the nation of the blight of slavery, sacrifice their safety and their lives in vain? If opposition to the blight of slavery was transformed by Lincoln's transcending rhetoric into an affirmation of the democratic principle of freedom, equality, and self-rule—if that rhetorical achievement spawned a new nation out of blood and trauma, as Wills suggests—did so much death, agony, and devastation set Americans on a new egalitarian course of human dignity?[89] Did the resort to arms accomplish more for such a cause than might have been achieved by compromise and reconciliation? Or was war simply rationalized and falsely glorified, rendering sheer savagery into intangible nobility?

A LESSON OF WAR

The answer to these questions is problematic at best, but surely no presumption of war's advantage over nonviolence is warranted. Lincoln himself knew that violence begets violence, that war outpaces a people's original intent and outstrips any rational purpose.[90] Whether or not civil war was, in William Seward's unfortunate phrase, an "irrepressible conflict," it failed to achieve a clearly progressive outcome, certainly nothing to match or otherwise justify so much devastation and such obvious carnage.[91]

Contrary to Tolstoy's vision of a Christian peace, to the one essential duty and meaning of a Christian life, to faith in a peace among divisive Christians in whom the kingdom of God resides, state violence was rationalized on both sides of the North-South divide. The command to serve humanity was severed from the command to return good for evil, to make peace rather than speak evil, to reconcile instead of succumbing to war. After the war, as Frank observed, the battles remained to be fought with one another and the world at large. The hazy line drawn between everyday adversaries and mortal enemies on the home front and the battlefield alike was forever shifting and always permeable, just as the brotherhood of arms forged in the deadly fire of combat could only partially alienate opposing sides from one another and temporarily blind them to an enemy's irreducible humanity. A common God had been made by wooly rivals to work at lethal cross purposes, and then only to resolve their differences in uncertain terms.

Emancipation itself, proclaimed in the midst of war, was a begrudging and qualified concession to military necessity rather than a ringing and principled endorsement of human equality extended to black Americans. It was a minimalist position taken by a President who did not believe in the social or political equality of the races, that was limited to the Constitutional authority of a Commander in Chief, and that was designed to minimize the affront to Southern sensibilities and institutions. Lincoln had made it clear nearly five years earlier in his contest with Douglas that he did not favor "bringing about in any way the social and political equality of the white and black races," that he opposed intermarrying with Negroes or allowing blacks to vote, sit on juries, or hold political office, and that physical differences between the races made whites superior to blacks.[92] Slavery was wrong simply because one human being cannot own another as one owns property, and thus it must eventually become extinct. The emancipation proclamation of January 1, 1863, was therefore as limited in scope as possible and devoid of moralistic sentiment or ethical principle. It freed slaves only in the South where they were being used as a resource of armed insurrection.[93]

Those like Frank Strain who fought to free the slaves and lived to form the Grand Army of the Republic did not even see fit to include among their ranks blacks who also were war veterans. The all-white GAR, which held its first national encampment in Indianapolis in 1866, in a state that had supplied 1,500 black soldiers in support of the Union cause, became a powerful cultural force of nationalism steeped in the martial spirit. Along with the Woman's Relief Corps, it succeeded in militarizing notions of patriotism and democracy and, as Cecilia O'Leary shows, ritualizing "an interpretation of the Civil War that narrowed its redemptive meaning from that of a war to end slavery to that of a war to preserve the Union."[94] Reconciliation with the

Southern white foe ultimately prevailed over Reconstruction's fleeting and forlorn gesture to racial equality, if it was even that. More than helping blacks, the radical reconstruction wing of the ruling Republican Party seemed bent on punishing the white rebels. Congressman G. W. Julian of Indiana liked neither Abraham Lincoln's nor Andrew Johnson's "tenderness to the Rebels," and the leader of this radical exercise in partisan vindictiveness, Thaddeus Stevens, told Congress that he was dedicating the remainder of his life to "the punishment of traitors."[95]

The plight of blacks in unreconstructed America remained little changed by war, and the prospects of racial equality stayed dismal at best. The carpetbag regimes of radical Republican reconstruction, motivated somewhat by idealism in the beginning, had soon degenerated into a racket and become an extension of the national spoils system in a gilded age. A weakly enforced fourteenth amendment to the Constitution, which formally forbade discrimination based on "race, color, or previous condition of servitude," was imposed on the Southern states as a condition of readmission to the Union. Yet, even as the radical wing of the ruling Republican Party demanded equality for blacks, Andrew Johnson, like his assassinated predecessor, considered the end of slavery sufficient and the preservation of the Union paramount.

The majority of Republicans were moderates not interested in a program of social engineering, but Johnson's stubborn and clumsy politics enabled the radicals to assume control of the national government for a time and to impose radical governments in the South. Newly enfranchised blacks did not dominate these carpetbagger regimes, however, and the subsequent backlash of Southern whites eliminated most of any modest gains that had been made. Reconstruction lost favor even in the North relatively quickly, within less than a decade after the end of the Civil War, and without blacks securing their political rights. Instead, the Ku Klux Klan terrorized former slaves, and defiant, vindictive Southern white supremacists began rebuilding a segregated society in which blacks were subordinated, disenfranchised, impoverished, and brutalized in the lasting image of Jim Crow.

The nation's memory of emancipation just slipped away, no longer the great cause of Civil War that had moved even declared pacifists to abandon their religious principles of nonviolence. In its place, through the sustained efforts of the WRC and the GAR, consistent with dominant cultural representations, and drawing heavily on religious imagery, Memorial Day was established as a holy day symbolizing the white man's heroic struggle to save the nation; "aggressive virility and militarism [were made] the core of national character."[96] Racism had prevailed despite the nation's battlefield sacrifices: "No longer a war of secession and treason, the Civil War was recast by orator after orator as a heroic struggle between brothers whose blood had strengthened the nation."[97] Slavery was formally abolished, but emancipation was forgotten in the mainstream of white culture where the blight of racism remained strong and palpable.

Not only was the cause for which soldiers had died lost to memory and posterity, but the cult of militarism was reinforced rather than chastened by the bloody ordeal. National unity was purchased at the expense of social equality by valorizing war. North and South were reunified over several decades of a cultural process that drew most immediately on the annihilation of the Plains Indians to articulate a common, non-white enemy against which former Civil War foes could begin bonding with one another. This racist bond against a common enemy was subsequently solidified in the Spanish-American War and the heroic adventures of aggressive imperialism.[98]

White America was being fashioned into a national brotherhood of arms even as Tolstoy was insisting that God's kingdom of peace could be realized on earth only by nonresistance to violence and refusing to bear arms against the enemies of the state. The national trajectory toward militant patriotism was directly opposed to Tolstoy's vision of peace. Americans had convinced themselves that God favored them to Christianize and civilize the world at the point of a bayonet and later to make the world safe for democracy by force of arms. Even peace activists began to abandon the Gospel's call for reconciliation, turning instead to a secular vocabulary of arbitration, conflict resolution, and social justice, a critique of war on economic grounds, and the advocacy of international agreements to outlaw certain weapons and to protect innocent noncombatants. This was deemed to be a realistic turn from "religious rhetoric…based on the teachings of Jesus Christ and to rational, pragmatic, and legalistic arguments" that would establish "a rule of law among civilized nations."[99]

Where does this leave us? What lesson, if any, can we draw from Frank Strain's story? Are we a nation of Christian hypocrites who glorify war rather than commit to peacemaking? Are we so vain that we cannot acknowledge our guilty indulgence in the human slaughter? Are we so blinded by our own rationalizations that we cannot learn even from brutal experience that nothing of value is gained by the turn to violence, that much of what is most dear to us is lost in armed conflict, and that our problems are compounded, even perpetuated and mutated, rather than alleviated or solved by the killing? Does our faith in Christian love amount to mere rhetoric with no rational purchase or claim to pragmatic force?

I do think the Christian call to love and peacemaking is a rhetorical response to life's deep quandaries and difficult challenges. It is an interpretation of the perplexed and perplexing human condition that aims to persuade us toward our better inclinations, an expression of a moral point of view that is compensatory to hate and violence. It is an articulation of elevated perspective, a vantage point for seeking alternatives to social alienation. It is a symbolic inducement to traverse the rocky terrain of political discord with uncommon forbearance. It is a poetic appeal to the spirit of humanity, a soul-searching gesture and irrepressible aspiration to transcend the attitude of war. As such, this is a rhetorical practice to embrace rather than to abandon. It is an indispensable incentive to check our ingrained habit of war by working toward a culture of reconciliation. It is an honest rhetorical appeal and a sincere expression of hope that points us toward, and challenges us to pursue, nonviolence without issuing a false guarantee of positive results or absolving us from responsibility to persist despite our shortcomings and failures. It is our collective conscience speaking in dark times. It haunts us even when we succumb to the rhetoric of war. As war's countervailing rhetoric, this mediating language of faith and humility alerts us to the arrogance of violence. It is a precious gift to nurture a dreadfully conflicted but richly diverse humanity through recurring cycles of hostility and insecurity that all too easily devolve into warfare. Nothing could be more reasonable or pragmatic or important than to remain faithful to, and become more practiced in, a rhetorical discourse that troubles our collective conscience even in throes of battle. We should hope ultimately to be persuaded to peace rather than to war.

This, I think, is the lesson of Frank Strain's story of war, a compelling but fractured story that is troubled relentlessly by irrepressible tensions and motivated throughout by unresolved quandaries despite its allegiance to a just cause. The contradictions of his maddening experience are relentlessly sobering from the beginning of the tale to its end, with no relief in between for us to distinguish absolutely or clearly between friend and foe, war and peace. Who could make out the difference between Federal and Confederate forces in the heat of deadly battle and under cover of darkness, even when one party was absent, or while listening to the groans of dying men in the night, or looking at the upturned faces of slain soldiers on both sides in the befuddling daylight of victory, or watching with troubled astonishment as the other side's infantry is hacked down from above and behind by one's own cavalry, or chatting across the lines in the lulls of battle? Was the enemy the Confederate rebel or was it disease, poor planning, bad weather, and political bickering among Union leaders? Was he friend or foe with the rebel warriors whom he fought and nurtured, and who fought and nurtured him? Were the Southern civilians an enemy he policed or helpers he trusted to guide him home safely? Were his neighbors in southern Indiana conspirators or defenders of the homeland, political adversaries or traitors? Was he friend or foe to the black man whom he would fight to emancipate but not invite into the fraternity of Union veterans? Was the comradeship of fellow soldiers more satisfying in war and peace than the conflicts of civilian life? Where was the vague, shifting line between friendship and enmity, and how did he know when he had crossed it in one direction or the other?

It is not my sense that Frank wrote his story deliberately to reveal the human failure of war, but instead that the fissures just below the surface of his narrative are inescapable and that they cue us to look deeper for what we might discover there about the rhetorical configuration of fellowship and enmity. This is the nuanced work of a mature writer experienced in human affairs from which we might rightly draw useful inferences about the language of alienation and the idiom of reconciliation, both from what is present in his memoir and what is absent, what is manifest in his words and what is missing. It is an unwitting record of a troubled Christian conscience and a haunting desire to find a better way. No matter how Frank might have tried to tell an honorable tale of military service about which he could be "proud" to have heeded the call of his country "in the hour of its supreme need" and could be "glad" to have had "a little part in carrying the flag to final victory," he could not help but leave behind for posterity a record of disenchantment with simplistic Manichaean distinctions between the righteous Us and evil Them.[100] That story just did not ring true to experience nor did it meet the spiritual standard of reconciliation.

It is as if the Christian exemplar of peacemaking had become culturally engrained enough to serve as an archetype of people reaching out to one another and a reminder that excuses for hating and slaying are ultimately transparent. It is the appeal to the God of war that, by this measure, seems labored and never fully convincing, that requires incessant rationalization, memorializing, propagandizing, and coercing. Without such a moral model— Christ or another archetypal image that resonates within one's given culture— we could not know what to expect of narratives of discord. We could not sense or surmise the absence of adequate gestures of reconciliation, but from the culturally elevated vantage point of such a deeply ingrained paradigm of reconciliation we can envision what went wrong, and what was not done consistent with the dictates of conscience.

What lurks in the shadow of Frank's unsettled and unsettling account of lethal estrangement is a profoundly humane sentiment, a residual impulse to reconnect the broken circle of humanity. His story resists being elevated from the trying experience of a down-to-earth "ordinary citizen" fraught with unresolved contradictions to a heroic adventure of good conquering evil. It is in this way a cautionary tale for his children's children to ponder, a tale of conscience that confounds the simplicity of simplistic disaffection among antagonists.

There are no sheer enemies in this chronicle of war, except the deadly missiles themselves that bonded soldiers into a brotherhood of survivors. Frank left his gun behind when he jumped to safety from a sinking military transport to begin the journey home on foot—penniless, lost, and vulnerable in devastated Georgia and dependent on help from comrades and adversaries alike to make his way through an alien land. He took comfort from the kindness of a former enemy, who shared a soldier's knowledge of hardship, and he promised in return to help the next unfortunate man he met. Even before he abandoned his gun and while still engaged in combat, Frank shared his own provisions with a starving foe, listened to the piteous moans of agony from the mortally wounded on a darkened battlefield of intermingled humanity, and looked into the upturned faces of men he had killed to grasp the true horror of war and the cost of victory. Even at war's end, the reward of victory was as illusive as the prospect of a pure and redeeming peace. Slavery was technically ended in its old, restricted form, but the "blight" remained, and Frank moved onward, feeling suddenly alone, to fight the endless "battles" of civilian life in the world at large.

Placed in the context of its time, Frank's memoir of conflated enmity and amity among warring whites segues to the blighted relations between whites and blacks. Robert Strain built a home in southern Indiana to harbor runaway slaves secretly on their uncertain journey north to freedom. The world was his country, just as working for the good of humankind was his religion. The son shared the father's faith in a universal humanity, for which he risked his young life on behalf of enslaved blacks and because of which he could not afterward tell a vain story of vanquishing an evil Confederate enemy. Yet, the stereotyped face of blacks in North and South was not so recognizably human to whites before or after the Civil War, certainly not as recognizable as whites were to one another even across enemy lines during the Civil War. White America fought an internecine war over a debased image of African Americans, and then set about reconciling its internal differences at the expense of nominally free, but brutally repressed, blacks and other enemies of color, including Native American and Filipino "savages" who resisted the forward march of white "civilization." What are we to make of such agonizing irony?

The incongruity of violating our values should give us pause no less than it prevented Frank Strain from leaving behind a seamless saga of total victory over the forces of evil. As a matter of common conscience, it should cause us to reflect more deeply on where our ancestors fell short of professed values and acted too little on the religious conviction of peacemaking. Americans desire peace and abhor war, or so we insist. We are reluctant warriors, we believe, who resort to arms only in self-defense and for good causes when there is no viable alternative. Yet, we know war compounds the problems and exacerbates the conditions that tempt us to fight in the first place—the means contradict the end, and the original purpose of resorting to hostilities is defeated by the dreadful consequences of belligerence itself, both during the bloody struggle and in its ugly aftermath. Anti-slavery began as a nonviolent movement and morphed into a cause for civil war that killed and maimed vast numbers of combatants without necessarily improving the condition of black Americans. Moreover, white America healed its self-inflicted wounds and licked its guilty conscience by valorizing militarism and by relegating people of color to the subjugated position of Jim Crow or the threatening status of uncivilized enemy. What lesson might be drawn from the paradox of committing violence in the name of those whom a Christian people would thereafter continue to violate?

The Civil War is not a war to like, but it is one from which we should be able to learn something about where we can go wrong by our own cultural standards and despite good intentions. At the point of declaring hostilities, a considerable body of white public opinion in both sectors of the divided country still preferred some kind of reconciliation and hoped for an eventual resolution of differences through peaceful contestation. They fought each other to the death with lingering regret and forsook their responsibilities to an abandoned black populace in the end. They did not see their own image, the full likeness of humanity, in the black face of a people they had despoiled and that they wished either to emancipate or continue to enslave but not to embrace as one of their own kind. Blacks were a race apart, a fallen race, a lesser race in the common white worldview, including the liberal worldview of the time. White America, North and South, could not imagine black America as its equal. Black chattel was property to be disposed of one way or another, but under neither circumstance, whether emancipated or not, was it to be fully humanized.

Here we see the cost of racial arrogance and prejudice to everyone concerned, victimized and victimizer included. The chain of humanity was broken by the physiognomy of color. Emancipation was a radical proposition, not an inadequate gesture, from the prejudiced perspective of whites throughout an embittered land, whether or not they had an economic interest in abolishing or prolonging slavery. They could not reconcile black to white enough to envision an obligatory condition of equality, regardless of race, that was incumbent upon everyone to work toward achieving sooner rather than later. Their low expectation of racial justice intensified their differences over property rights and embittered them toward one another, leaving them without a common motive to work for the higher purpose of securing human rights. They killed one another reluctantly over slavery (an issue that was disembodied and dissociated from the color black in Lincoln's abstract notion of equality) and disunion (Lincoln insisted that the struggle was over preserving the union), and they cooperated with one another to subjugate rather than to liberate the object of their common disdain.

Thus, the killing that was for naught—because it militarized the national ethos and reinforced a debilitating regime of racial prejudice—would have been rendered unnecessary and unwarranted from a different perspective. That is, from a perspective animated by the beatitude of peacemaking, the Christian commandment to love and serve all humankind, and a corresponding ethic of egalitarianism, a society rent by racism would be motivated to reclaim the wholeness of humanity in its rich diversity. That alternative perspective, which did not ultimately prevail even among the majority in the initially nonviolent movement against slavery, might well have guided the nation toward more constructive compromises and greater progress in human relations instead of the destruction and regression that actually occurred. This is a lesson we can extract from our ancestors' principal shortcoming: the terrible price they paid for disregarding their better conscience.

A LOCUS OF PEACE

My purpose is to identify what went wrong (not to determine whether the Civil War might have been prevented) so that we can better appreciate the relevance and challenge of reconciliation in our own troubled time and tangled circumstances. We cannot afford to lose sight of the face of humanity or fail to recognize its diverse manifestations if we aim to keep the normal state of contested relations from escalating into deadly hostilities. It would be a mistake to think we could or should eliminate the differences and distinctions that constitute the human divide and make conflict endemic to politics. The challenge is to manage that conflict constructively by addressing opponents as equals despite their palpable differences. The tendency instead is to turn divisive affairs into relations of hostility by speaking of enemies in caricature. A people might be expected to persevere with one another and with those they deem to be outsiders only in the degree to which they recognize each other's humanity. We know that because it is an ethic deeply ingrained in a common religious heritage that resonates with the highest values of other religious traditions.

This is the work we can and should undertake if we wish to make more peace and less war. I take heart from the evidence in Frank Strain's memoir of war, written from the vantage point of a practiced citizen. His consciousness of a declared enemy's humanity could never be fully suppressed, not even on the battlefield, at least not in retrospect. I am encouraged to discover there a sensibility that resists valorizing or naturalizing the condition of war, or even justifying his personal battles in no uncertain terms. The haunting voice of irony reverberates throughout a story disenchanted with simplistic representations of good and evil. The incidents in his soldier's life are titled "A Family Matter," but they are told in the broader sense of the human family and conveyed in the spirit of his parents who made kindness a virtue, doing good a religion, and the world their country. Frank was proud of his military service, but not prideful or deluded by victory, or even certain of where to mark the boundary of fellowship. We would do well to ponder his plebeian example and to consider what his humble gesture reveals.

Tolstoy's complaint is heroic by comparison, his vision pure. Even a sincere Christian may consider Tolstoy's revelation an impractical guide to everyday peacemaking. It does, however, call us to consciousness about what can be done to dissent from war, and it would be hypocritical to attempt less than is feasible.

A feasible and meaningful dissent from war may take many forms, but the essence of Frank's unassuming example is to speak as humanely as possible of one's adversaries. Indeed, speaking more rather than less humanely of everyone who figures into our stories of strife is no small challenge when we are confronted by the daily uncertainties and persistent anxieties of secular affairs. Frank's example is merely indicative of the task at hand. It is not perfect in scope or execution. Its imperfection is itself instructive. Its honest inadequacy encourages us to try as well. It illustrates an option somewhere between becoming boisterous and belligerent with unwarranted conviction in a purportedly righteous cause or remaining silent and acquiescent for lack of compelling answers to haunting questions of conscience. It resists perfection, certainty, and even closure, and thus it invites an attitude of open-mindedness and critical reflection on the matters at hand. It is the persona of a fair and impartial Judge Strain that would persuade us to consider and weigh opposing perspectives to the best of our abilities. As a single, delimited iteration of a muffled, yet resilient attitude of human affinity, Frank's story cautions us against impulses to alienate and degrade one another and beckons us to articulate an attitude of reconciliation in our own time and circumstances. Such an attitude might be amplified and extended in countless expressions, each short of perfection but in that way also more feasible for anyone who would heed the call of conscience.

War is fundamentally dehumanizing. It is an expression of lost empathy for, extreme alienation from, and utter debasement of one variety of people by another. It perfects and perpetuates the very process of dehumanization that enables and sanctions it. It is in this sense a degraded and degrading discourse of diminished human relations. There are many interrelated causes of war—economic, ideological, geopolitical, psychological, accidental, and more—that pressure us to dehumanize and violate one another.[101] Yet, recognizing the common dignity of human beings inhibits the killing reflex and cultivates a compensatory attitude of nonviolence. Indeed, such recognition, when we can achieve it, undermines the traditional premise—from Saint Augustine forward—on which Christians distinguish between just and unjust wars, the premise that the enemy is a barbarian or some other version of a subhuman, decivilized being. The image of the enemy's savagery has been the trope basic to American justifications of war, from declaring independence to fighting terrorism and everything in between.[102] It is the standard rhetorical move that rationalizes war and quiets, but never fully settles, a troubled conscience.

Humanity is so interconnected that degrading one group brings harm to another. In the case of the Civil War, black America was so thoroughly dehumanized by white America that the nation split asunder, whites alienated from one another in a death struggle over an issue of black property. Blacks were reduced to a condition of property that either would be liberated or enslaved. They were not recognized as fellow human beings to be embraced as equals and empowered as citizens. If whites North and South had been able to perceive the face of humanity where they saw only a debased and lesser being, they would have been inclined more by conscience to work peacefully together toward the rehabilitation of black America rather than to demonize and kill one another while continuing to repress blacks.

Rationalizing our failure to articulate better human relations dooms us to repeating the mistakes of the past and keeps us from learning what we might do differently to resist the pull of war. Acknowledging the mistakes of the past, identifying what went wrong, and listening to expressions of conscience where they can be found helps us to appreciate what kind of ordinary actions on our part can make a small but positive difference. Perhaps more than anything, apprehending our ghostly conscience teaches us a quotidian way of making peace that we citizens cannot evade without shirking our responsibility to one another or succumbing to hypocrisy. Our only honest option is to insist on speaking as humanely as possible of others at home and abroad. The most immediate way to make headway toward peace under circumstances of continuous political struggle is to dissent from caricatures that dehumanize. That, at least, is a decent starting point for developing a public opinion more inclined toward reconciliation and increasingly skeptical of violence.

There are, of course, other rhetorical and institutional factors to consider in developing a democratic practice of peacemaking, but they cannot operate absent a collective articulation of conscience. Thus, when we turn to reflect on additional requirements of peace, we cannot afford to forget the practical lesson extracted from an ordinary soldier's tale of ambivalence about sheer enemies. It is a conflicted story that invites us to ponder rather than celebrate the call to arms. It teaches us to question the jaded image of savagery that legitimizes a persistent presumption of war—that justifies the killing fields regardless of the devastation inflicted and the problems compounded by the fighting, and despite the unwelcome consequences that exceed any realistic expectation of benefit or reward. It is a precious glimpse of what might be achieved by modest acts of empathy, a revealing glimpse of the presence of conscience—its location and its operation. Here within our reach is the first and basic locus of dissent from war, which is to *resist dehumanizing anyone.*

NOTES

1. W. Norwood Brigance, "The Backwash of War," *Vital Speeches of the Day,* December 1, 1945, 105–08.

2. Leo Tolstoy, *The Kingdom of God is Within You,* trans. Constance Garnett (1893; New York: Barnes and Noble Books, 2005), 335.

3. Tolstoy, *Kingdom,* 95, 89–90, 98, 105, 113, 118. Tolstoy quotes C. D. Bartlett on p. 113 regarding the notion of playing at Christianity so long as we ignore the problem of war.

4. Tolstoy, *Kingdom,* 234, 193, 228.

5. Tolstoy, *Kingdom,* 100–01.

6. By point of departure, I mean much the same as Michel de Certeau, the French Jesuit and cultural scholar who also taught literature at the University of California, San Diego, when he wrote: "A place is needed if there is going to be a departure, and departure is possible only if it has a site from which it can proceed: the two elements—the *place* and the *departure*—are correlative in that a distancing allows the closure of the initial localization to be perceived, but nonetheless this closure makes possible all new investigation." Quoted in Luce Giard, "Introduction: How Tomorrow is Already Being Born," in Michel de Certeau, *The Capture of Speech and Other Political Writings,* ed. Luce Giard and trans. Tom Conley (Minneapolis: University of Minnesota Press, 1997), xiv. Emphasis in the original. For an elaboration of this point as it applies directly to one's Christian standing, see Michel de Certeau, "The Weakness of Believing: From the Body to Writing, a Christian Transit," in *The Certeau Reader,* ed. Graham Ward (Oxford: Blackwell, 2000), 214–43.

7. These commonly reported figures will not be surprising to most readers. They can be conveniently accessed online at sources such as the following: Samuel Huntington, "Are We a Nation 'Under God'?" *American Enterprise* (July–August 2004); "What We Think, What We Believe, How We Act," reprinted from the New Watch column of the *Christian Research Journal* 25:1 (2002) by the Christian Research Institute; Adelle M. Banks, "Gallup Poll: American Link Faith to Everyday Life," March 5, 2003, *The Foundation for Religious Freedom*; and "Religious Identification in the U.S.," *Religious Tolerance.org.*

8. James Hillman, *The Terrible Love of War* (New York: The Penguin Press, 2004), 190, 216.

9. Jim Lobe, "Conservative Christians Biggest Backers of Iraq War," published October 10, 2002 by Inter Press Service and reprinted in *Common Dreams News Center.*

10. John 13.34–35 (NRSV).

11. Matthew 5.9 (NRSV).

12. Ira Chernus, *American Nonviolence: The History of an Idea* (Maryknoll, New York: Orbis Books, 2004), 1.

13. Franklin Strain, *A Family Matter: A Brief Story of the Strain Family and Incidents in the Life of Frank Strain* (Phillipsburg, Kansas: Privately Printed, Undated), 3. This 23-page pamphlet was "written by request of the family" sometime after Frank's retirement from an active life in and around Phillipsburg, Kansas. I hold a copy of the original pamphlet. The portion of it dedicated to his account of his service in the Civil War is excerpted in Appendix B of Mary Strain Cowgill, *Franklin and Susan C. Strain, Kansas Pioneers: Four Centuries of their Roots and Branches* (Baltimore, Maryland: Gateway Press, Inc., 1999), 307–18.

14. Cowgill, *Franklin and Susan Strain*, 4.

15. The preceding information about Robert and Elouisa Strain is drawn from Cowgill, *Franklin and Susan Strain*, 214, 216–17, 226–27, 232–36, 242–43. The house Robert designed and built still stands. When I visited it in 2004, it was the home of a couple that knew it had been the Strain homestead and part of the Underground Railroad.

16. Cowgill, *Franklin and Susan Strain*, 235.

17. James H. Madison, *The Indiana Way: A State History* (Bloomington: Indiana University Press, 1986), 107.

18. Howard H. Peckham, *Indiana: A History* (Urbana: University of Illinois Press, 1978), 65–66.

19. Gregory P. Lampe, *Frederick Douglass: Freedom's Voice, 1818–1845* (East Lansing: Michigan State University Press, 1998), 186–89, 301.

20. Levi Coffin, *Reminiscences of Levi Coffin, The Reputed President of the Underground Railroad*, 2nd ed. (Cincinnati, Ohio: Robert Clarke and Company, 1880), 108–09.

21. Coffin, *Reminiscences*, 116.

22. Melvin E. Strain, *Family Life in These United States, 1750–1964: A Story of the John Strain and Kindred Families* (Wichita, Kansas: Privately Published, No Date), 4; Franklin Strain, *Family Matter*, 4. Melvin Strain was the great grandson of John Strain.

23. Frank Strain, *Family Matter*, 22–23.

24. This statistical summary, provided by The United States Civil War Center, was compiled by Al Nofi: "Statistical Summary [of] America's Major Wars," available online.

25. Peckham, *Indiana*, 71, 75.

26. Chernus, *American Nonviolence*, 43–44.

27. John Louis Lucaites, "The Irony of 'Equality' in Black Abolitionist Discourse: The Case of Frederick Douglass's 'What to the Slave is the Fourth of July?'" in *Rhetoric and Political Culture in Nineteenth-Century America*, ed. Thomas W. Benson (East Lansing: Michigan State University Press, 1997), 52.

28. Chernus, *American Nonviolence*, 41.

29. Alix Kates Shulman, ed., *Red Emma Speaks: An Emma Goldman Reader*, 3rd ed. (Atlantic Highland, New Jersey: Humanities Press, 1996), 253–54; quoted in Chernus, *American Nonviolence*, 67.

30. Frederick Douglass, *My Bondage and My Freedom* (1855; New York: Barnes and Noble Classics, 2005), 293–94.

31. Frederick Douglass, "No Union with Slaveholders: An Address Delivered in Boston, Massachusetts: 28 May 1844," reprinted in Lampe, *Frederick Douglass*, 315–16. Emphasis in original.

32. *Declaration of Sentiments of the American Anti-Slavery Society, Adopted at the Formation of said Society, in Philadelphia, on the 14th day of December, 1833* (New York: American Anti-Slavery Society/William S. Door, 1844), cited in Stephen John Hartnett, *Democratic Dissent and the Cultural Fictions of Antebellum America* (Urbana: University of Illinois Press, 2002), 13.

33. Frederick Douglass, *Narrative of the Life of Frederick Douglass, An American Slave* (1845; New York: Barnes and Noble Classics, 2003), 100. Emphasis in the original.

34. Douglass, *Narrative*, 26; Robert O'Meally, "Introduction," in Douglass, *Narrative*, xiv, xxxii.

35. Douglass, *Bondage*, 131–32.

36. Lucaites, "Irony," 55.

37. Brent Hayes Edwards, "Introduction," in Douglass, *Bondage*, xxvii, xxxviii.

38. Douglass, *Bondage*, 48.

39. Edwards, "Introduction," xli.

40. Frederick Douglass, "The Anti-Slavery Movement," extract from a lecture delivered in 1855, in Douglass, *Bondage*, 356, 358–62, 364.

41. Kenneth Burke, *A Grammar of Motives* (1945: Berkeley: University of California Press, 1969), 514.

42. Stephen John Hartnett, *Democratic Dissent*, 16.

43. Hartnett, *Democratic Dissent*, 58–59, 65–66.

44. Ernest G. Bormann, *The Force of Fantasy: Restoring the American Dream* (Carbondale: Southern Illinois University Press, 1985), 179.

45. Bormann, *Fantasy*, 180.

46. Bormann, *Fantasy*, 194.

47. David Zarefsky, *Lincoln, Douglas, and Slavery: In the Crucible of Public Debate* (Chicago: University of Chicago Press, 1990), 183; see 166–97. Douglas quoted in Zarefsky, *Lincoln, Douglas, and Slavery*, 170

48. Merle Curti, *Peace or War: The American Struggle, 1636–1936* (New York: W.W. Norton and Company, 1936), 47.

49. James Darsey, *The Prophetic Tradition and Radical Rhetoric in America* (New York: New York University Press, 1997), 75, 82.

50. J. Jeffery Auer, "Preface," in *Antislavery and Disunion, 1858–1861: Studies in the Rhetoric of Compromise and Conflict*, ed. J. Jeffery Auer (New York: Harper and Row, 1963), v.

51. Charles Chatfield, "Introduction," in *Peace Movements in America*, ed. Charles Chatfield (New York: Schocken Books, 1973), xi. "Here and there," Chatfield notes, "individuals kept the faith of absolute pacifism, but organized work abated" (xi). The Universal Peace Union, organized in 1866, renewed the quest for nonviolence and against hatred under the long-term leadership of Alfred Love (xi–x).

52. Charles DeBenedetti, *The Peace Reform in American History* (Bloomington: Indiana University Press, 1980), 33.

53. DeBenedetti, *Peace Reform*, 33, 58.

54. "Document 2.1, Noah Worcester: The Custom of War, from *A Solemn Review of the Custom of War, 1815*," in *Peace/Mir: An Anthology of Historic Alternatives to War*, ed. Charles Chatfield and Ruzanna Ilukhina (Syracuse, New York: Syracuse University Press, 1994), 89.

55. Curti, *Peace or War*, 36.

56. Garrison quoted in DeBenedetti, *Peace Reform*, 41. Emphasis in the original.

57. Stearns quoted in DeBenedetti, *Peace Reform*, 55.

58. Cowgill, *Franklin and Susan Strain*, 213.

59. Frank Strain, *Family Matter*, 21.

60. For an insightful discussion of the cultural work of the Woman's Relief Corps and the Grand Army of the Republic, see Cecilia Elizabeth O'Leary, *To Die For: The Paradox of American Patriotism* (Princeton, New Jersey: Princeton University Press, 1999).

61. The details of Frank's and Kate's lives after the war are drawn from Frank Strain, *Family Matter*, 21–22, and Cowgill, *Franklin and Susan Strain*, 236, 243–44, 251–60.

62. Frank Strain, *Family Matter*, 4.

63. Frank Strain, *Family Matter*, 5.

64. Frank Strain, *Family Matter*, 6.

65. Shelby Foote, *The Civil War, A Narrative: Fort Sumter to Perryville* (New York: Vintage Books, 1958), 89–99; J. G. Randall and David Donald, *The Civil War and Reconstruction*, 2nd ed. (Boston: D. C. Heath and Company, 1961), 37–72.

66. Frank Strain, *Family Matter*, 6–7.

67. Frank Strain, *Family Matter*, 7–8.

68. Frank Strain, *Family Matter*, 9.

69. Quoted in Foote, *Sumter*, 293; for a detailed description of the battle, see Foote, *Civil War*, 280–93.

70. Frank Strain, *Family Matter*, 10.

71. Randall and Johnson, *Civil War*, 406, 409, 411–12.

72. Frank Strain, *Family Matter*, 12.

73. Shelby Foote, *The Civil War, A Narrative: Fredericksburg to Meridian* (New York: Vantage Books, 1963), 385–86.

74. Frank Strain, *Family Matter*, 12–13.

75. Foote, *Fredericksburg to Meridian*, 613.

76. Foote, *Fredericksburg*, 613–14.

77. Frank Strain, *Family Matter*, 13–14.

78. Frank Strain, *Family Matter*, 14.

79. Frank Strain, *Family Matter*, 14–15.

80. Frank Strain, *Family Matter*, 16.

81. Frank Strain, *Family Matter*, 17–18.

82. Frank Strain, *Family Matter*, 19.

83. Frank Strain, *Family Matter*, 19.

84. Frank Strain, *Family Matter*, 20.

85. Frank Strain, *Family Matter*, 1.

86. Garry Wills, *Lincoln at Gettysburg: The Words that Remade America* (New York: Simon and Schuster, 1992), 20.

87. Wills, *Lincoln*, 162, 148–49; see also 37, 62, 88.

88. Wills, *Lincoln*, 88; see also 62, 78, 89, 177, 179–80, 183–85, 187.

89. Wills, *Lincoln*, 175.

90. Wills, *Lincoln*, 179–81.

91. Seward delivered his regrettable speech on October 25, 1858 in Rochester, New York. As Robert T. Oliver observes, it "stirred a fever of excitement across the nation and provided one of the key phrases in the history of our country." Robert T. Oliver, "William H. Seward on the 'Irrepressible Conflict,' October 25, 1858," in *Antislavery and Disunion*, 29.

92. Wills, *Lincoln*, 91–92, quotes this segment of Lincoln's speech in Charleston, Illinois, when he was campaigning against Douglas for a seat in the U.S. Senate.

93. On Lincoln's attitude toward emancipation, see Wills, *Lincoln*, 137–47.

94. O'Leary, *To Die For*, 134–35; see also 29.

95. Randall and Donald, 568–69.

96. O'Leary, *To Die For*, 55; see also 50, 53, 103, 107–08, 133, 134–35, 148, 192–93, 195.

97. O'Leary, *To Die For*, 203.

98. O'Leary, *To Die For*, 111, 116, 137, 142–43, 146.

99. Chatfield and Ilukhina, *Peace/Mir*, 87.

100. Frank Strain, *Family Matter*, 22–23.

101. For a useful discussion of the complexity of the determinants of war, see Seyom Brown, *The Causes and Prevention of War* (New York: St. Martin's Press, 1987).

102. Robert L. Ivie, *Democracy and America's War on Terror* (Tuscaloosa: University of Alabama Press, 2005), 30–31, 46; also Robert L. Ivie, "Images of Savagery in American Justifications for War," *Communication Monographs* 47 (1980): 279–94.

3

A Question of Redemption

We are in a conflict between good and evil, and America will call evil by its name.

George W. Bush[1]

At the root of all war is fear.

It is not only our hatred of others that is dangerous but also and above all our hatred of ourselves.

We drive ourselves mad with our preoccupation [with evil] and in the end there is no outlet left but violence.

Hell is where no one has anything in common with anybody else except the fact that they all hate one another and cannot get away from one another and from themselves.

Thomas Merton[2]

If the basic lesson of war—that is, the first locus of dissent from war—is to resist dehumanizing anyone, including one's enemy, the primary locus of the call to arms is to vilify the nation's adversaries. Rendering the enemy evil and savage is the war propagandist's way of identifying a threat of sufficient magnitude to justify the carnage of armed hostilities. It is a way of escalating debatable and secular questions of collective security ultimately into a compelling and sacred concern of redeeming the nation's soul. The political sacrament of redemption by vilification and victimization purifies the deadly sacrifice, precludes any reconciliation with adversaries, and perpetuates a state of perceived insecurity that motivates continued warfare.

The US invasion of Iraq, although troubled by controversy from the outset and bedeviled by unpopularity during a prolonged period of brutal occupation, is indicative of an enduring sense of national insecurity fixed in a prevailing culture of war. The desire for security runs deeper than considerations of military and civilian casualties, concerns over depleting the public treasury, issues of irrelevance to an ostensible war on terror, evidence of lies told by public officials, questions regarding violations of international law, worries about curtailments of civil liberties, or unease over alienating world opinion and provoking more terrorism. These are all grave matters for thoughtful appraisal and serious reconsideration of preventative war as a prophylactic for terror.

55

Yet, the mounting costs, the swelling criticisms, and the lessons that might be learned, as a long war runs its jaded course from dauntless beginning to disconcerting end, mostly aggravate a gnawing sense of collective anxiety instead of engendering wise counsel against the perils of hate, arrogance, and militarism. The nation's shriveled worldview remains rigid—unyielding to experience, closed to reflection, and habituated to an anxious impudence regardless of (and even because of) any and all recalcitrance encountered along the way to fulfilling its self-proclaimed destiny. Impervious to countervailing experiences and disconfirming consequences, US war culture feeds on self-induced and overinflated expressions of national peril that transcend particular situations and transform specific exigencies into ritualized pretexts for violence.

What, we may venture to ask, are the habits of discourse that jangle the nation's belligerent nerves? Through what rhetorical formulation is American insecurity amplified beyond the limits of critical thinking and thus placed outside the reach of pragmatic political critique, and what is the possibility of rehabilitating such a troublesome construct in search of a peacebuilding alternative? That is, how might a violent and ongoing quest for national redemption through victimization, which reflects and perpetuates a culture of terror and war, develop into a pursuit of collective redemption through reconciliation? This is the central question that any dissent from war must answer if it aims to further a culture of peace.

APPREHENSIONS OF EVIL SAVAGERY

The stubborn issue of national peril and security, which always confounds and often preempts or subsumes and subordinates any immediate aspiration of peace, is itself provoked by a rhetoric of evil savagery, which envelops all considerations of safety and well-being in a swirl of fear and hatred. The ubiquitous sign of savagery converts the secular quest for security into a prayer for redemption and a sacrament of atonement through the sacrifice of "a scapegoat in whom we have invested all the evil of the world."[3] Safety becomes a matter of salvation in the rhetorical universe that is US war culture. No other equation casts such a deadly spell on an embattled people confronted by a deeply troubled world.

America's lethal preoccupation with evil precedes the tragedy of 9/11 and George W. Bush as presidential spokesman-in-chief. Certainly, Ronald Reagan was eager to proclaim the Soviet Union an evil empire, and the dark memory of Adolph Hitler is forever fixed in the national imaginary as the personification of archetypal evil. The image of evildoers evoked by President Bush after the fall of Manhattan's twin towers resonated not only with rightwing Christian fundamentalism but also with mainstream political culture rooted in the secular religion of mission and American exceptionalism. A deep and wide channel of patriotic piety was cut over centuries of spilling blood in the name of the Almighty and the Redeemer. As a matter of history and of living custom, a Manichaean divide between good and evil—civilization and savagery—came to separate righteous patriots from enemies of the state. Thus, Bush's belabored and hardly deft, but certainly compelling, rhetoric of evildoers merely channeled already strong cultural predispositions to render any enemy palpably savage and essentially diabolical.[4]

The image of the enemy as a savage is much older than the United States but nevertheless intimately linked to the nation's identity and defense. The incomprehensible babble on the other side of the defensive walls surrounding democratic Athens was the threatening sound of the barbarian in ancient Greece. The Roman Empire fought barbarians, too, those hordes of crude Germanic tribes who were the mortal enemies of culture and the negation of civilization. Indeed, throughout the ages, the archetype of the barbarian enemy has served to legitimize war and empire—Athenian, Roman, British, Japanese, Soviet, American, and other such exercises in dominion and domination—whether in defense of democracy or, in the case of Nazi Germany, to justify the rule of the Third Reich and the extermination of Jews.[5]

After winning its independence from Great Britain and then taking a continent (or all of the northern part of the continent that it wanted) by decimating indigenous peoples and invading its neighbor to the south, America next set out to Christianize and civilize the savages of the Philippines. The mission of an exceptional nation now reached beyond manifest destiny to encompass the rest of the world. The beginning of an American century soon was dramatically announced with the atomic bang over Hiroshima and then extended through four decades of bipolarizing Cold War. Today, American empire has become a unifying project in globalizing the world economy and democratizing all nations in order to secure a universal peace and thus the end of history.[6]

Pronouncing itself the world's one essential nation, post-Soviet-era America shortly thereafter declared war, again in the name of civilization and under the banner of fighting for a democratic peace. Monarchy, fascism, and communism had been conquered, each in its turn, in order to make the world free of barbarous tyranny and thus safe for democracy. After the tragedy of 9/11, however, terrorism was proclaimed the new savagery threatening America's empire of democracy. Civilization would be rescued this time from an international conspiracy of militant Islamist extremists who wished to destroy freedom and to instill the tyranny of an evil theocracy. The discourse of savagery versus civilization—deeply rooted in the American political lexicon, its culture, and collective psyche—was easily pressed into service to rally the nation, quell dissent, and inoculate the public against any alternative perspective.[7]

Indeed, the ruling trope of evil savagery is indigenous to American war rhetoric. The United States was born in a new world that European settlers cleared tribe by tribe, nation after nation, of its native savages. British rule was overthrown in the colonies with a call to arms against English monsters that thirsted for American blood.[8] The War of 1812, considered by many to be America's second war of independence, was justified in Congress and to the nation by increasingly intense cries of British diabolism and by resort to decivilizing metaphors of force that conveyed the image of a people being trampled, trodden, and bullied by an enemy portrayed variously as a beast of prey, common criminal, ruthless murderer, haughty pirate, and crazed tyrant.[9] Similarly, the expansionist war declared against Mexico in 1846 was portrayed by a partisan President Polk, with a disciplined majority party in Congress, as a reluctant act of national defense in response to an irrational and evil Mexican aggressor, a belligerent foe that was easily inflamed and was as unstable as a violent storm.[10] President McKinley's justification of commercial imperialism five decades later, as the US was about to enter the twentieth century, was that America, by God's grace, would "uplift and civilize and Christianize" those who "were unfit for self-government." These savages of the Philippines would be the beneficiaries of America's "noble generosity" and "Christian sympathy and charity."[11]

The savagery of war itself, as well as the rationalization of slaughter, was marked particularly in the modern age by the trope of the machine. War became "the mechanical human beast," adding yet another metaphor to the heritage of "discursive support for military conflict" and to the language of "common sense" that legitimized its destructive reality. A "delirium of technology" transformed the machine into a deranged and destructive monster. The national character of the evil enemy was contained in this image of mechanized madness, with expansionist Germany representing the perfectly oiled war machine, its individual citizens reduced to uniform mechanical cogs. The beast became a rampaging automaton, an anarchic machine, an abdication of individuality and human responsibility, an uncontrolled threat to democracy that transformed the savage lust of the masses into the modern menace of civilization. Indeed, the "broad distinction between 'civilization' and 'barbarism'" that was so central to the language of World War I rested heavily on the pejorative characterization of Germany as a perversion of progress, a degeneracy of "overrapid development," a mechanical mentality that elevated atrocity to "a science and a technology." The modern primitive had become a "murdering machine," stripping its victims of their humanity, reducing them to raw material—its mechanical ethos making war into an inevitability, into "the Frankenstein's monster of the twentieth century."[12] Thus, Woodrow Wilson called for a war against Germany to make the world safe for democracy, with "civilization itself seeming to be in the balance" because the menace of "auto-cratic governments backed by organized force" had taken control "of the will of their people."[13]

The very militarization of America led next, under this technological shadow of war, into a second world conflagration. Franklin Roosevelt, as Michael Sherry observes, "did not merely perceive the importance of technol-ogy in modern warfare, he seized on it as fitting the nation's strengths and he deepened the American impulse to achieve global power through technologi-cal supremacy." Such was his "ideological construction" of national security. Europe's war-mad barbarians were the product of a technological determin-ism that assaulted "the foundations of civilization" and required the United States to adopt "strategies of annihilation" as the measure of its own security against the danger of new technologies and ideologies.[14] Thus, FDR called on America, as the world's arsenal of democracy, to lead a crusade against the evil Axis of fascist power, a diabolical enemy that feigned peaceful intentions even as it ravaged the world in the most shocking, brutal, and criminal acts of treachery. The Japanese aggression at Pearl Harbor on Sunday, December 7, 1941 was a cause for indignation, an affront to a God-fearing nation, and an exigency for defending civilization by vanquishing rampant evil. Roosevelt's war rhetoric condensed belligerency to its pure form for a technological age and enemy.[15]

War itself became, even for Americans who prided themselves on their indi-vidualism, a "mindless, anonymous" expression of "machine-age dehuman-ization and cosmic purposelessness." The bombing of cities was portrayed "as a process of surgical destruction administered by cool-headed Americans." This was an image of war rendered benign and a sense of power inflated into a technological arrogance that culminated in the atomic extermination of Japanese treachery and savagery.[16] The mindset of Hiroshima among the American public was "a collective form of psychic numbing" that carried for-ward into a regime of Cold War nuclearism. The atomic bomb, President Truman announced in triumph, was repayment for Pearl Harbor manyfold, a "harnessing of the basic power of the universe," for which Americans were rightly "grateful to Providence" that decent people possessed and with which they had righteously vanquished an evil enemy.[17]

The World War II American image of the enemy, although technologized into a numbing abstraction, retained its more visceral vehicles as well, includ-ing the raw emotions of racism captured in visions of atrocity. The Japanese were portrayed as subhuman, as apes and vermin, a primitive, childish, and mentally deficient threat to civilization that required extermination by a nation of reluctant warriors.[18] FDR merged the concrete with the abstract image of a barbaric enemy, blaming the "mechanized might" of the Axis powers for their "brutality" and condemning their "order of concentration camps" as a "savage and brutal" force "seeking to subjugate the world." America's "unscrupulous" enemies were condemned as "crafty" gangsters and powerful "bandits" harboring the morals of a predator, a lowly beast of prey.[19]

The rhetorical texture of the savage and evil enemy evolved in its time without losing touch with its history. Decades of Cold War, punctuated by hot encounters with communism in Vietnam and elsewhere, constituted a culture of fear premised on a multidimensional image of the enemy's evil savagery. Truman conjured a powerful Cold War spell by representing the Soviet savage in terms of fire, flood, and red fever to convey the threatening image of a communist epidemic and impending disaster for the free world. A metaphor of disease framed the inception, and infused the presentation and reception, of the Truman Doctrine speech at this formative moment, constituting a heroic expression of democratic America questing after total security by eradicating the communist infestation.[20]

Next in the line of presidential succession, Dwight Eisenhower cultivated an image of himself as the aspiring peacemaker, even as he affirmed Truman's vision of national vulnerability by totalizing the communist threat. The world's captive nations, Eisenhower insisted, had been "terrorized into a uniform, submissive mass." This "Red cancer" must "feed on new conquests—or wither." America could never rest until "the tidal mud of aggressive Communism receded." Civilization was imperiled by savagery—portrayed as primal, primitive, barbaric, monstrous, diseased, and brutal—with its insatiable lust for conquest. A voice of perpetual peril, speaking calmly and reassuringly behind a mask of peace, coaxed the nation down a path of nuclear deterrence, based on an insane logic of mutual assured destruction, and in search of a false security.[21] Elites as well as the public had become invested emotionally and intellectually in a visceral image of the enemy that provoked deeply repressed nuclear nightmares. "Just as empire did not look imperial to most Americans," Sherry observes, "the militarized state did not look militaristic."[22]

It is difficult to see something that is everywhere. War was becoming just that, a pervasive condition of American political culture, a habit of thought embedded in a manner of speaking, the cultural motif of an embattled nation. This militarized worldview extended to declaring metaphorical wars on poverty, drugs, disease, and crime, engaging in "trade wars" with foreign competitors, and fighting "culture wars" with one another. The agonizing task of Americanizing a lingering French colonial war in Vietnam drove the discourse of savagery ever more deeply into the national psyche in order to rationalize world hegemony as a defense of civilization. America would expel the godless Communist barbarian from the sacred garden of democracy in order to cultivate perpetual peace.

After the debacle of Vietnam drove the US into a temporary state of malaise, from which it quickly recovered following the Soviet invasion of Afghanistan, Ronald Reagan ascended to the presidential helm to reinvigorate the discourse of evil savagery versus pious civilization. Calling on Americans to defeat communism's "evil empire," Reagan drew upon a reified cluster of decivilizing terms that were the conventional idiom of an increasingly militarized culture of fear. This idiom of fear ranged from terms of natural menace, such as fire, flood, disease, tides, and storms, to the language of dangerous animals and predators, such as snakes and wolves, and progressed to figures of primitives and brutes, mindless machines, criminals, lunatics, ideologues and fanatics, culminating in references to the satanic and profane enemies of God. Each decivilizing term contributed to the depiction of an enemy by caricature, conveying an overall image of evil savagery by indirection and figuration. Thus, Reagan's Soviets were portrayed vividly in the language of light and shadow as a dark force, a gray monument to repression, a gale of intimidation, and an untamed adversary preying upon its neighbors, barbarously assaulting the human spirit, clubbing its victims into submission, bullying the world to submit to its unhappy fate, employing the machines of war to commit murderous crimes against humanity, cheating, lying, driven by psychotic fears and unbounded ambitions, immune to practical reason, and even denying the existence of God in the fanatical machinations of a menacing evil. This was the totalitarian onslaught against civilized ideas and the defenders of liberty of which Reagan spoke with such urgency in an idiom that expressed and shaped the common sense of a nation.[23]

The figurative nature of these tropes and their centrality to the recurrent narrative of war, necessitated each time by yet another savage and evil enemy, went unremarked and unrecognized for the most part. They were the thoroughly literalized elements of a long-told and often-repeated tale of American exceptionalism and mission. They were the plain-spoken and matter-of-fact words of a no-nonsense Harry Truman embedded in a language of rationality and a voice of reason handed down from the early republic. They were facts made certain and obvious within a narrow framework of interpretation.[24] Moreover, they were reified in their sheer opposition to everything that made sense about freedom, liberty, and democracy—the very terms of identity adopted by a peace-loving people to legitimize their warlike habits. Freedom, in the American political lexicon, was feminized and fragile, a risky experiment in a dangerous world, and always vulnerable to the rape of the demonic and demented barbarian if left unprotected.[25]

Thus, the discourse of diabolical savagery informed but transcended the long era of Cold War and the eventual demise of the Soviet Union, further draining the nation's political imagination of any alternative to militarizing its domestic culture and foreign relations, and thereby constituting a people forever in search of new enemies and more wars to fight. The line between metaphorical and real war, Sherry maintains, had been blurred by now beyond recognition.[26] War had become the master trope of all things domestic and foreign and all issues economic and social. Everyone and everything was potentially an enemy. Saddam Hussein offered an irresistible temptation, not once but twice, in a simulated return engagement with evil under the symbolic shadow of Hitler and Stalin. But it was the sheer savagery of terrorism that put America back on its steady rhetorical course of defending civilization with all its surplus military might. Whether or not there was a demonstrable connection between Saddam and the terror of 9/11, there would be an open-ended "war" of terror on the axis of evil, a different kind of war that acknowledged no political or territorial bounds within or between states.

Thus, the reified trope of savage evildoers depicted the post-Cold War era as a perpetual condition of ubiquitous violence, a Hobbesian state of nature and vicious warfare on civilians that would seem to indicate the fall of civilization or signal the arrival of a modern leviathan of imperial peace.[27] Conditions seemed ripe for realizing Kant's vision of perpetual peace among a world federation of republican states, now called liberal democracies (or just democracies in shorthand).[28] This so-called "democratic peace" was a peace that would be achieved through the agency of, in Kant's words, "a powerful and enlightened people" who had formed a republic that could serve as "a focal point for a federal association among other nations that will join it in order to guarantee a state of peace among nations that is in accord with the idea of the right of nations, and through several associations of this sort such a federation can extend further and further."[29] This vision of peace was akin to a biblical prophesy of world salvation by virtue of an American ascendancy; a chosen people would lead the world toward the final realization of an empire of democracy where evil was forever vanquished.[30]

Terrorism as the legitimizing sign of American empire—the reigning symbol of demonic savagery opposed to a civilizing empire of democratic peace—grew out of a long tradition of war discourse. "Combating terrorism," Jeffrey Simon observes, "would now be a top priority for the United States." Like fighting the evil of the communist empire, combating terrorism was portrayed by Ronald Reagan and his presidential heirs in strict black-and-white terms and as a matter of war.[31]

RIGHTEOUS WAR OF REDEMPTION

George W. Bush, the rhetorical and ideological son of Reagan, filled in the blanks after 9/11, drawing on the time-honored language of demonic savagery to justify an open-ended war on international terrorism. As a medium of American war culture, Bush spoke to a Christian America as a Christian man crusading for a righteous cause by declaring an unrestricted war on evil. Much like the Puritan rhetoric of covenant renewal, as Denise Bostdorff explains, Bush's rhetoric of evil depicted Americans as a special people watched over by God, represented 9/11 as a test of national character, and advanced a righteous call to arms with a renewed sense of mission, making clear "that the evil character of an external enemy was to blame, [and] thereby absolving US citizens and the US government of any guilt."[32] Bush's post-9/11 rhetorical world was "governed by theistic essence," John Murphy observes. It was filled with heroes and villains, divided by good and evil, and given purpose by God's will, which was to be fulfilled by people of faith and character opposed to evil.[33] "Bush's providential certainty" and "prophetic dualism," David Noon concludes, supplanted critical thought with the righteous pursuit of "moral security" against evildoers.[34]

There was nothing secret or sophisticated about President Bush's basic rhetorical strategy. In "The Gospel According to George," *Newsweek* reporters Howard Fineman and Tamara Lipper observed that the President believed his faith would "guide" him in Iraq. In biblical cadences, he preached time and again a simple secular sermon to the receptive public that he would lead by faith and vision into holy battle in order to bestow freedom on an otherwise evil world.[35] Billy Graham's son, the Reverend Franklin Graham, affirmed the President by declaring Islam an "evil and wicked religion," while the administration's deputy undersecretary of defense for intelligence and war-fighting support, Lieutenant General William Boykin, professed that America was fighting Satan in Islamic Iraq on behalf of the real, Christian God.[36]

Indeed, the integrating theme of Bush's post-9/11 presidency was that any and all means were justified by holy ends in what amounted to a redemptive war on Islamic terrorism. One must wonder, along with Wes Avram, if the President's early reference to fighting a "crusade" was "an accidental gaffe at all."[37] Despite his later differentiation between terrorism and Islam as a faith based on peace, love, compassion, and tolerance, the President and his supporters persisted in the use of "coded Christian language," as Stephen Chapman argues, to invest the nation and its war with "*messianic* meaning."[38] America was endowed by the Creator with moral ideals, Bush proclaimed, and, "as the greatest force for good in history," was now fighting in Afghanistan and Iraq "to the glory of God."[39] America had entered a "Third Awakening" of religious devotion in its war on global terrorism, the President suggested on the day after the fifth anniversary of 9/11, a spiritual awakening to this stark "confrontation between good and evil."[40]

Michael Hyde insists we should remain skeptical and not acquiesce uncritically "in the land of democracy" to a heroic rhetorical stance that is so rotten with moral perfection.[41] Such an obsession with evil, Thomas Merton observes, such a preoccupation with punishing and exorcising it, is motivated by guilt that makes a people see their own evil in others and unable or unwilling to see it in themselves. Distrust of the other is a deflection of distrust of self. To minimize our own faults and avoid "shouldering responsibility for it," we exaggerate the faults of others. The enemy as scapegoat becomes the receptacle of all collective self-hatred, malice, and evil and thus "the cause of every wrong."[42] Such is the fear that Merton sees at the root of all war, which is a fear of damnation. Rhetorical practices that invoke the sign of evil cannot be banished entirely if for no other reason than, as John Campbell attests, evil is a trope deeply embedded in political culture.[43] Yet, James Aune rightly insists that the incantation of radical evil "is inherently corrosive of democratic politics" and, we might add, overly conducive to war.[44]

The rhetoric of religion informs political culture in just this way, as we have learned so well from Kenneth Burke. The ritual of "victimage" in secular affairs, he explains, is the "logological" equivalent of a theology of redemption through sacrifice and thus an "insight into the nature of language itself as a motive": Order leads to guilt which involves redemption through victimage. Thus, the cult of the kill pervades the language of sociopolitical relations, especially in the secular religion of a chosen people whose covenant with God implies the possibility of a fall from grace and entails, as a condition of redemption, some punishment or payment for wrongdoing. This logic of atonement allows redemption through vicarious sacrifice, which is the principle of mortification by transference or scapegoat that "is particularly crucial to conditions of empire," Burke insists, when purification is achieved by venting conflict through a sacrificial vessel. In this sense, "the role of the sacrificial principle...[is] 'logologically inseparable' from the idea of dominion," and thus, the scapegoat principle is "basic to the pattern of governance."[45]

As a basic principle of symbolic action, then, the idea of "redemptive sacrifice" follows from the repression of conscience-laden guilt and in response to the condition of sociopolitical order. Victimage, or "redemption by vicarious atonement," is "intrinsic in the idea of guilt" just as "guilt is intrinsic to the idea of a covenant." Moreover, terms for order, fall, and redemption imply one another in a cyclical logic that can be reversed so that, for example, "the terms in which we conceive of redemption can help shape the terms in which we conceive of the guilt that is to be redeemed." Accordingly, the name by which we designate a "curative victim" to cleanse our guilt not only reflects but also reflects back upon our sense of order and a concomitant fear of damnation.[46] The more fearful and sinister the image we paint of our enemy, the greater our corresponding sensation of endangerment and the stronger our need for redemption through vicarious sacrifice. It may well be that simply naming the enemy is, per se, sufficient cause for war, or as James Hillman writes, "Once the enemy is imagined, one is already in a state of war."[47]

The cycle of interconnected and symbolically charged terms makes it strictly impossible to sort out a simple linear progression from empirical threat or actual necessity to measured or just response and thus unrealistic to assert that issues of national security can be calculated and assessed objectively. At least in the case of US war culture, the articulation of good and evil suffuses and distorts every reason, every calculation, every perception, and every dimension of motivation for choosing armed hostility over diplomacy or peace. The face of evil colonizes judgment, neutralizes arguments for pragmatic alternatives, and diminishes deference to ethical constraints. Even Michael Ignatieff, arguing for a "lesser evil approach," notes that just creating a space for "thinking about the terrorist problem means escaping the trap of moral perfectionism on the one hand and false necessity on the other."[48]

No such space for critical thinking about the challenge of terrorism or the invasion of Iraq was indicated by the President's categorical rhetoric of evil barbarism. From the beginning of Bush's war on terrorism, every consideration domestic and foreign became a matter of national security as viewed through the lens of an evil threat. In his first State of the Union address after 9/11, the President established a totalizing focus on evil that not only aimed to eliminate "terrorist parasites" who endangered civilization worldwide and to prevent an "axis of evil" in Iraq, Iran, and North Korea from threatening the world with weapons of mass destruction; it also endeavored to provide for comprehensive "homeland security," extending to increased research on bioterrorism, enhanced airport and border surveillance, better intelligence gathering by federal agents (and by "the eyes and ears of alert citizens"), and augmented police and firefighter training—all of which would improve public health, combat illegal drugs, and provide safer neighborhoods. Additionally, the President spoke of "health security," "retirement security," and a plan for "economic security" that would promote jobs, education, energy production, trade, and tax relief for the beleaguered nation. All of this added security would demonstrate to America's enemies that they "were as wrong as they are evil."[49]

Similarly, eight months later on September 20, 2002, Bush justified a doctrine of preventative war against the enemies of civilization and "the evil designs of tyrants," a doctrine that opened its third section with a quotation from the President speaking at the National Cathedral in Washington, DC three days after 9/11 and vowing to "rid the world of evil." On October 7, just over two weeks after announcing his strategy of "preemption," Bush applied the new doctrine directly to Saddam Hussein's regime in Iraq, saying that the US must presume the worst and must acknowledge "an urgent duty to prevent the worst from occurring."[50] Then, in his January 28, 2003 State of the Union address, the President insisted that America could not afford to trust in the "sanity and restraint" of, nor could it wait any longer to disarm, a "dictator" with access to "the world's most dangerous weapons" and a history of using them to kill and disfigure thousands of his own people. This was an "evil" man who tortured children and adults alike with electric shocks, hot irons, acid drips, power drills, amputations, and rape. "If this is not evil," Bush proclaimed, "then evil has no meaning."[51]

The image of Satan was Bush's rhetorical trump card in a case for preventative war that lacked strong evidence of a substantial or imminent threat to the US or to world security.[52] Fear and the perception of peril were themselves entailments of the sign of evil. The very soul of the nation was at risk of damnation and in need of redemption. A war to bring down the demonic Saddam Hussein was a war of atonement and salvation—a war, Christian Spielvogel argues, that Bush represented throughout his 2004 reelection campaign "as a test of national moral resolve in the face of evil."[53] Bush's born-again articulation of Christian moral orthodoxy and its daunting expectation of strict fidelity with God's law required the nation to go it alone in Iraq as an affirmation of faith. Thus, the moral logic of this pivotal symbolic form perpetuated war, as Spielvogel explains, because "fear of evildoers provides the impetus to sustain one's moral fortitude."[54] America's public faith ultimately was justified by a special covenant with God, and it was to God that the nation ultimately was accountable in what the President called, deep into the bloody occupation of Iraq, this "time of testing."[55] "Fellow citizens," he cautioned in the State of the Union address on January 31, 2006, "we've been called to leadership in a period of consequence."[56]

Any tragic appetite for war, Burke concludes, that is concocted by means of symbolic action—especially a longing for redemption by substitution, proxy, projection, sacrifice, or just plain passing the buck—can never be fully cured; it can only be processed and diverted, and then only by virtue of the comic corrective, that is, "in the spirit of solemn comedy."[57] Merton shares not only Burke's sense of the scapegoat but also his commitment to humility as the sole plausible answer to "universal self-hate." Humility, along with compassion and identification, Merton allows, are required to understand and face with equanimity the inevitability of failure and error. The "one truth that would help us begin to solve our ethical and political problems" is "that we are all more or less wrong, that we are all at fault, all limited and obstructed by our mixed motives, our self-deception, our greed, our self-righteousness and our tendency to aggressivity and hypocrisy." We must somehow come to accept, then, that everyone is a "mixture of good and evil." Only by such humility can humanity hope to "exorcise the fear which is at the root of all war."[58]

Such an abiding fear of damnation (that is, of a chosen people falling from grace) and incessant desire for redemption (that is, for reassurance of their exceptional status) is both a product of and motive for a tragic rhetoric of evil (in the logological sense of symbols cross-pollinating and mutually implicating one another). This potent mixture of fear and desire may very well evoke that elevated, menacing, and awesome aesthetic of the sublime, which Hillman refers to as a "terrible love of war."[59] War brings the Christian God to life, Hillman argues, in a conjunction of beauty and savagery, love and rage, life and death, desire, horror, attraction, and fear that is especially compelling in contemporary America.[60]

Yet, Hillman also maintains that the sublimity of this war sickness contains the key to its cure. The clues he draws from an ancient Greek "Hymn to Ares" include the power of imagination, the requirement of courage and contestation, a regard for justice, a capacity for tolerance and restraint, and, perhaps most perceptive of all, a recognition that wars begin "in the shrill voice" of political leaders, the press, and members of the public "who perceive 'enemies' and push for a fight." Perceiving an enemy produces a threat. The constructive equivalent and fitting answer to war's sublimity—the rhetorical response to war from within the symbolic universe of war itself—is a regimen of "aesthetic passion," an "aesthetic intensity" that overcomes "peacetime monotony" and turns war inside out by countering inhuman with humane relations of identification and difference, thus providing a reason to pause and reflect, a way of taming haste, of motivating restraint, of cultivating prudence.[61]

GUILTY TRANSGRESSIONS

If enemy-making is the sublime expression of a chosen people's tragic fear of damnation and their collective desire for redemption by vicarious sacrifice, then humble peacemaking might properly begin by reflecting courageously and intensely on the image of their terrifying antagonist so that they might discover therein the sins for which they seek atonement. What guilty transgressions are sublimated in the depiction of an abominable adversary? What does a menacing caricature reveal to those in whose own image it is formed, and how might such a revelation help to deter deadly, fear-inducing rituals of vilification? Is war a heroic nation's only path to salvation?

These questions cast a somewhat different light on Burke's notion of the comic corrective as it operates within tragic frames of acceptance, a notion typically understood as his antidote to the perverse enmity and factional strife that is an "almost tyrannous ubiquity in human relations."[62] The tragic line of development, which is endemic to the drama of political relations, readily leads to victimization unless a comic corrective is introduced strategically to complicate the matters at hand.[63] Caricature is the rhetorical instrument for converting necessarily mistaken adversaries whose wrongs (even terrible wrongs) are a function of foolishness and stupidity into diabolical and thus menacing enemies who perpetrate vicious crimes against humanity. The more charitable, reasonable, and realistic attitude is realized, Burke argues, in a "comic" widening of the operative frame of reference, a widening of perspective that broadens and matures "sectarian thought" in secular relations.[64] Thus, as William Rueckert notes, Burke's terms for the comic corrective stress the need for a broader, well-rounded frame—a terminology that amplifies rather than diminishes or reduces, that acknowledges irony, respects ambiguity and ambivalence, and deploys metaphor to peek around conceptual corners and to relax rigid boundaries.[65]

This way of understanding Burke's comic corrective focuses attention primarily on rounding out narrow, inordinately threatening caricatures of adversaries. Perhaps there is something also to be gained by contemplating the caricature itself, that is, by examining it closely for the traits and transgressions it discloses about those who seek absolution indirectly through vicarious sacrifice. What unwanted qualities and guilty lapses of their own would they cast off symbolically in the image of a wicked foe? From this perspective, we might be able to penetrate more deeply into the dark recesses of a nation's guilty conscience and gauge more realistically the intensity of its impetus for redemption. We may even discover additional correctives and alternatives to rituals of vilification and victimization by confronting sublimated motives from this reverse angle.

In this regard and for this purpose, George Bush's unmitigated rhetoric of good versus evil is a perfect specimen on which to experiment. He spoke extensively, explicitly, and consistently about evildoers to justify total war on terrorism, and he did so in a polarizing manner of speaking that completely vindicated the US, cleansing it of any and all guilt by equating the enemy with utter depravity. A rhetorical discharge this uninhibited would seem to function as a welcome purge and great relief to the body politic. What it suggests about the state of the nation's soul, however, may be somewhat less satisfying. Indeed, Douglas Kellner has argued forcefully that Bush administration rhetoric, "coded as an apocalyptic battle between good and evil," mirrors Al Qaeda rhetoric all too closely and thus that the president's "war on terrorism" would be more accurately called a "Terror War" that uses "aggressive military force and terror as the privileged vehicles of constructing a US hegemony in the current world (dis)order."[66]

The following sampler of Presidential portraits of evildoers should suffice for the purpose at hand:

January 23, 2007

The evil that inspired and rejoiced in 9/11 is still at work in the world. And so long as that's the case, America is still a nation at war.... These past five years have given us a much clearer view of the nature of this enemy... possessed by hatred and commanded by a harsh and narrow ideology.... They preach with threats, instruct with bullets and bombs, and promise paradise for the murder of the innocent.[67]

January 10, 2007

The terrorists and insurgents in Iraq are without conscience, and they will make the year ahead bloody and violent.... Our cause in Iraq is noble and necessary.[68]

September 11, 2006

Since the horror of 9/11, we've learned a great deal about the enemy. We have learned that they are evil and kill without mercy, but not without purpose.... We have learned that their goal is to build a radical Islamic empire where women are prisoners in their homes, men are beaten for missing prayer meetings, and terrorists have a safe haven to plan and launch attacks on America and other civilized nations. The war against this enemy is more than a military conflict. It is the decisive ideological struggle of the 21st century and the calling of our generation.[69]

January 31, 2006

By allowing radical Islam to work its will—by leaving an assaulted world to fend for itself—we would signal to all that we no longer believe in our own ideal, or even in our own courage.

When they murder children at a school in Besian, or blow up commuters in London, or behead a bound captive, the terrorists hope these horrors will break our will, allowing the violent to inherit the Earth.[70]

January 23, 2006

These [Saddamists] are the thugs that kind of control the country. They loved power; they don't want to give it up.

Their vision of the world is dark and dim. They have got desires to spread a totalitarian empire.... They have no heart, no conscience. They kill innocent men, women and children to achieve their objective.[71]

January 18, 2005

After the swift fall of Baghdad, we found mass graves filled by a dictator.

The terrorists will continue to have the coward's power to plant roadside bombs and recruit suicide bombers.

These terrorists view the world as a giant battlefield.

Pulling out of Iraq before our work is done... would cause tyrants in the Middle East to laugh at our failed resolve.[72]

May 28, 2005

We see the nature of the enemy in terrorists who exploded car bombs along a busy shopping street in Baghdad, including outside a mosque. We see the nature of the enemy in terrorists who sent a suicide bomber to a teaching hospital in Mosul. We see the nature of the enemy in terrorists who behead civilian hostages and broadcast their atrocities for the world to see. These are savage acts of violence.

The terrorists believe that free societies are essentially corrupt and decadent, and with a few hard blows they can force us to retreat.

The terrorists who attacked us . . . murder in the name of a totalitarian ideology that hates freedom, rejects tolerance, and despises all dissent. Their aim is to remake the Middle East in their own grim image of tyranny and oppression.[73]

June 2, 2004

Like other totalitarian movements, the terrorists seek to impose a grim vision in which dissent is crushed and every man and woman must think and live in colorless conformity.

In all these threats we hear the echoes of other enemies of other times: that same swagger and demented logic of the fanatic.

Our country must never allow mass murderers to gain hold of weapons of mass destruction.[74]

May 24, 2004

The terrorists' only influence is violence and their only agenda is death.

We've also seen images of a young American facing decapitation. This vile display shows a contempt for all the rules of warfare and all the bounds of civilized behavior.[75]

May 15, 2004

This week, our nation was sickened by the murder of an American civilian, Nicholas Berg. The savage execution of this innocent man reminds us of the true nature of our terrorist enemy, and of the stakes in this struggle. The terrorists rejoice in the killing of the innocent, and have promised similar violence against Americans, against all free peoples, and against any Muslims who reject their ideology of murder. Their barbarism cannot be appeased, and their hatred cannot be satisfied.[76]

April 13, 2004

Now is the time and Iraq is the place in which the enemies of the civilized world are testing the will of the civilized world. We must not waiver.

We have seen the same ideology of murder . . . in the merciless horror inflicted upon thousands of innocent men and women and children on Sept. 11, 2001.

All [of these acts] are the work of a fanatical political ideology. The servants of this ideology seek tyranny in the Middle East and beyond. They seek the death of Jews and Christians and every Muslim who desires peace over theocratic terror.... And they seek weapons of mass destruction to blackmail and murder on a massive scale.[77]

January 20, 2004

Having broken the Baathist regime, we face a remnant of violent Saddam supporters. Men who ran away from our troops in battle are now dispersed and attack from the shadows.... The once all-powerful ruler of Iraq was found in a hole, and now sits in a prison cell.... We are dealing with these thugs in Iraq, just as surely as we dealt with Saddam Hussein's evil regime.[78]

September 23, 2003

Saddam Hussein's monuments have been removed and not only his statues. The true monuments to his rule and his character—the torture chambers and the rape rooms and the prison cells for innocent children—are closed. And as we discover the killing fields and mass graves of Iraq, the true scale of Saddam's cruelty is being revealed.[79]

March 19, 2003

America faces an enemy who has no regard for conventions of war or rules of morality. Saddam Hussein has placed Iraqi troops and equipment in civilian areas, attempted to use innocent men, women and children as shields for his own military, a final atrocity against his people.[80]

The composite sketch of a terrorist threat to American security that can be drawn from these typical and very familiar presidential statements—so familiar, in fact, that they hardly call attention to themselves or draw comment any longer—is a crude and blunt profile of evil incarnate. Terrorists are wicked Islamists, religious fundamentalists and fanatics, who commit unspeakable acts of mass murder and mayhem against innocent civilians, including women and children; they are power-hungry thugs with a dark and dim vision of the world; they would remake the Middle East in their own grim image; lacking heart or conscience, these Saddamists rape, torture, and murder their hapless victims; they are shadowy cowards who hide in caves and holes, plant bombs along roadsides, explode car bombs on busy city streets and dispatch suicide bombers to hospitals, behead civilians, and routinely commit other savage acts of violence; they are totalitarian ideologues who, with contempt for morality and the rules of civilized warfare, perpetrate theocratic terror and intolerance; they hate freedom and crush dissent; their only agenda is death by violence, including the ruin of civilization with weapons of mass destruction; they are testing the will of America on the theory that freedom is too corrupt and decadent, too lacking in courage and resolve to defend itself or stand its ground after absorbing a few hard blows; the whole world is their battleground; their barbarism cannot be appeased or their hatred assuaged.

This stilted representation of a purely diabolical foe is easy to articulate and even reassuring to hear when a self-proclaimed exceptional nation is anxious over its world standing and apprehensive about its special virtue. "May God... continue to bless our country," the President prayed at the end of a speech on global terrorism.[81] If this ritualized invocation of a scapegoat is the expression of a guilty conscience and a misdirected cry for redemption within a Manichaean rhetorical universe of good and evil—if it is a projection of the nation's dark shadow, an unburdening of repressed self-hatred of the kind and in the manner to which Merton refers—what self-deceit does such a caricature of the enemy threaten to expose and how difficult might it be to look directly at, let alone reflect honestly upon, so raw and self-mortifying an image of malfeasance? Indeed, how difficult might it be to acknowledge and openly confront such a revelation of transgressions when America considers itself "the most Christian of nations," as Hillman has observed, and is historically, psychologically, and culturally Christian to the core, despite a felicitous mix of religious faiths and committed unbelievers?[82] Self-mortification is not the default response to guilty feelings under any circumstances, Burke attests, but especially not a circumstance like this, that is, like empire.[83]

What would Americans see if they could reflect the crude image they have made of their enemy directly back upon themselves? They would see a rogue nation of power-hungry religious fanatics attempting to remake the Middle East in their own image by perpetrating immoral acts of violence on a massive scale with criminal disregard for the rules of civilized warfare; a war machine that levels whole cities, condones torture, and hides behind superior technologies of death; decadent imperialists with an insatiable appetite for power, who detest freedom and dissent, and who hold the world hostage to their vast store of weapons of mass destruction, which they have deployed unconscionably against defenseless civilian populations; insecure ideologues determined to impose their rule and their way of life on the world; in short, wickedness personified.

Ridiculous? Absurd? Unthinkable? Weren't the abuses of Abu Ghraib an aberration, the work of a small number of low-level military miscreants—certainly not a reflection on the real America? "All Americans know that the actions of a few do not reflect the true character of the United States Armed Forces," insisted the President.[84] "Our enemies are brutal";[85] it was "the terrorists who beheaded an American on camera," not the US.[86] Yet, just drawing from headlines in the *Washington Post*, one wonders if these notorious photographs of US soldiers torturing Iraqi prisoners actually conjured up "A Wretched New Picture of America" that exposed "A System of Abuse" and exhibited "A Corrupted Culture" within an unsettling image of "George Bush as Saddam Hussein."[87] Would the selective prosecution of these few soldiers be enough to assuage the nation's guilty conscience and to fend off other criticisms of the nation's decent motives in this terrible war on terror? Should the public believe the President, or doth he protest too much? When the President said:

[T]here is no clash of civilizations.[88] This is not a clash of religions.[89]

We have no desire to dominate, no ambitions of empire.[90] They want to establish a totalitarian Islamic empire that stretches from Spain to Indonesia.[91]

The United States has no right, no desire, and no intention to impose our form of government on anyone else. . . . They seek to impose and expand an empire of oppression.[92]

And nobody in the Middle East should think that when the President talks about liberty and democracy, he's saying you got to look just like America, or act like America. Nobody is saying that.[93]

No act of America explains the terrorist violence.[94]

We're not going to lose our will to these thugs and murderers.[95]

The government does not listen to domestic phone calls without court approval. We are not trolling through the personal lives of millions of innocent Americans.[96]

[T]his government does not torture . . . [W]e adhere to the international convention of torture, whether it be here at home or abroad.[97]

Did he actually mean the opposite, that is, that Americans were proving their questionable mettle by perpetrating an imperial crusade abroad that imposes their civilization on the Middle East, even by murderous means such as torture that spawn more terrorism and even at the cost of their own liberties at home? Are the critics right when they accuse the US of imperialism, militarism, and fascism?[98]

Of course, nothing so starkly evil could be true of America, or at least believed by Americans, for those are the very charges that the satanic Osama Bin Laden and his world cadre of malevolent terrorists leveled against the US. Yet, this alter ego, this doppelganger in the guise of the Taliban, Saddam Hussein, Al Qaeda, Abu Musab al-Zarqawi, Muqtada al-Sadr, Hamas, or any number of other devilish personas, is the medium through which Americans would pay perpetual penance to justify themselves as an exceptional people in the eyes of God. Surely such symbolic subterfuge confuses and compounds whatever material threat to the nation actually exists, and vexes every peace-building effort. If the perception of national peril is largely a function of this ritualized making of evil enemies and seeking after vicarious redemption, then alternative ways of managing collective guilt should commend themselves to a seemingly demoralized and frustrated people.

RITUALIZING A LESSER EVIL

Most notably, this rhetorical cycling between the extremes of good and evil alienates the nation from an aesthetic of humility and, thus, from identifying with a common humanity. It produces what Merton reckons is hell: a condition in which Americans bond with one another only out of hate for others from whom they cannot escape, hate for others that is an expression of collective self-hate.[99] Americans can neither isolate themselves from the world nor fully master and tame it. Perhaps, then, the only choice that is both pragmatic and moral is to make enemies less evil and thereby reduce the blinding drive for redemption—the desperate fear of damnation—to a lower level of intensity so that the nation's collective capacity for tolerance, restraint, and genuine problem solving might improve.

The troublesome terms in the deadly cycle of guilt and redemption always implicate each other (logologically, as Burke would say) so that modifying one alters the rest more or less, directly or indirectly. Theoretically, that is, a comic corrective to an overly heroic and dangerously inflated national self-image would diminish any symbolic need for an equally overdrawn image of terrorist enemies. However, from a more linear perspective (or what Burke calls a "rectilinear" or narrative unfolding compared to a cyclical ordering of terms), critiquing arrogance would not appear to be the most likely place to start because, as David Campbell has argued so convincingly, national security (and insecurity) is not strictly an objective condition but instead is written in the language of an alien, dirty, sick, subversive, or similarly threatening representation of the enemy.[100] By this logic, one is more likely to begin productively by rewriting with aesthetic intensity the overdrawn and fear-inducing image of an utterly evil enemy than by moving directly to an appeal for humility.

Even the most determined and aesthetically intense efforts at rewriting the image of the enemy, one suspects, are unlikely to transform all evil into simple error, that is, to meet the Burkean standard of charitably attributing even the worst wrongs of an adversary to sheer stupidity and mistakenness rather than to viciousness and wickedness. The maximum opportunity for critically reworking political relations is more a matter of reforming, discounting, and modifying motives than of debunking them, Burke would agree, since he "considers human life as a project in 'composition'" an ongoing revision, an exercise in enhancing consciousness in order to cope better and more peacefully with the tragic "heroics of war."[101] We must do the best we can by advancing at an oblique angle instead of attempting a full about-face.

Michael Ignatieff's exploration of the political ethics of prudence in an age of terror seeks the path of "the lesser evil," that is, a balancing of competing necessities to defend the beleaguered state during a terrorist emergency and to preserve democratic rights and values throughout the process. The US war on terror failed to meet even this standard on a number of counts, he argues, including "its detention of nearly five thousand aliens, mostly single males of Muslim and Arab origin, after September 11."[102] Ignatieff's lesser-evil perspective is anti-perfectionist but committed to democratic accountability, which requires setting and monitoring standards for a war on terror by open adversarial review.[103] Thus, he would reinvigorate open forums of adversarial justification at home and abroad in the press, the courts, and legislatures in order to guard against such practices as torture and motives of revenge.[104] His sense of democratic values includes the notion that even enemies "deserve to be treated like human beings" and that liberal democracy privileges persuasion over coercion.[105]

The courage, however, to rely more heavily on persuasion and less on violence must be composed somehow, not just presumed and summoned. Toward this end, rhetoric persuades to peacemaking over warfare—assuages fear and self-loathing rather than overstating danger and projecting hate—most immediately by rehumanizing the hellish caricature of the enemy and thereby addressing by indirection the haunting question of redemption. The scapegoat is more than a barometer of angst; it is also a cultural device or ritual for articulating the nation's identity and defining its relation to the world.

As Allen Carter notes, language that is ethically surcharged and that tends toward moral perfectionism creates, by Burke's account, language-induced guilt that motivates a corresponding quest for self-justification through a surrogate victim.[106] There is a kind of symbolic cathexis and conflation of the scapegoat with the motivating source of fear, loathing, and guilt, much like the hated and feared Jew was confused with the "plague as a divine punishment" and became the first cause of the epidemic of Black Death. Thus, "to avert the plague," the guilt must be identified with and punished through the scapegoat. Mere mention of plague could therefore be cause for massacring Jews, who were thought, according to Guillaume de Machaut, to be "false, treacherous and contemptible swine," the "wicked and disloyal who hated good and loved everything evil," and thus who "poisoned" the rivers and caused the "mortal calamity" of Christians. Because of such "treachery," then, "every Jew was destroyed, some hanged, others burned; some were drowned, others beheaded with an ax or sword."[107] They were, in short, the evil terrorists of their medieval times, just as the present war on terror is a kind of legalized witch hunt "stimulated by the extremes of public opinion."[108]

American identity, as Campbell has underscored, intertwines secularism and spirituality with a special intensity so that throughout its history "an array of individuals, groups, beliefs, and behaviors have occupied the position of the Antichrist."[109] The representation of the Antichrist is deeply implicated in the expression of national identity and articulation of danger. Thus, Campbell observed at the beginning of the post-Cold War era that "the crisis of international politics is now very much a crisis of representation."[110] Specifically, we should add, it has become largely a crisis of representations of evil that foster deadly urges for redemption. This is the discourse of danger that fixes who we Americans are and tells us whom and what we most fear; it tells us even that guilty fear of damnation is the appropriate response to the situation at hand.

Rewriting this discourse of guilty fear is, then, a project of addressing sublimated self-hate in the guise of a terrorist scapegoat. It is a dramatistic exercise of a protagonist state re-imagining its global antagonists so that its resources and means are better calibrated to its democratic ethos and aims. While it is implausible to imagine a risk-free global environment, Campbell is right to suggest that the future of US foreign policy depends on whether America can reorient itself to an "inherently plural world" in a way that is not motivated by an overwhelming "desire to contain, master, and normalize" adversaries through violence.[111]

The aesthetics of reorientation most appropriate to this task of defanging the scapegoat—that is, the symbolic resource beyond Burke's indispensable emphasis on tropes of substitution, bridging and merging, transcendence, transformation, and the like—may well be René Girard's stress on repetition through ritual.[112] Rehumanizing rituals can cast a potent symbolic spell to counteract the ubiquitous gravitational pull of vilifying rituals. Certainly, in Eric Rothenbuhler's understanding of communication and social process, ritual is "necessary to humane living together."[113]

Rituals are dramatic performances that can draw upon verbal and nonverbal symbols jointly to enact and thereby reconstruct political motives with sufficient ambiguity to accommodate a diversity of otherwise conflicted identities and interpretations. As a recurring practice, each ritualized reiteration combines a familiar, reassuring sense of convention with a creative, experimental, individuating facet of improvisation, which together can facilitate over time both a renewal and modification of national identity, political attitude, and governing worldview. It is at once a conserving and reforming social practice. Appropriately, Roy Rappaport identifies ritual as "*the* basic social act."[114]

Thus, ritual is potentially a therapeutic exercise for generating and sustaining—through ongoing, inspired, and imaginative repetitions of dramatic enactments—a desire to reform demonizing and polarizing caricatures. Just as ritualized enemy-making caricatures dehumanize and demonize by stripping identities of their complexity, so that "the concept of good versus evil dominates people's understanding of identity" and the "good people believe they must kill or contain the bad people to rid the world of evil," Lisa Schirch insists that rehumanizing rituals can assist in the task of reconfirming the complexity and restoring the flexibility of identities essential to peacebuilding and contrary to warmongering inclinations.[115] Like rituals of vilification (which Girard argues is a way for a group to articulate its own identity in contrast to its "other"[116]), rehumanizing rituals invoke the sacred forces of the universe during disorienting and desperate secular times of peril and conflict, but to imagine relations of coexistence rather than of domination and destruction. They are, in short, vital to the dramatization of life over death.[117]

As motivational (that is, motive-inducing) dramatic performances, the ongoing and routine practices for ritually alleviating total terror and habitually easing unmitigated hostility toward adversaries involves all manner of theatrical considerations from staging to scripting. As Schirch observes, artful performances that employ the full range of "symbols, metaphors, myths, and symbolic actions remind participants of who they are, where they are, and what they are doing in a peacebuilding process."[118] The dramaturgy of performed myth enables a polity to preserve itself by transforming its most detrimental attitudes without destroying its venerable political culture.[119]

To appreciate myth's regenerating narrative and experience the impact of metaphor's reframing and web-spinning faculties—to translate potentially transforming words into actual performatives, making them true by speaking of them as true—requires their enactment in ritual. In Karen Armstrong's words, "Reading a myth without the transforming ritual that goes with it is as incomplete an experience as simply reading the lyrics of an opera without the music."[120] The performance of ritual, as ritual theorists understand and William Doty readily recounts, can place what *ought to be* in tension with what *currently is*; that is, as the acting-out of myth channels emotion, guides thought, restructures self-image, and organizes society, ritual's expressive and creative performance can operate on worldviews to identify social cleavages and elicit action that helps to restore more equitable relations.[121]

At the moment, however, ritual's performative power is severely underutilized for peacebuilding purposes and largely diverted to war-valorizing applications. War is ritualistically memorialized in any number of public media from carefully staged and regularly televised presidential encomiums to towering statues in central parks of capital cities throughout the land, patriotic performances in baseball stadiums, fulsome coffee-table books, glamorizing Hollywood films, stirring popular music, and awe-inspiring displays of weaponry in war museums.[122] The motive for war is staged and rehearsed daily in multitudinous forms and ubiquitous settings. War itself, Bell observes, is ritualized by rules that channel, shape, and legitimize violence, thus helping "to make the activities of killing appear civilized, humane, and expressive of important values such as loyalty, freedom or definitions of manhood" and "to rationalize war as in the service of the greater glory of God."[123]

Moreover, the most common rituals of war dissenters are mimetic, contrarian warlike practices of reverse recrimination, attributing the darkest motives imaginable (mirror images of the enemy's purported savagery and diabolism) to ugly Americans and especially to their diabolical leaders. One might hope, at least, for a more "comic" critique of the President as a "Burkean devil."[124] Criticism advanced from a more oblique angle than this stark turnaround of good and evil is less likely to aggravate stubborn (even desperate) crusades of national vindication and vicarious sacrifice. The more constructive approach would be for peacebuilding, anti-war dissenters to abandon demonizing rituals of dehumanization altogether and to develop instead lesser-evil and more prudential (perhaps even providential) rituals of rehumanization.

· In this way, motivated by ritualized expressions of shared humanity with its enemies, society might begin to transform the scapegoat mechanism into a positive salvation device, one that redirects the will, the resources, and the ingrained sensibility of an exceptional people into a productive (instead of destructive) pursuit of redemption by tending more to the alienating causes of terrorism and less to the killing of evil terrorists. The management of categorical guilt, not its elimination, is the issue at hand. Is it necessarily the case that making an enemy into a scapegoat is merely a way of affirming national identity and a product of the nation's guilty conscience, an overly convenient means of temporarily relieving alienation and dissipating excessive self-hate, or is it also possible that a scapegoat's representation as evil incarnate provokes as much as it alleviates the deadly urge for deliverance from damnation? If the relationship is truly reciprocal or bidirectional, as would seem to be the case, wouldn't it follow that radical enemy-making is in some measure tantamount to crafting an overstated and misdirected assessment of the danger at hand? Wouldn't prudence therefore dictate some lessening of attributions of evil for the sake of enhancing public policymaking? All of this, I submit, argues for taking seriously ritual's capacity for inducing political motives and grasping specifically its largely untapped potential for composing realistic, peacebuilding dramatis personae.

Taking seriously ritual's peacebuilding potential amounts to acknowledging that it is not a simple or magical solution to war and yet invoking it as a potent medium for articulating the community's ideals of identification and reconciliation—giving those ideals presence and immediacy in framing, channeling, and managing conflict and corresponding feelings of fear and enmity.[125] This is being realistic in the sense of adopting the lesser-evil approach of moderating and redirecting the communal desire for deliverance, rather than aiming to eliminate or bypass it. From an oblique angle (rather than a stark reversal), it is a realistic approach of publicly rehearsing and recontextualizing culturally embedded values, of steadily appropriating society's basic assumptions, firm beliefs, strong traditions, and condensed symbols to the purpose of reforming prevailing relations of hostility.[126] It is realistic in that it is regularly occurring social action—a recurring, marked, dramatic, participatory, and public event or practice, not primarily a passive shadowing or just an isolated moment of private contemplation—that is based on pre-existing, customary, and credible cultural constructions. Thus, drawing on Pierre Bourdieu's theory of human practice and cultural action, Bell observes that rituals and ritualizing are "strategic practices for transgressing and reshuffling cultural categories in order to meet the needs of real situations."[127]

RITES OF REMEMBRANCE

The need for peacebuilding—toward a positive peace strategically activated and maintained in regular and widespread rites of reconciliation that work to rehumanize the nation's adversaries and thereby moderate its nervous desire and excessive appetite for redemption—is a palpable cause for reallocating cultural capital in the all-too-real situation of chronic warfare. Peace is a real need in an actual condition of war that requires a practical way of activating a shared sensibility—a *sensus communis*—on behalf of a sane and prudent and more confident response to an embattled world. War is an expression of fear, misgiving, and self-doubt, not a manifestation of self-assurance or demonstration of confidence in the nation's cause, promise, and prospect. It is an expression of fear to which we have become habituated and that has been ritualized into an obsession, a compulsion to kill demons in exchange for the illusory safety of national salvation. War is a product of enculturation no less than a material response to a situation, an attitude or predisposition that shapes reality as much as it reflects a history of antagonism and strife, but a culture of war is not the sum total of political culture nor does it exhaust the full potential of political relations with adversaries or supplant the possibility of cultivating a culture of peace by practicing and proliferating rehumanizing rites of reconciliation.

Storytelling is a case in point, a cultural form that is "essential to collective memory" and can be made to serve as a ritualizing practice for rehumanizing adversaries and enemies on both sides of the divide.[128] In a war culture, disembodied abstractions and stone monuments supplant living memories of loved ones sacrificed for country and cause. Just as our enemies are dehumanized by rendering them into devils, our own soldiers are dehumanized by reducing them to depersonalized heroes. Flesh and blood is turned into inanimate statues of stone in cemeteries, on the squares of county court houses, and down the great avenue of war memorials in state capitals. We can find their names written on rows of flag-draped headstones in military cemeteries each Memorial Day and feel them engraved on solemn marble walls when we visit the nation's capital city. The stories of their lives—their lives both lived and lost— are secreted under the shadows of grand monuments to fallen heroes.

These abstract, stone-cold stories of war heroics written in lifeless concrete to ritualize continuous sacrifices on altars of condensed symbols as powerful as freedom, God, and country are everywhere. We encounter them near and far, in our daily lives, on vacation trips, and during holiday celebrations, and thus we are routinely reminded of (and reinvested in) the moral of their patriotic tale of human sacrifice.

When I visit Riverside Cemetery in my hometown, my eye is immediately drawn to Soldiers Memorial Pavilion perched prominently atop a grassy knoll. Designed by American sculptor E. M. (Earnest Moore "Dick") Viquesney (himself a veteran of the Spanish-American War) and dedicated to "the memory of those who served their country during the wars of the United States," the pavilion faces north, its backside protected by two Civil War cannons pointed south and its front guarded by a Revolutionary War cannon. The cannon dedicated "to soldiers of the Revolution" (seven of whom are specifically named) was donated in 1903 by the Spencer Chapter of the Daughters of the American Revolution. The two cannons "used in the war for the Union" were dedicated on July 4, 1905 "to the Union soldiers of Owen County." The grassy grounds, shaded by ageless trees and surrounded by historic headstones, are decorated by two mounted vases, each holding an array of red, white, and blue carnations, a soaring eagle affixed to the top of a memorial flag pole that is dedicated to all military veterans from Owen County, and six rows of cement benches facing, on either side of a center aisle, a podium that stands just inside the raised open front of the covered pavilion.[129] Matching cannon balls are mounted left and right of the steps leading up to the pavilion, which was constructed of rock and cement "through the efforts of the Women's Relief Corps of Spencer, Indiana in 1939" and restored in 1985 jointly by American Legion Post 285 and Veterans of Foreign Wars Post 1405. Hundreds of metal stars are mounted inside and outside the pavilion, each engraved with the name of a soldier or sailor, whether it was E. B. Marshall (Civil War), J. Cross (Spanish-American War), or C. E. Dunn (World War). Visitors to this war memorial stand on hallowed ground in the presence of heroes during special observances each Memorial Day and Veteran's Day.

When I stop by the city square on any given day to mail a letter at the post office, or twice a year to pay my property taxes at the courthouse, or annually to make merry at the Apple Butter Festival, I cannot help but notice the copper "Spirit of the American Doughboy" statue marking the northwest corner of the courthouse grounds directly below the main flag pole. This icon of World War I, sculpted and copyrighted by Dick Viquesney of Spencer, Indiana, appeared first on the campus of Furman University in Greenville, South Carolina, on June 7, 1921. A total of 140 original Doughboy statues are known to have been erected throughout the United States by 1943.[130] The statue in Spencer, funded by public contributions, was dedicated on May 29, 1927, with Viquesney present for the ceremony. A plaque on the front of the statue gratefully recognizes "the patriotic service rendered by the men and women of Owen County during the World War, 1917–1918," and a tablet on the back lists the eighteen names of "men of Owen County who gave their lives" in the war to end all wars.

Viquesney carefully crafted the lifelike Doughboy, seven feet tall standing on a six-foot pedestal of molded concrete, to honor Americans who served in the World War. This was not the image of a mighty military machine, but instead it personified the individual spirit of determination to preserve freedom. Thus, the Doughboy is erect and striding forward (rather than charging through) "no man's land." He is portrayed in perfect detail: his fresh uniform an impeccable fit, his flat steel helmet, backpack, gas mask pouch, bedroll, ammunition belt, canteen, mess kit, first aid kit, leggings, and boots realistic to the eye, his eyes and mouth both fully open, his left hand holding a Springfield rifle with bayonet attached, and his right hand poised to throw a grenade as he treads through stumps and barbed wire.

Walking down the west side of the courthouse square, I pass a block-long Owen County War Memorial. Its centerpiece is a mounted marble slab about five feet high and nine feet wide with the words "Lest We Forget" engraved on the street side, under which are listed a column of names of local soldiers lost in World War I, two columns of names for World War II, and a column divided between the losses suffered in the Korean War and the Vietnam War. The names of Civil War dead are engraved in seven columns on the back side of the slab. Three flag poles rise directly above the monument on the courthouse lawn. A wall that is about three feet high, running parallel to the sidewalk and dipping behind the marble slab of honored dead, contains over 1,000 six-inch-square tiles, each with the name of a man or woman from the county who served in the US military, with 50 feet of additional space being prepared for more tiles. One can easily imagine this wall of military honor being extended over time around the other three sides of the courthouse square, even in this sparsely populated county of 20,000 residents.

The courthouse square in neighboring (and much larger) Bloomington, where I drive daily to work at Indiana University, is similarly appointed with war memorials, and the state capital in Indianapolis is renowned for the number and scale of its war monuments in Memorial Plaza Historical District. The District begins with the Soldiers and Sailors Monument, made of gray oolitic limestone from Owen County quarries and located at the center of Monument Circle in the very heart of the city. Monuments extend due north for five blocks along Meridian Street to include the Indiana War Memorial, Veterans' Memorial Plaza, World War II Memorial, and more. These massive physical structures memorialize Civil War, World War, Cold War, the Vietnam War, indeed, all American wars up to and including the ongoing war on terror. The Indiana World War Memorial Building alone is a neoclassical structure that stands 210 feet high and flies a 17-by-30-foot American flag above the Altar of Consecration.

As Barbara Biesecker concludes, our collective memory is rhetorically claimed and represented, usually "as a more or less thinly veiled conservative response to the contemporary crisis of national identity, to our failing sense of what it means to be an American and to do things the so-called American way." These "memory texts" most often naturalize "traditional logics and matrices of privilege," but "it is possible to remember otherwise," she maintains, and in ways that can be "pressed into the service of a very different politics."[131] Commemorative rhetorics need not just be traditional stone-and-concrete rituals of dehumanization and redemptive violence. They might also become strategic rites of humanization and cultural resources for reconciliation.

Reconciliation can be imagined as an emergent norm of rhetorical practice—a tropological turn, a beckoning of storytelling, a matter of becoming, of remaking a collective state of mind and relationships—that invests heavily, as Erik Doxtader argues, in "the works of words" with an aim of turning "violence towards dialogue" and "deliberative controversy" so that we might at least "address the substantive question of what living in peace actually means." As such, he insists, reconciliation is a rhetorical concept with deep democratic import that makes a strong claim on the power of invention.[132] The rhetorical invention of reconciliation confronts and manages the ever-present tension between a comic corrective for peace and "the tragic cry for justice," in John Hatch's words, with "the potential to restructure unproductive debates in ways that remake the social order and the identities of adversaries for the better."[133] Humans, living within language and defined through symbolic action, may hope to reform their identities and relations to one another by means of tragicomic narratives and ritual dramas—that is, by inventing humanizing narratives and rites of reconciliation to remediate demonizing images of adversaries and deifying rituals of redemptive violence.

Like other county seats in Indiana, Terre Haute also features a Soldiers and Sailors Monument and a Vietnam Memorial on the courthouse grounds. Private First Class Jack R. Haley is one of the fallen warriors remembered there. He was killed in Germany on April 7, 1945, only three days after he had written his mother to tell her he was in good health and ready for more fighting. That last letter is one of 62 he wrote to his mother, Lucille Haley—letters now preserved in a shoebox by his two younger cousins, Carol Miller and Lewis Piepenbrink.[134] The story in that shoebox reveals much about a young soldier's humanity—his naivety, family cares, friendships, simple pleasures, trials and tribulations, his faith and love, his discipline, fear, and humor, his budding plans for life after the war—much, indeed, about his down-to-earth humility that necessarily is lost on any stone monument (no matter how large) or copper statue (no matter how detailed or tall), much that is worth telling now to make Jack Haley's blood sacrifice less abstract, more regrettable, and all too ordinary for the purpose of conjuring up extraordinary images of a demonic enemy in a deadly rite of collective atonement. The fact that Private Haley is remembered is important, but how he is remembered is crucial.

When we open the shoebox, the first object we see is a coffin-shaped black box, $6\frac{1}{2}''$ long, $3\frac{1}{2}''$ wide, and $1''$ deep, with scrollwork and the words "Purple Heart" etched in gold. The brilliant medal "for military merit" resting inside the case has the name "Jack R. Haley" engraved on it for posterity—a solemn symbol of the combat wound that killed him, the blood he spilled on the altar of consecration. In the words of Henry L. Stimson, Secretary of War, this posthumously awarded Purple Heart medal was sent to a grieving mother with "deepest personal sympathy" and "as a tangible expression of the country's gratitude" for her son's "gallantry and devotion." Her loss was "beyond man's repairing" and the medal itself was "of slight value," Stimson wrote, but "the message it carries" was evidence of "remembrance," evidence that Private First Class Jack R. Haley would never be forgotten and that "we are all comrades in arms in this battle for our country."[135]

How could a medal symbolizing one young man's sacrifice to a nation's great cause preserve the living memory of a boy his mother lovingly called "Sunny"? "Dearest Sunny," she wrote on February 27, 1945 (her birthday), the "nicest of all" gifts "was your letter which came yesterday wishing me a 'Happy Birthday.'" Her son had shipped out to Europe where he was about to see combat. A mother's deepest worry was expressed indirectly through "Grandma Haley," who had "called tonight and when I told her where you were she wept loudly as only she can do." Family relations were strained by Lucille's impending divorce from Jack's alcoholic father; she guessed that neither Jack's paternal grandmother nor his estranged "Daddy" had any intention of writing to Jack, since neither had requested his APO address. "You haven't lost anything though Sunny cause I have enough love for you to make up for Grandma and a Daddy too and then some left over." At Jack's request, Lucille had made a copy of his official Army photograph to give to a gal named Delores, "a swell girl" who "thinks an awful lot of you." Jack should send home more requests of things he wants and needs. A box of food and candy would be sent to him in a few days. "I am feeling fine Sunny and hope everything is O.K. with you. I am not going to worry because I know you are such a good soldier but write as often as you can darling and you can be sure I am writing every night even if you don't get them very often. Goodnight

Sunny and good luck. Love and kisses, Mother." Lucille's letter, which never found her son, was returned to her on July 26, nearly four months after he had been killed in action. He lay buried by then in Bensheim, Germany until moved sometime later by the Army to "a more suitable site"—"Plot EEE, Row 12, Grave 142 in the United States Military Cemetery St. Avold, located twenty-three miles east of Metz, France."[136]

Two pictures in the shoebox frame young Jack's short life. One is a snapshot of him at age ten standing next to his maternal grandmother, who is holding his six-month-old cousin Lewis on her lap. The other is an official Army portrait of him at age eighteen, published under the headline, "Killed in Germany," with a short obituary in the local newspaper. After graduating from Wiley High School, he had entered the Army in September, shipped to Europe in February, and was reported missing in action on April 7. Eighteen days later, on what would have been his nineteenth birthday, Lucille received a telegram from the War Department telling her that her son was lost forever.

A brown leather breast-pocket wallet with a bullet hole angling through it, the bullet that took Jack's life, sits on the bottom of the shoebox, next to a neat bundle of the letters he wrote to his mother. All but three of the thirteen cards and photos found in his wallet were pierced by the same projectile. Along with his high school library card, he carried snapshots of his pet dog Butch, his first cousins Lewis and Carol standing in front of their mother (Jack's aunt) Helen Piepenbrink, his second cousins Katherine and Raleigh Scott posing in front of a fenced yard, and his mother leaning against that same wooden fence. A small ($1\frac{1}{2}$'' by $1\frac{1}{4}$'') portrait of his mother dated August 22, 1942, was also tucked in his wallet.

Jack's index fingerprint on the back of a membership card affirmed that he was a De Molay brother in good standing in 1944, and a companion card renewed his membership for 1945. Another card certified that he had entered the Boy Scout's "Order of the Arrow" on December 31, 1943, when he was seventeen. From his Indiana driver's license, Social Security card, and Selective Service registration and classification cards, we learn that he was a white male with brown eyes and black hair who stood 5' $9\frac{1}{2}$'' tall and weighed 162 pounds; he lived at 2020 S. $10\frac{1}{2}$ Street, Terre Haute, Indiana when he registered on his eighteenth birthday with Local Board #2 of Vigo County. His middle name was Roy, which was his father's first name. He had a long scar on his left thigh. On May 26, one month and a day after registering with the Selective Service, Jack was classified I-A—fit for active duty—by his local board.

Jack's first four letters to his mother were written from Camp Attebury, Indiana, where he reported for duty and awaited orders for combat training. "I'm in the Army now," he wrote on September 10, 1944, after attending church services that morning. "Boy, it sure is swell here." The food wasn't as good as home cooking, but it wasn't bad, and his barracks had "its own showers, toilets & washroom." The beds were fine, and there was a PX that sold just about everything. His whole gang was in the same Company D. He wondered if his dad had come home that weekend or stayed in Evansville. "Don't worry about me cause I'm O.K."

Two days later, Jack asked about his mother's health and her move out of his father's house; he hoped she wasn't working too hard. He had gotten his uniform yesterday. "It sure is <u>swell</u>," and it fit "pretty good." His mother shouldn't worry about him too much because he was O.K. How was Butch? The next day, writing back to his mother, Jack reported that his arm was "a little sore" from shots he'd just gotten, but "Boy, I sure do like the Army." He would try to call home on Saturday if he hadn't already been "shipped" by then. He didn't need money because he would be paid $24.85, and "we had to take all of it to, whether we wanted it to ore not," he joked.

After a week at Camp Attebury, Jack was bored. He had been doing nothing but writing letters. He was tired of waiting to be shipped. He didn't really like standing an hour in a long line to get his meals at the big mess hall three-quarters of mile walk from his barracks, but he still liked the Army and had met some "swell fellows" from West Virginia, Kentucky, Ohio, and Indiana. He needed a sewing kit, a money belt, a pair of scissors, and some handkerchiefs. He thought his mother should sue for a divorce.

Jack wrote his first letter from Fort McClellan, Alabama, on September 22. He hadn't gotten a pass to come home before shipping to Alabama for basic training because, unlike the other guys, he didn't believe it was right to bribe the sergeant with gas stamps. Was everything O.K. at home? How was his mother's move progressing? "Boy, it sure is O.K. here. At first I didn't think it was going to be so good but its O.K. now." He was learning the Army drill and would be there for seventeen weeks. "They say there is a new law that says you can't be sent overseas till you are nineteen so you don't need to worry about me going for some time." He had just met the Chaplin, Captain White, who was "a swell guy." Jack was going to church every Sunday.

Twenty-five more letters were written home from Fort McClellan between September 27 and December 30. Jack worried a lot about his mother being sick, though Cousin Carol reports after the fact that Aunt Lucille was never severely ill while Jack was in the military. He was pleased that his mother was getting her new place fixed up. He wished she "wouldn't work so hard" at the Terre Haute Ordnance Depot and that she would take better care of herself because "I don't know what I'd do if something happened to you." She was his only "real parent. Dad would have been a swell father if he hadn't drank." Jack didn't drink or gamble. He got a "burr haircut," which he liked very much, and more shots, which he didn't like so much. His regular requests for packages from home included the Bible he'd been given by his church and more sweets from home; he missed home cooking. The weather was often wet and cold, but the scenery was pretty. He'd gotten a ten-page letter from Delores, who was a freshman at State, and he was pleased to learn that "Butchie" now had a blanket of his own to sleep on. He had received the first of what would be a number of gift boxes from his Aunt Helen. By early November, Jack was missing home and "sure wished he could have seen Carol Ann and Lewis on Halloween. I'll bet they looked swell."

In basic training, Jack was learning how to use a gas mask, shoot and clean a rifle, use a bayonet, throw hand grenades, carry a heavy backpack, march long distances in soggy weather, eat field rations, dig and sleep in a fox hole, crawl under barbed-wire fences, lay an anti-tank mine, shoot a bazooka, fire mortars, stand inspection, and more. That was military life; "you just grin & bear it. It may sound bad but its not when you think what the guys overseas are going thru," he wrote on October 15.[137] He and his buddies had learned to laugh when things went wrong. They just called each other "sad sack." They were getting up at 4:30 for rifle practice from sunrise to sunset. "I like to shoot," he wrote on October 24. "Boy, I'm sure glad I didn't get in the Navy now. They don't get half the training we get & from what I've heard we are even getting better training than the Marines." By October 30, he had qualified as a marksman on the M1 rifle, and by November 5 he'd made expert on the carbine. The training was good, he wrote on December 5, but "they say that all you learn here is just enough to take care of you for 2 days in combat & in those 2 days you learn enough to last the rest of the time."

All things considered, "I'm really glad I'm in the Army now Mother. I'm sure I wouldn't want it any other way but some day I hope to come home & I even think I'd like to go to college." That was late November. Much of his remaining time at Fort McClellan was spent on extended maneuvers in the final phase of basic training for an infantry soldier. On January 6, 1945, Brigadier General Howard E. Fuller certified that Private Jack R. Haley had successfully completed the prescribed course of training and was now qualified for MOS 745—Rifleman.

After graduating from basic training, Jack was stationed briefly at Fort Meade, Maryland in late January, where he received new equipment, underwent shakedown inspections to discard personal gear unsuitable for combat operations, marked and laundered his clothes, took an infiltration course, trained with his new gas mask, did "night problems," broke in his boots, and enjoyed sightseeing in Washington, DC. He worried about his mother's health and wondered if she had heard anymore from Dad; Jack hadn't. They were on alert to ship out at any time. He sure would miss going to the picture shows when he got over there. "Don't worry about me though cause I'm O.K.," he wrote from the troop train on January 29. "I think the war will just about be over when I get there, I guess they found out I was coming & knew they didn't have a chance." Dolores had asked for a picture he'd sent home. Could his mother get another made to give to her?

"You should see this ship.... It is the best boat in the world. They let us sleep all we want & its as if we were kings. I'm sleeping in a pretty ritzy stateroom & it sure is fun.... I wouldn't have missed this trip for anything Mother it sure is swell. I never dreamed it would be like this. Don't worry cause I'm as safe as a bug in a rug." That was January 31.

The Red Cross "has sure been swell to us." They handed out coffee and donuts and gave each soldier a special package. Jack's package came from someone in Clinton, Indiana. The troops got Pepsi Cola® twice a day and were given copies of *A Short Guide to Great Britain*, "so I guess that is where we are headed." That was February 2.

On February 9, "I am in France now.... I was only in Great Britain one day. Boy, this place is really blown up. We went through a town last night & most of the houses were all shot up.... The pack that we carry now is about 2 times as heavy as the one we trained with & I don't like it.... It won't be more than 2 or 3 weeks at the very longest before I see combat I guess. I've gone a long way since I left home & I've seen plenty.... Don't worry about me cause I'll always be O.K."

February 14. Valentines Day. "We are only a few miles from the front now & I'll probably be fighting very soon now.... There sure are a lot of things that I wish I could talk about but I can't... & don't worry to much cause I'll be O.K."

Three days later Jack had sent his mother memorabilia for her scrapbook, including some French money, his red meal ticket from the boat that took him from England to France, and his mess card and sleeping card from the troop ship to England. "I just came back from church so I guess I'm ready for whats ahead. You should go to a church Mother. I know you don't like Dad's church but there are a lot more in town besides that one." He had taken out a second war bond and was sending home some additional money. He knew which Regiment and Company he'd be joining soon. "They are on the front lines & have been there for over 3 months without rest. It sure is a tough outfit & I'm proud to be in it. I guess I'm scared stiff but everyone is at 1st. We sure are well equipped and I guess our training [is] O.K. so I don't think I have much to worry about." He would send home some German money as soon as they got into Germany.

By February 18, Jack's APO had changed permanently to 447. He hoped his mother was feeling fine. His pockets were full of more cigarettes than he could ever smoke, and he sure would like some cookies and "a can of fruit like peaches." He was now separated from all of his buddies.

On February 20, Jack wrote his Grandma Haley to tell her he was "just a few hundred yards back of the front now" and could "hear the shells as they go over us now." He had slept "in a German family's house last night & it sure is funny to here them talk."

On February 27, writing to his mother from a foxhole during a rainstorm, Jack confessed that, while it had been "a great thrill to cross the ocean," he was "looking forward to the return trip with more pleasure." He thought it would be "a couple of years yet before I get home.... Gosh, I sure do miss being home. Everything is so different over here. There never is anything funny to laugh at & in the towns there is no gayety, no bright lights. Everything is blacked out because of the war. Everywhere you turn you see nothing but destruction. It all seems like a dream & I'll sure be glad when it is over. Say, I wish you wouldn't work so hard.... I sure don't want anything to happen to you."

March 1. "I'm glad to hear that Billy got married but I think that he should have joined the Army & waited till the war is over. I don't see how he can want to stay home with everyone else gone." Jack assured his mother, though, that he would have taken her as his dependent if he could have, but they had told him at Fort Meade that he had to have proof he helped support her before he entered the service in order to get a deferment.

March 2. "Don't worry I'm O.K."

March 4. Writing after church, "We go back into the holes tonight so I guess it will be pretty tough. I don't think there is any need for you to send Dad my address, if he wants it he will ask for it but I don't think he will. He isn't interested in what happens to me at all. I don't care though cause I know that you will always love me & that I will always love you and that is all that counts. When you said I'll have a lot of experiences to talk about, when I get home that's no lie but I'll be more interested in forgetting some of them rather than talk about it. I'll sure be glad when this is over.... I'd like to have a small can of peaches & a fruit cake if you can send it."

March 6. "Don't worry about me cause I'm O.K. & I think this mess will end soon, I hope."

March 14. "I'm really in with a swell bunch of fellows. They've all seen plenty of action & are plenty tough. If anything ever happens to me I want you to know that I love you with all my heart Mother & sure appreciate everything that you did for me. You're the best Mother in the world and I wouldn't have had any other.... God bless you & keep you always."

March 18. "I'm way back in the rear & it seems good not to hear so much noise all the time. I'm still in a fox hole though.... I just came back from church & we had it on top of a hill. This sure is pretty country around here you can see for miles from this hill." He was glad his mother was going to church.

March 21. France. "Well, today is the 1st day of spring & it sure is a swell day here."

March 22. Germany. "Well, I'm in Germany now. It seems good to be here cause we know that we are just that much closer to the end of the war. The people here are very friendly, but we know that just a few days ago they were shooting at us so we can't trust them." They had stayed one night in a "Kraut" house and someone had played the piano. "It is the 1st music I've heard in a long time & gosh it really sounds good." Jack was proud of his mother's recent promotion at work: "Your sure are doing all you can for us over here & I know it.... I guess after this is over they won't be able to say that we didn't do our part."

March 25. "I've been awarded the Combat Infantry badge.... It also means $10 more pay a month."

April 2. "The funniest thing happened the other day. I was just standing out in the street watching the trucks go by when all of a sudden an Army officials car goes by & Marlene Dietrich the movie star was in it. She waved at me as she went by but I was so surprised I just stood there. It sure was good to see an American woman for a change.... Since I started this letter they told me I'm now a Private First Class (Pfc.). Not bad, huh? Promotions come pretty easy here. I also get $4.80 more on the month. My total pay is now $74.80 a month. Its more than I made at home."

April 4. Last letter. "We've got it pretty easy now & I'm sure glad.... Please send me more packages. That last one sure was swell.... I got a letter (Vmail) from Dad yesterday.... He makes me so mad I don't know what to do." Jack also got a letter from Dolores that same day.

That was young Jack Haley's story of war in a shoebox, told mostly in his own words. There were no grand causes, great heroes, or satanic foes. He was doing his part, and joining the Army was an adventure. He liked sweet things to eat, loved his mother, fretted about his father, bonded with his Army buddies, attended church regularly, and thought often of Dolores. He was afraid, but seldom said so directly. He didn't complain much and was a good soldier—brave, competent, and proud of his unit—but he wanted to forget much of what he had experienced and hoped to be home soon. He joked, mostly in a quiet way, and was saddened by the absence of music in the dark, cheerless landscape of destruction that was wartime France. The beauty of the spring countryside cheered him, and seeing an occasional movie was swell. The German foe couldn't be trusted, but they were friendly. Jack's world was more complicated than a simple struggle between good and evil, too palpable and ordinary to depict in stark contrasts of black and white, and largely incongruous with a drama of national redemption.

This was the son Lucille Haley lost to Secretary Stimson's "battle for our country," a son she would always remember in vivid flesh-and-blood terms, not as a name etched on the back of a medal or into a stone-cold monument of war. Was his blood sacrifice worth her loss? Is his memory, and the memory of other fallen soldiers, cause for conjuring up frightful images of foreign devils? Was America redeemed by Jack Haley's death? Many years later, when Lucille was confined to a nursing home, Lewis Piepenbrink asked his elderly aunt what she would do differently if she had her life to live over again. "I would find a way," she replied, "for my boy not to go to war."

HUMANIZING THE PROTAGONISTS

Isn't finding a way to keep all of our children from going to war just what every citizen and every political leader should want most to do? Our children remind us of a common humanity. They are our collective hope for a peaceful world, the manifest principle of love made deeply personal and immediately present. When we are mindful of them, we feel responsible to them, obliged to find a way—to do everything possible—to avoid war and make peace.

"No more war" was precisely President Jimmy Carter's aim for negotiating peace in the Middle East between Egyptian President Anwar Sadat and Israeli Prime Minister Menachem Begin.[138] He prepared for meeting with them at Camp David by learning as much as possible about these two "protagonists," having his advisors prepare biographies of the two leaders based on their public statements and writings, interviews they had given, and even their medical histories. Carter wanted to know as much as he could about Sadat's and Begin's motives and goals, their religious beliefs, political positions, and relations with other leaders and political constituencies, their attitudes toward one another, their individual strengths and weaknesses, and even their relations with family members.[139]

After a frustrating first year and a half of his presidency devoted to Middle East diplomacy and knowing full well that "generations of hatred and the vivid memories of recent wars could not be overcome easily," Carter approached the Camp David negotiations in September 1978 with substantial goals (including a peace agreement between Egypt and Israel) but with minimal expectations of success. He was rolling the dice by bringing Begin and Sadat together for an extensive, thirteen-day negotiation session with him. (Actually, the original plan was to meet for three days, maybe even a week if necessary.) Carter previously had developed "an easy and natural friendship" with Sadat—considering him to be a "close, personal friend"—but Begin was another matter. Israel's hard-line Prime Minister was courageous but more distant and had been less responsive to Carter's prior diplomatic initiatives. Going into the Camp David negotiations, Carter believed that Sadat trusted him "too much," Begin "not enough" and that "there was no compatibility at all between Begin and Sadat."[140]

The negotiations, as expected, proved to be very difficult. After the first three days, Sadat and Begin never again negotiated directly with one another at Camp David, working instead through Carter and other intermediaries. By the end of the tenth day, it appeared as though the negotiations had failed. Sadat packed his bags on the morning of the eleventh day and asked for a helicopter to transport him from Camp David. Carter drew on his friendship with Sadat to save the talks, telling Sadat that he would be breaking a promise he had made to Carter, undermining their mutual trust, and damaging their friendship if he left.[141]

On day thirteen, just as an agreement appeared to be secured, the talks suddenly broke down again, seemingly beyond repair, when Begin refused to accede to a letter by the US criticizing Israel's occupancy of East Jerusalem. Begin, though, was reminded of the children in time to return to the difficult task of achieving an accord. His timely remembrance was prompted by Carter, who brought to Begin's cabin an autographed photograph of Begin, Carter, and Sadat. Begin had previously requested signed copies for each of his grandchildren. Following a suggestion by Susan Clough, the President's secretary, Carter personalized the signed photos by writing each grandchild's name on one of the copies. When Carter handed the photos to Begin, the Prime Minister thanked the President and, upon noticing his granddaughter's name at the top, he

> spoke it aloud, and then looked at each photograph individually, repeating the name of the grandchild I had written on it. His lips trembled, and tears welled up in his eyes. He told me a little about each child, and especially about the one who seemed to be his favorite. We were both emotional as we talked quietly for a few minutes about grandchildren and about war.[142]

While this gesture did not end strife in the Middle East, it did speak to the heart of the matter, that is, to the humanity of the protagonists. All parties to an abiding conflict tend to lose sight of their enemy's humanity, founding their fearful quest for redemption on demonizing rituals. From the Palestinian perspective of Hanan Ashrawi—American-educated literary scholar and political activist in the first Intifada, an influential spokeswoman in peace talks with Israel, and a woman who happens to be Christian rather than Muslim—Israeli governments have made a practice of manufacturing "security fears," of "aggravating the fears of Israelis" and "creating a collective phobia among the Israelis," by delegitimating the Palestinians, by "stereotyping and labeling with the most demeaning, dehumanizing labels," by calling them vermin, cockroaches, snakes, and dogs. Through this process, she observes, Palestinians are perceived, even in the US, "as the aggressor, as the fanatics, and as the obstacle to peace." They have been "robbed" of their "most elemental of human feelings," including "the love of parents for their children."[143]

Shalumit Aloni, a recipient of the Israel Prize for service to her country, shares Ashrawi's basic understanding of the plight of Palestinian Arabs. Aloni is a veteran of the Israeli War of Independence. She was captured by Jordanian forces in Jerusalem. She has been a teacher, lawyer, columnist, radio producer, Knesset member, cabinet minister, human rights advocate, and founding member of the International Center for Peace in the Middle East. "What really needs to be fixed," she argues, "is the way Jews treat the Palestinians.... We are humiliating them." Treating "Arab women, men, and children as second-class human beings, not even as human beings," is a way for Israelis to see themselves as the true victims while behaving like the actual "colonialists," she insists. This "doublespeak" aims to prevent the Palestinians from achieving a sovereign state and is a mechanism for "brainwashing" Israelis into believing that Arabs want to throw the Jews into the sea. It is a formula for propagating war because no one, certainly not the Palestinian people, can "suffer humiliation for very long."[144]

"Terror against terror" may be emotionally satisfying momentarily, writes Wole Soyinka, recipient of the Nobel Prize in literature, but a climate of fear in a dehumanized world is nothing less than an assault on human dignity. "Once righteousness replaces rights in the exercise of power," he observes, "the way is paved for a permanent contest based on the primacy of the *holier-than-thou.*" This is nothing less than "rhetorical hysteria" to the exclusion of "dialogue." It is a "monstrosity" of absolutes that eventually consumes everyone, including its promoters, a "one-dimensional approach to all faces of reality," a "self-willed hysteria...induced by a deliberate exercise of blinding the mind to other considerations, *screaming doubts into silence*" (emphasis added). This "war-lust" of both Christian and Muslim fundamentalists is the triumph of monologues that devalue or deny human dignity. Thus:

> The monologue of unilateralism constantly aspires to the mantle of the Chosen and, of course, further dichotomizes the world, inviting us, on pain of consequences, to choose between "them" and "us." We must, in other words, reject the conditions George Bush delivered so explicitly in that ultimatum *You are either with us and against the terrorists, or you are on the side of the terrorists,* and in *We do not require the world's approval since we are divinely guided,* just as strongly as we repudiate Osama bin Laden's *The world is now clearly divided into two—the world of the followers of Islam against that of infidels and unbelievers.*[145]

The stories we tell each other can either promote humanizing dialogue or reiterate dehumanizing monologues. The World War II stories of Paul Fussell, himself a twenty-year-old Army lieutenant in a rifle platoon who survived severe wounds suffered in France in the spring of 1945, reveal the nation's wartime rationalizations that damaged intellect, honesty, complexity, ambiguity, and a collective capacity for irony and wit. Moreover, these rationalizations and euphemisms, perpetrated by "the sentimental, the loony patriotic, the ignorant, and the bloodthirsty," have since "sanitized and romanticized" a horrific war "almost beyond recognition."[146] We now remember it archetypically and simplistically as the good war, the great triumph over evil, a model for redeeming ourselves again against the evil of Islamist terrorism.

Where are the humanizing rites of peace to help "balance the scales," as Fussell has done and we might do routinely, so as not to ignore "the stupidity and barbarism and ignobility and poltroonery and filth of the real war"?[147] Where is the rehumanizing news of the day? The dramatization of protagonists' humanity in our poetry, art, literature, theatre, cinema, and music? The everyday speaking and the holiday oratory of our political leaders to cultivate peaceful relations with adversaries? The peace curriculum in our schools and universities? The public monument to reconciliation? The Sunday sermon of redemption by means other than vicarious sacrifice? These are the cultural resources of a beleaguered people for imagining the possibility of a less violent, more just world—the sites of storytelling rituals for remembering the humanity of protagonists on both sides of the divide and for motivating pragmatic acts of peacemaking over lethal habits of enemy-making. These are the humanizing rites that must be cultivated and promulgated in order to habituate the nation to a presumption for peace and a presumption against war, and to constrain stark dramatizations of good and evil that now torment the guilty conscience of a self-chosen people, dooming them to a cruel cycle of deliverance by violence.

NOTES

1. George W. Bush, "President Bush Delivers Graduation Speech at West Point," Office of the Press Secretary, The White House, June 1, 2002, available online.

2. Thomas Merton, *New Seeds of Contemplation* (1961; Boston: Shambhala Publications Inc., 2003), 114, 116, 126.

3. Merton, *New Seeds*, 116.

4. Robert L. Ivie, "The Rhetoric of Bush's 'War' on Evil," *KB Journal* 1 (Fall 2004), online at http://kbjournal.org.

5. For examples of how various regimes have visually caricatured their enemies as barbarians, see Sam Keen, *Faces of the Enemy: Reflections on the Hostile Imagination* (San Francisco, CA: Harper and Row, Publishers, 1986), 43–47.

6. See, for instance, Anonymous, *Imperial Hubris: Why the West is Losing the War on Terror* (Washington, D.C.: Brassey's, Inc., 2004); Jim Garrison, *America as Empire: Global Leader or Rogue Power?* (San Francisco, California: Berrett-Koehler

Publishers, 2004); Michael Mann, *Incoherent Empire* (London: Verso, 2003); Andrew J. Bacevich, *American Empire: The Realities and Consequences of U.S. Diplomacy* (Cambridge, Massachusetts: Harvard University Press, 2002); Chalmers Johnson, *The Sorrows of Empire: Militarism, Secrecy, and the End of the Republic* (New York: Metropolitan Books, 2004); Carl Boggs, ed., *Masters of War: Militarism and Blowback in the Era of American Empire* (New York: Routledge, 2003); John Newhouse, *Imperial America: The Bush Assault on the World Order* (New York: Alfred A. Knopf, 2003).

7. I discuss these points in Robert L. Ivie, *Democracy and America's War on Terror* (Tuscaloosa: University of Alabama Press, 2005).

8. Kurt W. Ritter and James R. Andrews, *The American Ideology: Reflections on the Revolution in American Rhetoric* (Falls Church, Virginia: Speech Communication Association, 1978), 7–10.

9. Ronald L. Hatzenbuehler and Robert L. Ivie, *Congress Declares War: Rhetoric, Leadership, and Partisanship in the Early Republic* (Kent, Ohio: Kent State University Press, 1983); Robert L. Ivie, "The Metaphor of Force in Prowar Discourse: The Case of 1812," *Quarterly Journal of Speech* 68 (1982): 240–53.

10. Robert L. Ivie, "Progressive Form and Mexican Culpability in Polk's Justification for War," *Central States Speech Journal* 30 (1979): 311–20.

11. McKinley quoted in Robert L. Ivie, "William McKinley: Advocate of Imperialism," *Western Speech* 36 (1972): 15–23.

12. Daniel Pick, *War Machine: The Rationalisation of Slaughter in the Modern Age* (New Haven: Yale University Press, 1993), 3, 11, 16, 49, 100–02, 106, 108–14, 153–55, 186–88, 203, 227.

13. Woodrow Wilson, "War Message," quoted in Robert L. Ivie, "Images of Savagery in American Justifications for War," *Communication Monographs* 47 (1980): 287.

14. Michael S. Sherry, *In the Shadow of War: The United States Since the 1930s* (New Haven: Yale University Press, 1995), 14, 38, 45, 83–85.

15. Robert L. Ivie, "Franklin Roosevelt's Crusade against Evil: Rhetorical Legacy of a War Message," in *Great Speeches for Criticism and Analysis*, ed. Lloyd Rohler and Roger Cook, 4th ed. (Greenwood, Indiana: Alistair Press, 2001), 98–105.

16. Sherry, *Shadow*, 96–98, 114–15.

17. Robert J. Lifton and Greg Mitchell, *Hiroshima in America: A Half Century of Denial* (New York: Avon Books, 1995), xiv; Truman quoted in Lifton and Mitchell, *Hiroshima*, 4–6.

18. John W. Dower, *War Without Mercy: Race and Power in the Pacific War* (New York: Pantheon Books, 1986), x, 9.

19. Roosevelt quoted in Ivie, "Images of Savagery," 287, 289.

20. Robert L. Ivie, "Fire, Flood, and Red Fever: Motivating Metaphors of Global Emergency in the Truman Doctrine Speech," *Presidential Studies Quarterly* 29 (1999): 570–91.

21. Eisenhower quoted in Robert L. Ivie, "Eisenhower as Cold Warrior," in *Eisenhower's War of Words: Rhetoric and Leadership*, ed. Martin J. Medhurst (East Lansing: Michigan State University Press, 1994), 14–15.

22. Sherry, *Shadow*, 132–34, 139.

23. Robert L. Ivie, "Speaking 'Common Sense' about the Soviet Threat: Reagan's Rhetorical Stance," *Western Journal of Speech Communication* 48 (1984): 39–50.

24. See, for instance, Ivie, "Metaphor of Force," and Robert L. Ivie, "Literalizing the Metaphor of Soviet Savagery: President Truman's Plain Style," *Southern Speech Communication Journal* 51 (1986): 91–105.

25. Robert L. Ivie, "The Ideology of Freedom's 'Fragility' in American Foreign Policy Argument," *Journal of the American Forensic Association* 24 (1987): 27–36.

26. Sherry, *Shadow*, 431–32, 441–42, 445–46, 461, 464, 467, 497.

27. See, for instance, Quentin Skinner, *Reason and Rhetoric in the Philosophy of Hobbes* (New York: Cambridge University Press, 1996), 320–21.

28. Immanual Kant, "To Perpetual Peace: A Philosophical Sketch," in *Immanuel Kant: Perpetual Peace and Other Essays on Politics, History, and Morals*, ed. and trans. Ted Humphrey (Indianapolis, Indiana: Hackett Publishing Company), 107–39.

29. Kant, "Perpetual Peace,"117.

30. There is a substantial literature on the current appropriation of the idea of a democratic peace, much of which is critically reviewed in Robert L. Ivie, "Democratizing for Peace," *Rhetoric and Public Affairs* 4 (2001): 309–22.

31. Jeffrey D. Simon, *The Terrorist Trap: America's Experience with Terrorism*, 2nd ed. (Bloomington: Indiana University Press, 2001), xx, 8, 167, 178–79, 185, 195.

32. Denise M. Bostdorff, "George W. Bush's Post-September 11 Rhetoric of Covenant Renewal: Upholding the Faith of the Greatest Generation," *Quarterly Journal of Speech* 89 (2003): 303; see also 29, 302, 305–07.

33. John M. Murphy, "'Our Mission and Our Moment': George W. Bush and September 11th," *Rhetoric & Public Affairs* 6 (2003): 626–27.

34. David Hoogland Noon, "Operation Enduring Analogy: World War II, The War on Terror, and the Uses of Historical Memory," *Rhetoric & Public Affairs* 7 (2004): 357–58.

35. Howard Fineman and Tamara Lipper, "The Gospel According to George," *Newsweek* 26 April 2004: 18–21.

36. Eric Alterman and Mark Green, *The Book on Bush: How George W. (Mis)leads America* (New York: Viking, 2004), 332.

37. Wes Avram, "Introduction," in *Anxious About Empire: Theological Essays on the New Global Realities*, ed. Wes Avram (Grand Rapids, Michigan: Brazos Press, 2004), 14.

38. Stephen B. Chapman, "Imperial Exegesis: When Caesar Interprets Scripture," in Avram, *Anxious About Empire*, 95–96. Emphasis in original. To see how the President's messianic language plays in the broader public and popular culture, see Debra Merskin, "The Construction of Arabs as Enemies: Post-September 11 Discourse of George W. Bush," *Mass Communication and Society* 7 (2004): 157–75.

39. "President Bush Delivers Commencement Address at Oho State University," White House, Office of the Press Secretary, June 14, 2002, available online; "President Delivers Commencement Address at Concordia University," White House, Office of the Press Secretary, May 14, 2004, available online.

40. Peter Baker, "Bush Tells Group He Sees a 'Third Awakening,'" *Washington Post*, September 13, 2006.

41. Michael J. Hyde, "The Rhetor as Hero and the Pursuit of Truth: The Case of 9/11," *Rhetoric & Public Affairs* 8 (2005): 25–26.

42. Merton, *New Seeds*, 114–17.

43. John Angus Campbell, "Evil as the Allure of Perfection," *Rhetoric & Public Affairs* 6 (Fall 2003): 525.

44. James Arnt Aune, "The Argument from Evil in the Rhetoric of Reaction," *Rhetoric & Public Affairs* 6 (2003): 518.

45. Kenneth Burke, *The Rhetoric of Religion: Studies in Logology* (1961; Berkeley: University of California Press, 1970), vi, 1–2, 4–5, 174–76, 181, 190–91, 196, 200.

46. Burke, *Rhetoric of Religion*, 208, 218–19, 223–24.

47. James Hillman, *A Terrible Love of War* (New York: Penguin, 2004), 25.

48. Michael Ignatieff, *The Lesser Evil: Political Ethics in an Age of Terror* (Princeton, New Jersey: Princeton University Press, 2004), viii.

49. George W. Bush, "State of the Union Address," Office of the Press Secretary, The White House, January 29, 2002, available online.

50. "The National Security Strategy of the United States of America," The White House, signed by the President on September 17, 2002 and released to the public on September 20, 2002, available online; "President Bush Outlines Iraqi Threat," Office of the Press Secretary, The White House, October 7, 2002, available online.

51. George W. Bush, "State of the Union," Office of the Press Secretary, The White House, January 28, 2003, available online.

52. For a more extended discussion of Bush's use of the theme of evil to justify the invasion of Iraq, see Ivie, *Democracy and America's War on Terror*, 158–66.

53. Christian Spielvogel, "'You Know Where I Stand': Moral Framing of the War on Terrorism and the Iraq War in the 2004 Presidential Campaign," *Rhetoric & Public Affairs*, 8 (Winter 2005): 552.

54. Spielvogel, 561.

55. George W. Bush, "State of the Union Address," Office of the Press Secretary, The White House, January 31, 2006, available online.

56. Bush, "State of the Union," January 31, 2006.

57. Burke, *Rhetoric of Religion*, 235–36.

58. Merton, *New Seeds*, 117–19, 121.

59. Hillman, *Terrible Love*, 118–19.

60. Hillman, *Terrible Love*, 185, 106–09, 190, 196.

61. Hillman, *Terrible Love*, 202–05, 211–14.

62. Kenneth Burke, *A Rhetoric of Motives* (1950; Berkeley: University of California Press, 1969), 20.

63. For a more extended discussion of the comic corrective, see Ivie, *Democracy and America's War on Terror*, 38–41.

64. Kenneth Burke, *Attitudes toward History*, 3rd ed. (Berkeley: University of California Press, 1984), 41, 102–03, 106–07.

65. William H. Rueckert, *Encounters with Kenneth Burke* (Urbana: University of Illinois Press, 1994), 119.

66. Douglas Kellner, *From 9/11 to Terror War: The Dangers of the Bush Legacy* (Lanham, Maryland: Rowman & Littlefield Publishers, Inc., 2003), 6–7.

67. George W. Bush, "State of the Union Address," Office of the Press Secretary, The White House, January 23, 2007, available online.

68. George W. Bush, "President's Address to the Nation," Office of the Press Secretary, The White House, January 10, 2007, available online.

69. George W. Bush, "Text of President Bush's Address to the Nation," *Washington post.com* September 11, 2006, available online.

70. Bush, "State of the Union Address," January 31, 2006.

71. George W. Bush, "President Discusses Global War on Terror at Kansas State University," Office of the Press Secretary, The White House, January 23, 2006, available online.

72. George W. Bush, "Transcript of President Bush's Remarks on Iraq," *Washington post.com*, December 18, 2005, available online.

73. George W. Bush, "President Addresses Nation, Discusses Iraq, War on Terror," Office of the Press Secretary, The White House, June 28, 2005, available online.

74. George W. Bush, "Transcript: Bush Casts War on Terrorism in Historic Terms," *Washingtonpost.com*, June 2, 2004, available online.

75. George W. Bush, "President Bush's Address at the Army War College," *The New York Times*, May 24, 2004.

76. George W. Bush, "President's Radio Address," Office of the Press Secretary, The White House, May 15, 2004, available online.

77. George W. Bush, "President Bush's Opening Statement on Iraq: 'We Will Finish the Work of the Fallen,'" *The New York Times*, April 14, 2004.

78. George W. Bush, "State of the Union Address," Office of the Press Secretary, The White House, January 20, 2004, available online.

79. George W. Bush, "President Bush Addresses United Nations General Assembly," Office of the Press Secretary, The White House, September 23, 2003, available online.

80. George W. Bush, "President Bush Addresses the Nation," Office of the Press Secretary, The White House, March 19, 2003, available online.

81. Bush, "President Discusses Global War on Terror at Kansas State University."

82. Hillman *Terrible Love*, 190, 196.

83. Burke, *Rhetoric of Religion*, 190–91.

84. Bush, "President's Radio Address."

85. Bush, "President Addresses Nation, Discusses Iraq, War on Terror."

86. Bush, "Transcript: Bush Casts War on Terrorism in Historic Terms."

87. Philip Kennicott, "A Wretched New Picture of America: Photos From Iraq Prison Show We Are Our Own Worst Enemy," *Washingtonpost.com*, May 5, 2004, available online; Editorial, "A System of Abuse," *Washingtonpost.com*, May 5, 2004, available online; Editorial, "A Corrupted Culture," *Washingtonpost.com*, May 20, 2004, available online; Jefferson Morley, "George Bush as Saddam Hussein: Abuse Photos Prompt Comparison to Former Iraqi Leader," *Washingtonpost.com*, May 3, 2004, available online.

88. Bush, "Graduation Speech at West Point."

89. George W. Bush, "President Bush Speaks at Air Force Academy Graduation," Office of the Press Secretary, The White House, June 2, 2004, available online.

90. George W. Bush, "State of the Union Address," Office of the Press Secretary, The White House, January 20, 2004, available online.

91. George W. Bush, "President Discusses War on Terror and Upcoming Iraqi Elections," Office of the Press Secretary, The White House, December 14, 2005, available online.

92. George W. Bush, "State of the Union Address," Office of the Press Secretary, The White House, February 2, 2005, available online.

93. George W. Bush, "President Bush Discusses Global War on Terror," Office of the Press Secretary, The White House, April 6, 2006, available online.

94. Bush, "President Bush Speaks at Air Force Academy Graduation," June 2, 2004.

95. Bush, "President Discusses Global War on Terror at Kansas State University, January 23, 2006.

96. George W. Bush, "President's Radio Address," Office of the Press Secretary, The White House, May 13, 2006, available online.

97. George W. Bush, "President Meets with McCain & Warner, Discusses Position on Interrogation," Office of the Press Secretary, The White House, December 15, 2005, available online.

98. See, for instance, Andrew J. Bacevich, *The New American Militarism: How Americans Are Seduced by War* (New York: Oxford University Press, 2005); Stephen John Hartnett and Laura Ann Stengrim, *Globalization and Empire: The U.S. Invasion of Iraq, Free Markets, and the Twilight of Democracy* (Tuscaloosa: University of Alabama Press, 2006); John B. Judis, *The Folly of Empire: What George W. Bush Could Learn from Theodore Roosevelt and Woodrow Wilson* (New York: Scribner, 2004); Kellner, *From 9/11 to Terror War*; Clyde Prestowitz, *Rogue Nation: American Unilateralism and the Failure of Good Intentions* (New York: Basic Books, 2003); and Gore Vidal, *Imperial America: Reflections on the United States of America* (New York: Nation Books, 2004).

99. Merton, *New Seeds*, 126.

100. On rectilinear or narrative style compared to the cycle of terms, see Burke, *Rhetoric of Religion*, 183; on the matter of danger and security, see David Campbell, *Writing Security: United States Foreign Policy and the Politics of Identity*, rev. ed. (Minneapolis: University of Minnesota Press, 1998), 1–8.

101. Burke, *Attitudes*, "Introduction," 173.

102. Ignatieff, *Lesser Evil*, 8–10.

103. Ignatieff, *Lesser Evil*, 1, 23–24.

104. Ignatieff, *Lesser Evil*, 153–55.

105. Ignatieff, *Lesser Evil*, 167, 169. Even though initially a supporter of the U.S. invasion of Iraq, saying he had witnessed the torture and seen the massacre when touring Iraq in 1992, center-left political candidate Ignatieff subsequently disavowed the President's war strategy, saying "George Bush has made every mistake in Iraq and then some" (CP, "Ignatieff Under Fire Over Iraq," *EdmontonSun.com*, September 18, 2006, available online.)

106. C. Allen Carter, *Kenneth Burke and the Scapegoat Process* (Norman: University of Oklahoma Press, 1996), 86–87.

107. René Girard, *The Scapegoat*, trans. Yvonne Freccero (Baltimore, Maryland: The Johns Hopkins University Press, 1986), 3. Girard, *Scapegoat*, 2, quotes Mahaut's *Judgment of the King of Navaree*.

108. Girard, *Scapegoat*, 12.

109. Campbell, *Writing Security*, 133.

110. Campbell, *Writing Security*, 169.

111. Campbell, *Writing Security*, 252.

112. Carter, *Kenneth Burke*, 21–22

113. Eric W. Rothenbuhler, *Ritual Communication: From Everyday Conversation to Mediated Ceremony* (Thousand Oaks, California: Sage, 1998), xi, 129–31.

114. Roy A. Rappaport, *Ecology, Meaning and Religion* (Richmond, California: North Atlantic Books, 1979), 174. Emphasis in original.

115. Lisa Schirch, *Ritual and Symbol in Peacebuilding* (Bloomfield, Connecticut: Kumarian Press, 2005), 125.

116. Catherine Bell, *Ritual Perspectives and Dimensions* (New York: Oxford University Press, 1997), 16.

117. The respective characteristics of ritual as ambiguously inflected, sacred, conventional and improvisational, reorienting in desperate times, constructing relations of coexistence, and dramatic are reviewed in Schirch, *Ritual and Symbol*, 17, 19, 21, 23–24, 26–28. Other useful overviews of the key characteristics of ritual (formal, traditional, rule-governed, performative, voluntary, recurring, social, subjunctive, aesthetic, symbolic, transformative, and serious or sacral) are provided by Bell, *Ritual Perspectives*, 138–164, and Rothenbuhler, *Ritual Communication*, 7–27.

118. Schirch, *Ritual and Symbol*, 165; on the dramaturgy of rituals, see also Schrich, *Ritual and Symbol*, 1, 31–32, 65–72, 85, 94, 101–04.

119. Schirch, *Ritual and Symbol*, 147.

120. Karen Armstrong, *A Short History of Myth* (New York: Cannongate, 2005), 35; also see Schirch, *Ritual and Symbol*, 85, and for general discussions of the myth and ritual schools of thought, see Bell, *Ritual Perspectives*, 5–8; Robert A. Segal, *Theorizing About Myth* (Amherst: University of Massachusetts Press, 1999), 37–46; and Robert A. Segal, *Myth: A Very Short Introduction* (Oxford: Oxford University Press, 2004), 61–78.

121. William G. Doty, *Mythography: The Study of Myths and Rituals*, 2nd ed. (Tuscaloosa: The University of Alabama Press, 2000), 335, 339, 345–46, 357–59.

122. One might cite any number of studies of public war rituals, from Carole Blair, Marsha S. Jeppeson, and Enrico Pucci, Jr., "Public Memorializing in Postmodernity: The Vietnam Veterans Memorial as Prototype," *Quarterly Journal of Speech* 77 (1991): 263–88 to Michael L. Butterworth, "Ritual in the 'Church of Baseball': Suppressing the Discourse of Democracy after 9/11," *Communication and Critical/Cultural Studies* 2 (June 2005): 107–29.

123. Bell, *Ritual Perspectives*, 154.

124. See, for example, Ivie, "The Rhetoric of Bush's 'War' on Evil."

125. Bell, *Ritual Perspectives*, 235, 252.

126. For a relevant discussion of ritualizing condensation symbols, see Rothenbuhler, *Ritual Communication*, 16–19.

127. Bell, *Ritual Perspectives*, 78. See also, Catherine Bell, *Ritual Theory, Ritual Practice* (New York: Oxford University Press, 1992), 82; and Pierre Bourdieu, *Outline of a Theory of Practices*, trans. Richard Nice (Cambridge: Cambridge University Press, 1977), 3–9, 79, 96, 106.

128. Rothenbuhler, *Ritual Communication*, 12, reports the general observation about storytelling as a ritual form "essential to collective memory."

129. E. M. Viquesney is himself buried in Riverside Cemetery, along with and between his beloved first and second wives.

130. For background information on the statue, see Earl Goldsmith, "The Statue: The Spirit of the American Doughboy," available online.

131. Barbara A. Biesecker, "Remembering World War II: The Rhetoric and Politics of National Commemoration at the Turn of the 21st Century," *Quarterly Journal of Speech* 88 (2002): 406.

132. Erik Doxtader, "Reconciliation—A Rhetorical Concept/ion," *Quarterly Journal of Speech* 89 (2003): 267–70, 278, 280–81, 284–86.

133. John B. Hatch, "The Hope of Reconciliation: Continuing the Conversation," *Rhetoric & Public Affairs* 9 (2006): 263–66.

134. Carol Miller, a fellow member of the Spencer (Indiana) Presbyterian Church who kindly allowed me access to the shoebox and gave me permission to write about its contents, is the younger sister of Lewis Piepenbrink. Their mother, Helen Piepenbrink, was Jack Haley's aunt—his mother's sister.

135. Secretary of War Henry L. Stimson to Mrs. Lucille Haley, May 26, 1945, personal correspondence, filed in the shoebox.

136. First Lieutenant William E. Reid to Mrs. Helen Piepenbrink, July 22, 1946, War Department, Army Service Forces, Office of the Quartermaster General. Filed in the shoebox. Helen Piepenbrink was Jack's aunt. She had written the Army to find out where her nephew had been buried.

137. Jack wrote, on October 22, "Boy a tank doesn't have a chance against an infantry man, they may look like they would be hard to get at the crew, but they teach us how to make any tank say 'Uncle.'"

138. Jimmy Carter, *Keeping Faith: Memoirs of a President* (Toronto: Bantam Books, 1982), 267.

139. Carter, *Keeping Faith*, 320.

140. Carter, *Keeping Faith*, 283–84, 316–17, 321–22, 328.

141. Carter, *Keeping Faith*, 392.

142. Carter, *Keeping Faith*, 399.

143. Quotations are from an interview of Ashrawi by Scott Hunt, reported in Scott A. Hunt, *The Future of Peace: On the Front Lines with the World's Great Peacemakers* (New York: HarperSanFrancisco, 2004), 122–24; see also 119–20.

144. Quotations are from an interview of Aloni by Hunt in Hunt, *Future of Peace*, 139–40, 143; see also 136–37.

145. Wole Soyinka, *Climate of Fear: The Quest for Dignity in a Dehumanized World* (New York: Random House, 2005), 10, 28, 38, 64–65, 73–74, 81, 100, 134–35.

146. Paul Fussell, *Wartime: Understanding and Behavior in the Second World War* (New York: Oxford University Press, 1989), ix.

147. Fussell, *Wartime*, ix, 297.

4

A Question of Communication

No subject is more basic to peace than communication. Dissenting from war means nothing less than communicating a bond of humanity to mitigate fractious relations between disputing parties. Absent the expression of such a bond, enemies emerge where parties in dispute can no longer abide differences between them. Their differences become increasingly alienating and are made to appear progressively more threatening across a lengthening line of division. In this way, discord escalates all the more readily into systematic and sustained violence, which is the scourge of our technologically sophisticated world. We have learned to kill with unprecedented proficiency, to engage in total violence, killing without limit and transforming war into annihilation. As Jonathan Schell envisions our plight, "If an evil god had turned human society into an infernal laboratory to explore the utmost extremes of violence, short only of human extinction, he could scarcely have improved upon the history of the twentieth century."[1]

Many affirm that the twentieth century was the most violent in human history, and few would attest that the prospects of an already vicious twenty-first century are any better. We live in an age of terror and counter-terror, an escalating cycle of self-perpetuating violence.[2] For many disparate voices to cohabitate peacefully in one shrinking world, we must ascertain an order of communication that resists relations of sheer hostility and imparts compensating points of affinity. This is the very kind of information and communication world order that UNESCO's International Commission for the Study of Communication Problems envisioned in 1980 with the publication of its MacBride report.[3]

DEMOCRATIC MEDIA AND MESSAGES OF PEACE

The image of peacemaking through communication that is projected in the MacBride report is strikingly humane and strongly committed to a democratic ethic. It is a hopeful view of a better world in the making, a vigorous expression of our right to communicate, and a frank avowal of our obligation to exercise such a readily available means of strengthening human relationships that is so basic to democratic self-governance. As Andrew Calabrese says clearly and candidly in his forward to the 2004 edition of the report, "By our humanity, and as citizens of the world, it is our birthright and our duty to speak, write, read, listen, watch, assemble, and associate as a means to better understand one another and our shared and separate histories, needs, and interests."[4] Amadou-Mahtar M'Bow, writing as the Director General of UNESCO, understood when the report was first released that "communication is at the heart of all social intercourse." He believed it was not wishful to think or imagine that people around the world could come to understand better how "their national destinies are closely intertwined," even though they were still vulnerable to and tempted by old habits of enmity and coercion. They might "seek to develop ties of growing fellowship" and "establish little by little relationships based on mutual respect and co-operation," he suggested, unless they "enlist" the media of communication instead to "assault" human dignity and "aggravate" existing inequalities "in the service of narrow sectarian interests." The emergence of a new communication world order could help humankind to take "a decisive step forward on the path to freedom, democracy and fellowship."[5]

Sean MacBride, paraphrasing H. G. Wells, likewise understood that humanity was in "a race between communication and catastrophe."[6] As president of the commission that produced the report, he recognized that the chances of peace and human betterment were most at stake. The report itself understood that the key to overcoming obstacles to peace and mobilizing the resources of communication for human benefit was to make the public's voice heard by infusing communication systems and practices with "the spirit of democracy."[7] In an era of economic globalization, media consolidation, self-censoring by journalists, and one-way, vertical flows of information, the commissioners conceived of communication anew as *a powerful means of promoting democratization of society and of widening public participation in the decision-making process.*"[8] Democratic communication would quicken mutual awareness and *"the supreme interest of all humanity in peace"* at a time when *"the dangers of war are heightened by intolerance, national chauvinism, and a failure to understand varying points of view."*[9]

The MacBride report was rejected by powerful Western interests for its vision of social justice and its criticism of corporate control of media flows. Indeed, the US, followed by the UK, withdrew from UNESCO, insisting that the MacBride report's criticism of the one-way flow of information amounted to support for censorship of Western media by authoritarian regimes in the non-Western world. The Non-Aligned Movement understood the call for a new world information and communication order as resisting cultural colonization and affirming economic development, peace, and democracy. The US government and corporate media interests distorted these aims by claiming falsely that the MacBride report proposed to license journalists and by misrepresenting the report's desire for equity and balance as an attack on the free flow of information and the free marketplace of ideas.[10] Other critics identified with the MacBride Commission's aims, but criticized it for defaulting to the forces of centralization and accommodating too readily to statist inclinations without adequately taking into account the diversity of viewpoints operating within civil society. Caught in a rhetorical crossfire, the report appeared to fall ironically short by the measure of its own democratic standard, even as it called for "new attitudes for overcoming stereotyped thinking and to promote more understanding of diversity."[11]

The commissioners understood and rightly insisted that better answers to the challenges of the new world communication order would not be premised on the development of increasingly advanced technologies. A more just and democratic social order would require instead greater attention to the conceptual and political foundations of human development. The penetrating question the commission report asked, but could only begin to answer, was: "What type of communication practices and structures are needed to institute truly active involvement by the people in making global, overall development their own responsibility?"[12] For, as Vincent Mosco later noted, information technologies, including computer communication systems, do not by themselves create a more peaceful and equitable world; they require instead an expression of will and exercise of inventiveness by citizens dedicated to democracy in order to convert the technologies of a war system into instruments of a just peace.[13]

The vitality of communication was appropriately understood by the MacBride Commission to extend to the formation of community and to encompass the ordinary activities and personal responsibilities of everyday people. It was not conceived narrowly as just a process of conveying information, transmitting knowledge, disseminating culture, or providing other such neutral mediations. Human understanding, mutual appreciation, and social cohesion could be produced in communication when differing viewpoints were engaged widely in debate and discussion.[14] Yet, nowhere in the report was a richly democratic practice of dissent described, conceptualized, or otherwise explained. Instead, the more or less centralized modalities of communication media, well removed from the grassroots of everyday political participation, were featured by the commission. Attention was focused throughout on matters such as the protection of journalists, the democratization of media management, inequities of communication facilities, impact of new media, and in general the infrastructure, economics, advanced technologies, organization, and operation of mass media, all of which are important considerations of media institutions and media policy. While the MacBride commissioners recognized the role of symbols, gestures, language, and images in the makeup of messages, they did not pursue the question of how these elements of discourse can work in the interactions of common citizens to constitute and strengthen cultural investments in peace.[15]

Here, then, at the intersection of media and messages is where we need to look more closely at how the discourse of ordinary people can enrich the democratic practices of society. Media messages are consumed and attitudes are articulated into public opinion at the grassroots of society. Collective attitudes about war and peace are composed in public discourse, not simply adopted in the form transmitted by governing elites. The threatening images of foreigners, which are packaged and conveyed in mainstream media, ultimately must pass muster with the people. Public talk reconstitutes menacing images into commonplace terms that may or may not conform to the will of economic and political elites. Democratic communication shapes media messages one way or another into civic attitudes that favor hostilities or, alternatively, resist war. Ruling images can continue to rule, then, only if they make sense at the grassroots of society as expressed in commonplace terms. The vernacular of political talk among the citizenry is a potential source of recalcitrance to the governing discourse of reigning authority.

Thus, a decent regard for human diversity expressed in the discourse of ordinary people can be a hedge against the whirlwind of prejudice and can provide a basis of public disenchantment with fear-mongering propaganda. We should ask, therefore, how the mesmerizing rituals of vilification and the governing discourses of victimization that are conjured up so readily by media institutions in the service of controlling authorities might be held more accountable to the articulated conscience of the citizenry. What are the tactics of dissent that can make public opinion more responsive to an ethic of peace and more resistant to war and, conversely, how are the tactical configurations of antiwar discourses vulnerable to reconfiguration by mainstream media and to recapture and control by the disciplining structures of power? Is there a way to make discourses of dissent more robustly democratic in an age of globalization and violence?

The MacBride report's remarkable and lasting achievement is the seriousness it attributes to the role of communication in matters of democratization and peace. It challenges us to probe further and deeper into the workings of democratic communication and peacemaking. As such, it is a firm foundation on which to build a better understanding of the everyday tactics of dissent and corresponding resources of media within the larger framework of a world communication order and for the purpose of enriching democratic culture to resist war.

(RE)HUMANIZING TACTICS OF DISSENT

Dissent from war is usefully thought of as a tactic, or set of tactics, of ordinary communication employed by everyday citizens who interact in settings that are saturated by media of one kind or another at every point in the process. Thinking of dissent in this way is critical to determining how a people might feasibly resist the ubiquitous caricatures and dehumanizing images that goad them to kill a phantom enemy or to defend a vague symbol such as freedom that has been emptied of any significant meaning. Tactics are all that a people have at their disposal in a political system of representative, rather than direct, democracy. Power is wielded most immediately by political elites. Collective self-governance is achieved only indirectly, if at all, by pressuring elected and appointed officials.

The latent power of the people resides in their ability to resist that which delegated authority is empowered to initiate. The main remaining check on the measures undertaken by political elites—the principal counterweight to the initiatives of governing authorities—is the recalcitrance of articulated public opinion. The governing principle of the commonwealth is to distribute direct political power—the power to formulate, carry out, and justify or rationalize policy—to executive, legislative, and judicial authorities in various amounts and types. Little to none of this direct authority to originate policy and to author courses of action is granted to, or reserved for, the people themselves.

On matters of foreign relations generally and war specifically, executive license to act prevails over all other political authority. The presidency not only sets and directs policy in this domain but also formulates the official rationale for engaging in warfare. The presidential persona speaks to and for the state on matters of national crisis. It is given license to act with minimal interference from the legislature, the judiciary, and the mainstream press. The president—or whoever wields executive authority in a given system of representative democracy—is presumed to be in charge of defining the crisis and assumes responsibility for leading the way to its eventual resolution.

This is a system of governance that would lull the citizenry into mental passivity and encourage political quiescence, except to impel the people to participate in public displays of patriotic fervor or otherwise to affirm, sanction, endorse, or consent to official policy and its justification. It would co-opt the people's power to withhold assent, especially their potential to resist an official rationale for war, to hold executive authority to a higher standard of justification, and to insist on an alternative to warfare. It would relegate to itself the sole power to establish the prevailing framework of sense-making because that is the hinge of interpretation most vulnerable to resistance.

The guiding perspective from which governing authority would have the people see warfare as the nation's only realistic option is vulnerable because it is subject to daily challenge by ordinary people in small and large venues distributed throughout the land. The people, who are not well-positioned to formulate war policy, are capable of reacting against it. Indeed, they are called into existence as a collective entity on the subject of war by the executive authority's very efforts to vindicate armed hostilities. With the people so constituted, presidential strategy is rendered publicly accountable and subject to citizen tactics that can make war propaganda problematic.

This distinction between presidential strategy and citizen tactics is much like the general differentiation Michel de Certeau has made between strategies and tactics in his analysis of politics and communication in everyday life. A strategy is a maneuver, a calculation, or a manipulation from an established position or place of strength in which someone or some agency can operate with a substantial accumulation of symbolic and material resources. This is an operation available to someone or to an institution or other entity (such as an army, a presidency, a multinational corporation, or a discipline of scientific knowledge) that is endowed with significant power on a given terrain of social contestation and political conflict. These empowered authorities aim to establish and maintain a proper place for every relevant element of thought and action. Strategy functions as a discipline of power.[16]

Tactics, on the other hand, are mobile operations devised and executed on the fly by a weaker party to oppose the strategies of a stronger opponent. They are calculated actions of resistance taken in a space or on a terrain that is occupied, controlled, organized, defined, and imposed on an inferior force by a dominant authority. The weaker party does not have the opportunity to plan a general strategy and therefore must maneuver in an ad hoc manner and opportunistic fashion under the scrutiny of the controlling force. "In short," Certeau writes, "a tactic is an art of the weak" that "is determined by the *absence of power* just as a strategy is organized by the postulation of power."[17]

Communication and politics—not just military operations—consist of strategies and tactics. Tactics require an operation of insight or wit that reveals the apparently better position staked out by the controlling authority to be the worse stance to assume on the matter at issue. In this sense, tactics are derived from rhetorical twists and turns. They are tropes of language, "a *different* use of a language *already used*," the tricks or maneuvers of "linguistic combat."[18] These "manipulations of language" in the "interplay of forces" are "ways of speaking" that correspond to "ways of operating" against established authority.[19] Such rhetorical modes of moving about and speaking, Certeau explains, are characteristic of "tactical ruses and surprises: clever tricks of the 'weak' within the order established by the 'strong,' an art of putting one over on the adversary on his own turf."[20]

Language tactics, in this sense, provide the people with a vehicle of maneuver and a means of resistance when they are called into being and put into place as a subordinate political body by a controlling regime of war propaganda. Tactics are a common resource with which the people can develop liberating insights and articulate reasons for opposing war. But the counter-tactics of the dominant regime, consistent with its strategy of placement and superior material and symbolic resources, also operate linguistically and rhetorically to discredit opposing discourses and recapture the mind of the public. Maneuvers and counter-maneuvers remain in play until a controlling authority recuperates its position and achieves a "return to order," or unless and until a resistant citizenry attains a position of ascendancy by producing "a new *cultural and political unity*," a new or revised structure of discourse that puts in place a "different order" of meaning, rather than just an immobilizing negation or rhetorical inversion of the original regime of interpretation.[21] Such a different unity or new order, if and when it is achieved, provides an alternative understanding of available options and/or a revised interpretation of threatening circumstances that can be acted upon to supplant a damaged and discredited framework of war propaganda.

What kind of a new unity or synthesis of understanding or revised perspective might erode the authority of war propaganda? Given that the strategy of war propaganda is to dehumanize adversaries so that they can be portrayed as utter enemies, *the tactics of resistance are most aptly focused on expressing the unity of humanity*. By means of a dehumanizing and decivilizing rhetoric of savagery, executive authority goads the citizenry to dissociate themselves completely from an alien identity or estranged population that is marked as barbaric, irrational, aggressive, and coercive. Stereotyped and dehumanized enemies can be killed more or less freely as if they are demons or mere animals and without the dissonance of recognizing their complex human identity or acknowledging that they share a world in common.[22] The people are prompted to feel threatened and victimized by uncivilized evildoers. This has been the traditional strategy for justifying hostilities throughout US history, and it is the heart of the rationale for a blanket war on terrorism.[23] The struggle between executive authority and public resistance is over the strategic projection of and tactical opposition to a simplistic but culturally indigenous image of a free and just Us mortally threatened by a hateful and hostile Them.

Myriad tactics to resist such caricatures of victim and victimizer may and must be devised in democratic communication, but the chance of ultimately prevailing over a regime of war depends on more than just negating stereotypes or, worse yet, merely reversing oversimplified attributions of guilt and innocence. Such tactical maneuvers, consistent with Certeau's analysis, are subject to recapture within the strategic perspective of political authority, thus risking a reversion to the hostile imagination rather than moving forward constructively toward a humanizing vision of reconciliation. The most viable and hopeful way to dissent from war is to articulate an alternative order of understanding, a way of grasping the common humanity of those who would otherwise be designated as mutual enemies and/or made the subjects of deadly struggle. To communicate this bond of humanity, moreover, requires a dissenting discourse that avoids vilifying or in other ways alienating the identity of the very people it would constitute as peacemakers.

This is not to suggest that politics and peacemaking operate free of struggle or without the discord of rivalry. Politics, by definition, is a realm of constant contestation, limited agreement, and irreducible contingencies. It is the alternative to warfare in which opponents are not relegated to the status of enemies but nevertheless remain adversaries.[24] One's political adversaries are deemed wrong in the sense of being mistaken—necessarily and even profoundly mistaken—whereas one's mortal enemies are considered wrong in the sense of being downright evil, vicious, and barbaric. Persuasion, rather than coercion, is the operative mode of political contestation and the means by which one attempts to correct a mistaken rival rather than to eradicate or neutralize an evil threat.[25]

In short, rivals have to establish some minimal degree of identification with one another in order to engage in nonviolent political contestation over their differences instead of outright warfare. They have to perceive some shared substance to avoid becoming sheer enemies. Their communication, as Kenneth Burke has observed, must make them sufficiently "consubstantial," which is not the same as identical but instead is a strong enough basis of identification with one another to bridge the substantial differences that divide them.[26] Peaceful and robust political contestation requires the artful articulation of consubstantial rivals—the rehumanization of enemies—which allows tensions to be managed, not eliminated.[27] Diversity is expected, not effaced or perceived as inherently threatening. One's political rivals are never stripped of their common humanity, whereas one's mortal enemies are reduced to reptiles, insects, germs, beasts of prey, barbarians, lunatics, demons, and the like.[28] The choice between war and peace, as Burke understood, is a function of numerous persuasive acts that add up over time to construct a social texture of one kind of cooperation or the other, a cooperative attitude of violence or a social web of constructive contestation.[29]

THE DOUBLE GESTURE OF NONCONFORMING SOLIDARITY

Similarly, political dissent is a double gesture of nonconformity and solidarity, difference and identification, division and consubstantiation. The very credibility of democratic dissent, especially in a political system that is troubled by controversy during times of war and crisis, depends upon a capacity to criticize, argue, protest, object, or remonstrate in a manner that is connected to, based on, and developed from within a common political culture.[30] Accordingly, a sharp critical thrust against governing opinion or official policy must be balanced by an equally firm footing in the underlying culture of values, beliefs, and accepted ways of acting.

The legitimacy of democratic dissent is a double-sided notion of constructive criticism, qualified deference, or conflicted confirmation that defines a loyal opposition. Without the sharp edge of criticism, dissent fails to challenge existing attitudes, conventions, and policies. Without a reassuring embrace, dissent is readily dismissed as alien and ill-willed—thus, the necessity of a faithful or trustworthy embrace to reduce the distance between dissenters and the ruling formation of authority they wish to challenge. Yet, the gap cannot be fully closed without conforming entirely to the contours of a political regime that is committed to coercion and warfare. The possibility of credible dissent relies on achieving a certain productive tension between affirming and disconcerting the political order. Optimal credibility, by this account, implies a kind of rough equivalency between, and synthesis of, the two gestures of nonconformity and solidarity.

This double gesture of dissent is evident, for example, in a political documentary that entered the fray of an already heated 2004 presidential campaign season to criticize the Bush administration's preemptive invasion of Iraq. *Uncovered*, directed by Robert Greenwald, was circulated to the public first as a DVD and then as a film. Sharply challenging the presidential rationale for war, it argued that the claim of a threat from Iraqi weapons of mass destruction was not just wrong but also deceitful. It challenged the administration's strategic representation of conventional wisdom and attempted to realign the dictates of common sense. Examining this particular documentary as a concrete example of how nonconforming solidarity can be articulated in popular media reveals in the basic gesture both a tactical potential to make antiwar dissent credible and a strategic limitation when it operates sans a rehumanizing theme.

Uncovered initiated its critique of the Bush administration by assembling a cast of insiders, introduced as "The Experts," whose credentials leveraged their repudiation of governing authority on the issue of Iraq's alleged threat to American security. Administration political figures were juxtaposed visually and verbally throughout the documentary, on matters related to Iraqi weapons of mass destruction, with this cast of dissenting experts, whose expertise ranged from military intelligence to arms control, diplomacy, warfare, and defense policy. Sharp criticisms of government claims were embedded in calm and cogent narratives of fact and perspective, which were systematically contrasted with clips of administration spokespersons in progressively compromised positions. Images of truth, reason, balance, judgment, openness, and democracy were rearticulated to the ends of the documentary's critique and dissociated from the prevailing political position by multiple accounts of the administration's dishonesty, distortions, manipulations, propaganda, theatrical performances, obsessions, dirty tricks, and illegalities.

Completed in November 2003 and initially released the following December as a 56-minute DVD under the full title of *Uncovered: The Whole Truth about the Iraq War*, Greenwald's critique of the war reportedly sold nearly 100,000 copies on line by May. *The Village Voice* identified it as a "documentary of dissent." The liberal advocacy group, MoveOn.org, widely publicized the DVD and actively organized home screenings of it nationwide. It was designed for grassroots consumption and discussion, but it was also watched by opinion leaders and policymakers in Washington, DC through the auspices of the Center for American Progress.[31] The DVD version was then expanded into a 90-minute, 35-millimeter film for worldwide distribution by Cinema Libre Distribution, to open in August in theaters in New York, Boston, and Washington, DC under the shortened title, *Uncovered: The War on Iraq*.

The press release for the film version stated that Greenwald's documentary "deconstructs the administration's case for war through interviews with US intelligence and defense officials, foreign service experts, and UN weapons inspectors—including a former CIA director, a former ambassador to Saudi Arabia and even President Bush's Secretary of the Army."[32] The documentary's basic formula for turning the tables on executive authority was to combine an edgy act of deconstruction with a heavy cast of authoritative insiders. Not surprisingly, then, it was described by reviewers as a damning and devastating critique that was honest, as sober as a legal brief, and uncorrupted by the flamboyancy of Michael Moore's *Fahrenheit 9/11*.[33] It adopted the tactic of a straightforward and intellectual approach to contest claims of fact and interpretations of evidence.

The documentary's credibility as an exercise in dissent rested on both its devastating criticism of the war and its diligent conformity to the broader cultural values of reason and rationality. It made itself consubstantial with the larger political culture in the very manner it rivaled the Bush administration, studiously adopting a persona of reasonableness to convey a contrasting image of executive manipulation and misrepresentation. A principal vehicle of this tactic for turning the tables on the administration was an array of recurring visual and verbal metaphors of political "theater" and obsessive "propaganda." Director Greenwald's stinging criticism was delivered by his large cast of expert characters with a demeanor that was consistently calm, never agitated.

The number and credentials of Greenwald's cast were featured throughout the documentary, which devoted a long opening segment to introducing "The Experts," who appeared one by one and spoke in the following manner:

> MILT BEARDEN, Thirty years with the CIA from 1964 to 1994; RAND BEERS, I worked for the government for 35 years starting with the Marine Corps from 1962 to 1968 with some service in Vietnam; GRAHAM FULLER, I was 25 years as a professional intelligence officer with CIA; KAREN KWIATKOWSKI, Almost 5 years in the Pentagon and the last almost 3 of that working in the office of the secretary of defense; JOHN BRADY KIESLING, I spent almost 20 years with the state department. Three years in Athens as a political counselor for the chief of the political section; PATRICK LANG, I'm a retired colonel in the United States army, military intelligence special forces; LARRY JOHNSON, I was previously with the state department's office of counter-terrorism from 1989-1993. Prior to that I worked with the Central Intelligence Agency. . . . RAY MCGOVERN, For 27 years I was an analyst first of Soviet affairs and then of wider responsibilities; JOSEPH WILSON, I served for 23 years in the American Foreign Service as a diplomat. . . . SCOTT RITTER, I'm a former weapons inspector with the United Nations in Iraq. I served in that capacity from 1991 until 1998. . . . ADMIRAL STANSFIELD TURNER, I never expected that I'd leave the navy and become chief spook of our country, director of Central Intelligence, but that happened.[34]

Each time these and the other experts appeared throughout the documentary, their credentials were displayed on screen.

The veracity of this expert testimony was expressed in numerous subtleties of speech and manner, such as Milt Bearden's resort to ironic understatement when he said:

> Preemptive war by its very nature is something that is entirely new to the United States of America and to what we call the Western Alliance. You go back through history and at the Peace of Westfalia in 1648 a group of nations that had just killed most of each other off decided that isn't quite the way to do it and they came up with a set of laws that we've all lived by fairly well since then which doesn't much allow for preemptive war.[35]

These subtleties were bolstered by overt claims to special knowledge, such as Scott Ritter contradicting Secretary of State Powell and other administration figures by saying:

> There were never any chemical weapons in that facility. I'm intimately familiar with that facility. I've inspected it a number of times. Other inspectors have inspected it many more times than I have.[36]

Ray McGovern, commenting similarly from his experienced vantage point on "Colin Powell's [UN] debut as an imagery analyst," found it to be "highly embarrassing for those of us who know something about the business." Joe Wilson told of being sent by the CIA to check out, at the request of Vice President Cheney, a report of Niger's government authorizing the sale of uranium yellowcake to Iraq, which Wilson reported back to the CIA "could not have happened." Yet, the administration insisted after that on citing the bogus report as evidence of Iraq's development of weapons of mass destruction. When a clip was next played of Condoleezza Rice denying that the administration knew the Niger report was bogus, Ambassador Wilson trumped her denial with his own unique authority as the administration's source of corrected intelligence: "Given what I knew about where the question had originated and given what I knew about the way the government works, I knew that people in her circle did know" the Niger report was bogus.[37]

Against this uniform display of expert knowledge and controlled rationality, Greenwald showed a presidency determined to distort reality to its own ideological ends. He had UN arms inspector Scott Ritter comment on a visual image of Secretary of State Colin Powell, who was making the administration's case for war at the United Nations, by saying in a voice over, "First of all it should be noted that Colin Powell's speech to the United Nations was theater, a masterful theater, effective theater at the time." A few shots later, intelligence expert Ray McGovern characterized Secretary Powell's UN speech, specifically the faulty evidence of Iraqi weapons of mass destruction, as "a masterful performance, but none of it was true." CIA Director George Tenet, McGovern observed, was placed directly behind Powell "as a prop . . . as if to say that the Central Intelligence Agency stands behind, or in this case sits behind, everything that Colin Powell says." Even the images of mobile labs that Powell used to dramatize his case for Iraqi possession of weapons of mass destruction, Ritter pointed out, were not photographs but instead "artist's renditions" because "we have no proof they exist." In another expert voice over toward the end of the documentary—as President Bush was shown emerging from a fighter aircraft outfitted in flight suit after staging an aircraft carrier landing to declare the end of major fighting in Iraq—viewers were told that "you don't want your president to be seen as a hot dog. . . . I mean you want a sign of kind of maturity and not testosterone blasting through."[38]

Besides relegating the administration's case for war to theatrical display, Greenwald had his experts frame it variously as *propaganda* (David Albright, scientist and weapons inspector: ". . . it borders on propaganda to argue that the small number [of chemical weapons] that have been found by inspectors imply that, in this case, over 29,000 exist"); as *rhetoric* (Ritter: the media "bought into the Bush Administration's rhetoric"); as *manipulation* (Senator

Ted Kennedy: "...what has happened was more than a failure of intelligence, but a manipulation of the intelligence... to justify the decision to go to war"); as the *one-sided* case-making of an unchecked prosecuting attorney (Albright: "It was a prosecutor making a case, using what benefited his case, ignoring evidence that would undermine his case, and there was no defense attorney to give us the other side"); as *misleading, distorting,* and *criminal* (John Dean, who served in the Nixon "dirty tricks" White House: "The most troubling thing about the... distortions and the misleading statements that Bush gave Congress is that it is a federal felony, it's a crime to mislead and distort information to present to the Congress").[39]

As Greenwald's experts refuted the administration's case point-by-point, clips were repeatedly shown of George W. Bush, Dick Cheney, Donald Rumsfeld, Colin Powell, Condoleezza Rice, Ari Fleischer, and Paul Wolfowitz reasserting their now-deconstructed case for war, until finally they began to stumble, bluster, and backpedal when no weapons of mass destruction could be found in occupied Iraq. In one instance, at the end of a series of clips conveying the image of a progressively unraveling Secretary of Defense, Donald Rumsfeld was seen saying that he could not think of anyone who "contended that the Iraqis had nuclear weapons."[40] The veracity of expert dissenters stood in bold relief to the administration's theatrics as the documentary closed on the theme of upholding the Constitution, questioning authority, and recognizing the patriotism of dissent. The tables had been turned on the administration, at least within the confines of the documentary itself.

By these kinds of rhetorical operations, *Uncovered* captured and re-appropriated cultural capital to challenge a privileged narrative of war. It articulated the legitimacy of its own dissenting voice as a democratic rival to a ruling executive by displaying deference to the public values of transparency, honesty, and reasonableness, the very values that it accused the Bush administration of abandoning in favor of political theater. Metaphors of deceitful theatrical production helped to convey the image of a ruling regime placed at odds with the substance of a democratic people and contrasted directly with the democratic persona of Greenwald's cast of well-credentialed war dissenters.

The point here is not to suggest that these were the only tactics used in *Uncovered* to turn the tables on a war president, his cabinet, and advisors. Nor do I mean to suggest that *Uncovered* was superior overall to other documentaries of dissent (such as Moore's *Fahrenheit 9/11*). Instead, my purpose is to illustrate one way in which the double gesture of nonconforming solidarity can operate to articulate credible dissent. Achieving a rough equivalency between affirming and disrupting the political order leverages dissent in circumstances that otherwise demand overt assent or silent compliance, even against one's better judgment. The tactics for transforming and reallocating political and cultural capital will vary from one dissenting voice, medium, genre of communication, and set of circumstances to another, but in general they will operate in the manner of a rhetorical twist or turn that exposes and unsettles a governing authority's rigidified and violence-engendering propaganda. Dissent understood in this way returns human struggle to the realm of everyday politics made accessible and accountable to the citizenry.

Still, these tactical negations, inversions, and reversals are rhetorical maneuvers short of advancing an alternative order of understanding or new unifying perspective. As negative tactics of dissent, they are susceptible to recapture within the strategic framework of political authority. They tear at the fabric of the prevailing order of interpretation without producing a new structure of meaning to replace the damaged rationale for armed hostilities. If perspective serves to frame attitudes and attitudes are predispositions to act one way rather than another, then tactics must contribute to the articulation of a perspective that transcends the hostile imagination; that is, they must contribute to an alternative perspective that reorients and motivates the people to support humane measures over human slaughter. Anti-war tactics, such as those illustrated in *Uncovered*, are badly handicapped and cannot ultimately prevail unless the double gesture of dissent also affirms the common order of humanity in culturally apt terms even as it dismantles particular aspects of the official pretext for war. Tactics must contribute to a palpable and present sense of human solidarity, not only to justify nonconformity to the dictates of a war regime but also to envision and motivate an optional course of action.

POLITICAL SURROGACY AND RITUALS
OF RECIPROCAL RECRIMINATION

Resisting a regime of war propaganda on its own turf becomes increasingly viable as the tactics of dissent maneuver away from the strategic disjunction of good and evil and begin to articulate a conjunction of humanity on both sides of the symbolic divide between Us and Them, ally and enemy, friend and foe, civilization and savagery, victim and victimizer. However, the tendency of dissenting tactics is to reverse the order of attributions rather than to transcend the disjunction itself. Thus, an officially designated enemy is typically re-inscribed in anti-war dissent as the victim rather than the victimizer, and the vaunted Us is transposed into an evil force. This inversion of good and evil leaves the citizenry to choose between its collective guilt and the guilt of an alien foe—between condemning its own or castigating an outsider—which makes it all the easier for a governing discourse to recapture ground previously lost to dissent. To avoid perpetuating rituals of recrimination that work strategically to the advantage of the war regime and to improve the chance of securing gains and making additional headway, anti-war dissent must bridge the differences between adversaries rather than just invert attributions of innocence and blame.

One must wonder, then, why dissent defaults so readily to the tactics of inversion and negation, preventing it from maneuvering away from a war regime's strategic talk of evil. An answer to that question can be found in a second example of anti-war dissent—the case of Ward Churchill, a professor of ethnic studies at the University of Colorado at Boulder. Professor Churchill exercised his academic freedom to blame Americans for the 9/11 terrorist attacks. His tactic of reversing the guilt (most people would say he was blaming the victims) played into the strength of the administration's strategy. He seemed to be lured, coaxed, and inveigled into making such counterproductive statements, as if the governing war discourse had invented a convenient fall guy to deflect anti-war dissent from the heart of the matter. To see how a ruling strategic discourse can contain dissent, minimize losses without losing position, and recapture its claim on common sense, we need look no farther than the orchestrated attack on academic freedom in which Ward Churchill was selected as an opportune and accommodating scapegoat.

This particular example of dissent is useful to examine because it illustrates not only how negative tactics of resistance can be readily recaptured and made to serve the strategic purposes of a war regime but also how a governing discourse operates through multiple conduits and intermediaries to regulate the outlook of the general public and thus contain dissent. It is not just the words uttered officially by formal authority that circulate strategically through mainstream media over the terrain of public opinion. A dominating discourse, especially in circumstances of perceived crisis and ongoing warfare, also asserts its will through unofficial and quasi-official surrogates—proxies, alter egos, stand-ins, proctors, cronies, operatives, delegates, and the like. Sometimes secretly—sometimes not—a political surrogacy is purposefully arranged and deliberately orchestrated, such as when the Department of Education covertly prearranged to pay a prominent African-American political commentator, Armstrong Williams, to condemn the National Education Association and other critics of the administration's "No Child Left Behind" policy as if he were speaking and writing independently.[41] Other times, unofficial surrogates of power operate parallel to, but without immediate or specific direction from, central authority. One cannot know for sure in any given instance how or whether official and unofficial operatives are closely coordinated or if they are simply functioning as parallel and congruent agents of a governing discourse. Thus, the contest over which perspective will dominate

the nation's political imagination and prevail upon collective public opinion
can be delegated and become strategically decentralized in any particular case.

Culture Wars, Terrorism, and Academic Freedom

Political authority operates on a base of articulated public opinion. The controversy over Ward Churchill and corresponding attack on academic freedom
in the immediate context of the administration's declared war on terrorism
worked in just this way, that is, as an extension of the ongoing culture wars.
The culture wars had been raging since the 1980s, well before the dramatic
events of 9/11 propelled neo-conservatism into the forefront of American politics at all levels of governance. After 9/11, neo-conservative ideology rapidly
became the agenda-setting discourse of politics on foreign and domestic
policy. As George Lakoff observed about moral politics in America:

> Conservatives want to change American culture itself. They want to change
> the idea of what counts as a good person and what the world should be
> like. Conservatives understand that this means starting with the family. But
> it also means changing such things as who gets what jobs and what ideas
> dominate our culture … over a range of cultural issues, from affirmative
> action to the nature of art.[42]

The political battleground over conservative and liberal values extended to
a cluster of interrelated subjects and defining issues such as homosexuality
and gay rights, multiculturalism, affirmative action, feminism, abortion,
family values, religion and public morality, moral education, church-state
relations, welfare, gun control, environmentalism, postmodernism, political
correctness, funding for the arts, and so on. It became a site of moral conflict
and power politics aimed at imposing one ideological agenda over another
instead of negotiating differences.[43] The right wing advanced a politics of
social conservatism and assumed an aggressive moralist posture toward foreign affairs. This take-no-prisoners attitude extended easily after 9/11 to an
open-ended war on terrorism, an overt policy of preemptive warfare, and a
thoroughgoing exercise in American unilateralism and imperialism under the
guise of spreading democracy.

In this ideologically heated and polarizing environment, the right-wing
surrogates of political authority targeted America's institutions of higher
learning for special attention. This was not the first time in US history that
university professors and the principle of academic freedom had come under
attack. Attempts to suppress academic freedom came in the late nineteenth
century from religious fundamentalists among university trustees and administrators; at the turn of the twentieth century it came from trustees who were
unfettered capitalists; during World War I it came as an outbreak of jingoism

accompanied by widespread suppression of civil rights; before and after World War II it came in waves of anti-communism, including the notorious era of McCarthyism. As an extension of the culture wars, the post-9/11 attack on academic freedom from the ascendant right combined all these elements of ideological, religious, and economic fundamentalism within a supercharged context of militant patriotism. The assault was made viciously ironic by alleging that professors themselves were destroying academic freedom.

The university curriculum—especially in the arts, the humanities, and the social sciences—was already an object of scrutiny and censure in the ongoing culture wars before the terrorist strikes on the twin towers and the Pentagon. Right-wing ideological vigilantes such as Accuracy in Academia had set themselves up as watchdog outfits to report miscreant professors, and the American Council of Trustees and Alumni was launched in 1995 by the likes of Joseph Lieberman and Lynne Cheney (the former chairwoman of the National Endowment for the Humanities and ultraconservative spouse of "neocon" Vice-President Dick Cheney) with the aim of mobilizing "concerned alumni, trustees, and education leaders across the country on behalf of academic freedom, excellence, and accountability at our colleges and universities."[44] ACTA charged that the threat to academic freedom came from within academia, that is, from professors, not from external sources: "The barbarians are not at the gates; they are inside the walls." Trustees should protect the academic and financial well-being of their institutions, ACTA warned, by "ensuring that their campus maintains a genuinely open intellectual environment when faculty and administrators fail to do so." Everyone, including state officials, should work to return campuses to their "intellectual moorings" and to "reaffirm the search for truth" because "no fanaticism, no ideology, no political passion has the right to suppress free minds in the pursuit of truth."[45]

ACTA's rhetorical stratagem set the tone of the times. While in reality it was an instrument of the ideologically extreme and politically empowered right-wing, ACTA masqueraded as the protector of truth, balance, openness, excellence, accountability, and intellectual freedom. It posed as an unbiased defender against a horde of fanatical professors whom it accused of manipulating student minds, instead of educating them, and of turning students into agents of social engineering.

Following 9/11, ACTA quickly established what it strategically called a "Defense of Civilization Fund." The fund's first project, released in November 2001, was a 43-page report entitled "Defending Civilization: How Our Universities Are Failing America and What Can Be Done about It."[46] ACTA proclaimed that college and university professors were the weak link in the war on terror. It named 117 scholars, students, and administrators who had uttered supposedly unpatriotic sentiments when suggesting, for example, that war may not be the best means of fighting terrorism. Unwilling to distinguish between explanation and justification of the 9/11 terrorist attacks, ACTA dogmatically insisted that any intellectual accounting for terrorist attacks amounted to a terrorist-sympathizing act of blaming America first.

ACTA's threat-from-within-academe, barbarian-within-the-walls-of-civilization stratagem carried forward the reactionary anti-political correctness campaign of the 1980s culture wars. This resurgence of fundamentalism, Henry Giroux observed, attacked the teaching of critical thinking and social responsibility that is crucial to the enrichment of democratic culture. These fundamentalist reformers, he argued, infantilized students in the name of defending ortho-doxy against the imagined onslaught of radical PC professors. This far-right version of academic correctness promoted a traditional curriculum and upheld an elitist sensibility of national unity by excluding information on oppression and suppressing knowledge of alternative perspectives. Whereas teaching the traditional canon of knowledge was deemed neutral, introduc-ing issues of race, class, gender, culture, and perspective was considered polit-ical indoctrination. Yet, as Giroux underscored, so-called PC pedagogical ter-rorists were precisely the teachers who recognized the democratic values inherent in a pedagogy of disagreement, dissent, and debate over one of canonical indoctrination and the transmission of orthodoxy. Good professors promoted critical inquiry instead of performing as priests of supposedly unproblematic knowledge and universal truth. Developing a democratically appropriate critical consciousness required understanding how power oper-ates in the production of knowledge rather than succumbing to the dogmatic and doctrinaire rehearsal of received wisdom advocated by resurgent ultra-conservatives under the ironically inverse standard of anti-political correct-ness and in the false name of preserving academic freedom.[47] Calling such an ideologically-driven attack a defense of academic freedom was cynical at best; worse yet, it was an affront to critical thinking that made a mockery of democratic culture.

Inspired by ACTA's post-9/11 rehearsal of the right-wing myth of barbar-ians within the walls of academe, Daniel Pipes founded the Campus Watch web site as a project of the Middle East Forum. Its purpose was to criticize Middle East studies programs at American universities, which were accused of "analytical failures, the mixing of politics with scholarship, intolerance of alternative views, apologetics, and the abuse of power over students." These programs were deemed important to monitor because of their special rele-vance to public attitudes about the war on terror, the Arab-Israeli conflict, the invasion and occupation of Iraq, and related subjects. Middle East specialists were accused of analytical errors such as suggesting that Americans have an ethnocentric view of democracy, that Islamist movements are not necessarily anti-American, and that autocratic Arab regimes are precarious. They were condemned for extremism because, lacking an appropriate appreciation of American national interests, they criticized US foreign policy. They were denounced for being "almost monolithically leftist" and pilloried for engaging in apologetics to explain away "internal repression in Libya, Sudan, Syria, Iraq, Iran, and the Palestinian Authority," the suicide bombings against Israel, the aims of Islamist movements, and "the anti-American, anti-Christian, and anti-Semitic incitement that pervades state-run media through most of the region." They were derided for exercising abusive power over students whom they allegedly expected to embrace biased and partisan views and then punished with lower grades or weaker recommendations for resisting such unreasonable expectations. Campus Watch monitored institutions and individual scholars who manifested these problems, inviting students to file reports of abuse and publicizing its findings in various outlets. It alerted "university stakeholders," including administrators, alumni, trustees, parents, and state and federal legislators and challenged them "to take back their universities." All of this, Campus Watch insisted disingenuously, was in support of "unencumbered freedom of speech of all scholars, regardless of their views."[48]

Campus Watch also insisted that its campaign to root out anti-American bias in Middle-East studies differed entirely from McCarthyism because Campus Watch was not an official government activity or agency, it had no direct coercive power and no immediate authority over faculty members or universities, it documented its claims, it had no intention of depriving faculty members of employment or suppressing their freedom of speech, and it did not engage in name-calling. The legacy of McCarthyism resided instead, it asserted, in the antiwar movement and the tradition of left-wing academic McCarthyism, which relied on smear tactics to criticize Campus Watch.[49]

Despite its denials, disclaimers, double-talk, and rhetorical inversions, all aimed at portraying itself as a victim of unfounded incriminations and a defender of free speech, rather than a voice of orthodoxy and antagonist of academic freedom, Campus Watch was the instrument of political activist Daniel Pipes and his far-right associates. They initiated their presence on the World Wide Web by posting "dossiers" of scholars who had criticized US foreign policy in the Middle East, especially for America's one-sided support of Israel. As a consequence, the scholars featured in these dossiers received massive numbers of harassing e-mail messages and even death threats. Campus Watch removed the dossiers only after receiving a good deal of criticism, replacing them with a new focus on offending universities. Its "Keep Us Informed" section invited students to inform anonymously on their errant professors in Middle East and related studies. Pipes himself had written derisive comments over the years about Muslims and Arabs in the *National Review* and other places. One of his principal aims was to cut off Title VI funding to existing Middle East area studies programs in American universities and to redirect funding to create an alternative Department of Defense training program that would develop a new generation of politically reliable Middle East experts. He claimed his critics were biased against American interests. His critics responded that Campus Watch twisted their words, quoted them out of context, and stretched the truth in order to make them sound, for example, as if they blamed the US and not terrorists for 9/11. Indeed, the Campus Watch assault on academic freedom was so apparent to the American Association of University Professors that they formed a special Committee on Academic Freedom in a Time of Crisis to correct and counter its systematic misrepresentations.[50]

While Campus Watch aimed to discipline American scholarship on the Middle East in order to make it ostensibly more "balanced" and thus supportive of American foreign policy, NoIndoctrination.org was founded by Luann Wright, a former high school science teacher from southern California, to organize "parents who are disturbed that sociopolitical agendas have been allowed to permeate college courses and orientation programs" more broadly. Although they aimed to dilute or even eliminate progressive curricula, they expressed their goal in the doublespeak code of protecting students' academic freedom. Thus, they complained that universities allowed "ideological fiefdoms" to persist in indoctrinating students—a "blatant and oppressive bias" that they equated to "thought reform."[51] A supportive Stanley Kurtz reported in the *National Review* that Wright's motivation stemmed from her son being required to take a "politicized composition course" as a freshman at the University of California at San Diego, a course that critiqued "whiteness" and raised issues with "US centrism." Her response was to devise a web site that "gives moderates and conservatives a way around the radical's grip on our mainstream journalistic and educational institutions," a way to fight the oppression of "PC professors."[52]

The alleged plight of college students became the rhetorical focal point of the far-right assault on academic freedom.[53] The formerly militant Marxist and now-ultraconservative political pugilist David Horowitz made his proposed "Academic Bill of Rights" the centerpiece of a campaign to transform universities by eliminating "liberal bias" and replacing it with what he called "reasoned discourse." His Center for the Study of Popular Culture (CSPC) was "dedicated to defending the cultural foundations of a free society, a task made even more pressing by the attack on America of September 11th, the Iraq conflict and the internal opponents of freedom this attack has revealed." Toward this end, CSPC reported that it had distributed in one year alone "half a million books and pamphlets on the war on terror, the Middle East crisis and the anti-American left" and that during that same time period

Horowitz himself had made over 500 appearances on radio and television shows and delivered numerous speeches at multiple university campuses. Additionally, the Center placed ads against the "so-called peace movement" in over 50 college newspapers.[54]

Horowitz's web presence extended to *FrontPageMagazine.com*, an online magazine of ultraconservative opinion about such matters as the war on terror and the threat of multiculturalism.[55] A main web vehicle for promoting his "Academic Bill of Rights" was a group he set up under the name of Students for Academic Freedom, a self-designated clearinghouse for student organizations with the goal of ending so-called political abuse in the university and restoring "integrity to the academic mission as a disinterested pursuit of knowledge."[56] On this web site, one could find items such as listings of SAF campus chapters, "basic texts" such as the proposed "Academic Bill of Rights" and "Student Bill of Rights," various related articles by Horowitz, the AAUP critique of the "Academic Bill of Rights" and Horowitz's rebuttal, a featured essay by Stanley Fish and a substantial archive of other essays and reports, instructions on how to research faculty bias, an assessment of political bias at elite colleges and universities, information related to legislative hearings on academic freedom in Colorado and US Senate hearings on the disappearance of intellectual diversity in American colleges and universities, and more.

Horowitz campaigned vigorously and relentlessly for state legislatures and Congress to adopt his "Academic Bill of Rights," which aimed to hold tenure decisions, the development of reading lists, and the scheduling of campus speakers to the standard of achieving a so-called balance of political and religious beliefs on campus. His efforts were quickly rewarded by Republicans in the US Congress and the Colorado state legislature sponsoring such legislation. Such coercive measures were necessary, Horowitz argued, because universities had failed to act on their own to correct political bias on their campuses.[57]

Horowitz calculatingly depicted his "Academic Bill of Rights" as an anti-quota bill that would remove the political quotas supposedly existing in American universities, "quotas" he claimed that resulted in a "ten- or thirty-to-one" imbalance favoring professors left of the political center.[58] Stanley Kurtz echoed Horowitz on this point with the bald assertion that "the grander a radical scholar's accusation against his nonleftist colleagues, the more likely he is to get tenure."[59] Thus, a primary premise in the fabricated case against academia was the blunt allegation that a disproportionately large percentage of politically correct leftist radicals dominated the national professoriate, an accusation that was given the unexamined and undeserved status of fact by default.

Horowitz's unwarranted claim of leftist-radical domination was drawn from a loose study he conducted with Eli Lehrer and Andrew Jones under the auspices of his Center for the Study of Popular Culture, a detailed summary of which was posted on the Students for Academic Freedom web site.[60] Their report revealed a preset conclusion in search of supporting evidence. It put forward an audacious claim based on a skewed sample, shoddy data collection, slanted statistics, and presumptive attributions of cause.

One relatively brief example provides a sense of Horowitz's stratagem. After using a skewed sample and shoddy data collection methods to falsely document radical liberal bias in US universities, Horowitz and his co-investigators concocted slanted and misleading statistics, the basic finding of which was that the overall ratio of Democrats to Republicans among university faculty in six departments in the humanities and social sciences at elite institutions is 10 to 1, but as bad as 30–1 at Brown University and 17–0 at MIT. This alleged ratio of registered Democrats to registered Republicans later became the basis of Horowitz's audacious claim that "on any given university faculty in America, professors to the left of the political center outnumber professors to the right of the political center by a factor of 10–1 or more." Even if one were to accept the obviously confused argument that registered Democrats are leftists, the raw data on which the claim of imbalance was based simply did not support the conclusion that there was a 10–1 ratio, which itself implied that the percentage of Democrats among the faculty was 90 percent or higher: that is, that 90 percent of the faculty were Democrat/ leftist. In fact, the raw data (if it were not itself badly flawed by poor data collection methods) would support at most the conclusion that of the 4,255 faculty members studied in these selected departments and universities, 33 percent were identified as registered Democrats, 44 percent as unaffiliated, 3 percent as Republican, and an additional 19 percent could not be identified by party affiliation. That is, the largest category for even this skewed sample of faculty members in the humanities and social sciences at elite institutions was unaffiliated and nearly two-thirds were not identified as either Republican or Democrat, which certainly did not support the claim that leftists dominated political moderates by a ratio of 10–1 or more. Indeed, Neil Hamilton (another critic of the academy), acknowledged that probably only 4–8 percent of the professoriate were what he called extreme or far-leftists, and even then Hamilton complained only about the activities of a tiny subset of this estimated 4–8 percent.[61] Horowitz's overall obfuscating stratagem was to imply widespread left-wing bias throughout the American professoriate without actually documenting such bias; the supporting maneuver was to create a false façade of documentation.

This was part and parcel of a cynical campaign to mislead the public about American universities and their faculties. As Horowitz explained, he encouraged his allies "to use the language that the left has deployed so effectively in behalf of its own agendas." By this formula, right-wing propagandists should systematically invert political discourse by claiming that a radical professoriate was creating a "hostile learning environment" and undermining "intellectual diversity," that the conservative viewpoint was "underrepresented," that the university should be "inclusive" and intellectually "diverse," and that professors are the true enemies of "academic freedom."[62] Previously, and in the same spirit of deliberately misrepresenting those whom he targeted for attack, Horowitz had authored the pamphlet, "The Art of Political War: How Republicans Can Fight to Win." Then party-whip Tom DeLay distributed this pamphlet to all Republican members of Congress, and the Heritage Foundation (which also produced Newt Gingrich's "Contract with America") sent it to 2,300 conservative activists during election year 2000. Its argument, that politics is war by other means, required the aggressor to win by destroying the other side's ability to fight. Understandably, Horowitz was a favorite of Karl Rove, who recommended Horowitz's memoir, *Destructive Generation*, to George W. Bush as early as 1993 in preparation for the presidential campaign of 2000, a campaign organized around the deceptive theme of "compassionate conservatism."[63]

By these brazen means, Horowitz and his supporters perfected the art of reversal to project their own dogmatism onto others, while gazing into a mirror as if it were a window onto the actual academic world.[64] The American Association of University Professors understood clearly that Horowitz's proposed "Academic Bill of Rights" would infringe on the very academic freedom it purported to protect. This organization, founded by John Dewey and Arthur Lovejoy in 1915 and dedicated ever since to the preservation of academic freedom, underscored that decisions about the quality of scholarship and teaching must be made by faculty based on academic standards rather than by nonacademics based on political criteria such as an enforced "balance" of conservatives and liberals imposed on academics by right-wing ideologues external to the university. In the words of the AAUP, "The line between indoctrination and proper pedagogical authority is to be determined by reference to scholarly and professional standards, as interpreted and applied by the faculty itself" and based on their "scholarly expertise and professional training," not by a regime of administrative and legislative oversight.[65] Thus, the AAUP located the site of judgment within academic communities to be exercised there by academics.

Moreover, the AAUP's Committee A on Academic Freedom and Tenure noted that "controversy is often at the heart of instruction."[66] Thus, the AAUP's Special Committee on Academic Freedom and National Security in a Time of Crisis, which argued that "freedom of inquiry and the open exchange of ideas are crucial to the nation's security," maintained that "specific attention should be given to the freedom to invite and hear controversial speakers" without being constrained "by any notion of 'balance,'" to the "freedom of political utterance on and off the campus, and to freedom of teaching." Additionally, "institutional policy should recognize that as long as an instructor has observed professional standards of care in drawing conclusions on a subject and has treated students with respect, he or she is free to engage in passionate advocacy no less than in dispassionate dissection." The AAUP warned the professoriate not to abandon its essential liberties because, quoting Benjamin Franklin, "They that can give up essential liberty to obtain a little safety deserve neither liberty nor safety."[67]

Undeterred, Horowitz pressed ahead, targeting nineteen states in 2004–2005 for special attention and making noticeable headway here and there. His "Academic Bill of Rights" was reported out of committee in Florida by a vote of 8–2. It received further support from the Pennsylvania House of Representatives, which passed a resolution early in July that drew directly from the language of the "Academic Bill of Rights" to establish a special committee to investigate the hiring, evaluation, and promotion of faculty at public colleges and universities and to determine whether students were fairly evaluated if and when they expressed their political views.[68] Horowitz's bill was introduced as House Bill 1531 of the Indiana General Assembly by one of the state's most powerful political figures, State Representative Luke Messer, who was executive director of the Indiana Republican Party, which controlled both the Indiana House and Senate.

Although HB 1531 did not make it out of the Education Committee in the 2004–2005 session, the attack on academic freedom in Indiana by Horowitz and his Students for Academic Freedom organization was indicative of the political motivation that drove their cynical rhetoric. Among other targets, it assailed peace studies programs offered in Indiana colleges and universities, including those at Ball State, Purdue, and DePauw, but also peace studies programs throughout the nation. At Ball State, Professor George Wolfe, who taught an introductory course in peace studies, came under scrutiny by Horowitz and Students for Academic Freedom for allegedly being intolerant of conservative viewpoints. In response, the President of Ball State University, Jo Ann Gora, pointed out that Professor Wolfe's course included assignments such as a mid-term exam that asked students to write, first, an essay that supported the war in Iraq consistent with the five criteria of Just War theory and, second, an argument against the war using the same criteria.[69] Sara Dorgan, national director of Students for Academic Freedom, in an open letter to Indiana Legislators on December 7, 2004, observed that "there are at least a dozen Peace Studies programs at other Indiana colleges and universities, including at DePauw University, Notre Dame, Indiana University/Purdue University at Fort Wayne, Goshen College and Manchester College" that abuse students' academic freedom. With this observation, she called for the Indiana legislature and state education officials to adopt the Academic Bill of Rights.[70]

Horowitz added that all "250 peace studies programs in America teach students to identify with America's terrorist enemies and to identify America as a Great Satan."[71] Students for Academic Freedom even criticized Ball State University for offering a course of "left indoctrination" on the problem of poor nutrition, in a state that ranked third nationally in the incidence of childhood obesity, because offering such a course amounted to criticism of Indiana's food industry and therefore of the capitalist system.[72]

One had to hear Horowitz speak in person to appreciate fully the venomous tone and ideological tenor of his hateful attack on professors and their academic freedom. I was in the audience on April 7, 2005 when he spoke on my campus at Indiana University, Bloomington. His speech was polarizing and extreme from beginning to end. He called Democrats the racist party in America; referred to progressives as religious fanatics, labeled them the intellectual heirs of Hitler and Stalin, and attributed to them the deaths of 100 million people in our lifetime because they—that is, progressives—are filled with hate, because they think they can change the world for the better, and because they engage in a rhetoric of evil. Horowitz referred to Princeton University Professor Cornel West as a "pompous, incredibly inflated, affirmative-action baby" who thinks he is a prophet. Horowitz allowed that no one wants to leave the US, but everyone wants to get in, as in the case of refugees from Haiti—now there's a country run by blacks, he said. From Horowitz's extreme right-wing perspective, anyone who uttered an opinion one tick or more left of him was considered to be a radical leftist ideologue; any question raised or criticism offered of American foreign policy was verboten and downright unpatriotic.[73]

This really was quite silly drivel, a rambling rant consisting of extreme and sweeping assertions, name-calling, hateful attitudes, and downright polarizing, mean-spirited, hurtful demagoguery. Only true believers would be expected to cheer and take such nonsense seriously; everyone else should have been at least embarrassed if not outright offended. Yet, Horowitz was not the only voice from the ascendant political right speaking in this way, nor was the leadership of the majority party lining up to discredit him for his polarizing rhetoric. Instead, democratic dissent, free inquiry, critical thinking, unorthodox ideas—all of which are crucial to the health and well-being of a democratic public—were rendered suspect and subject to suppression, as in the notorious case of Ward Churchill at the University of Colorado.

Intellectual Freedom and Artful Dissent

Professor Churchill was made notorious for views he expressed soon after 9/11 about the culpability of Americans, including the victims of the terrorist attacks at the World Trade Center and the Pentagon. They were "little Eichmanns," he said, not innocent civilians. When this statement was brought into focus three years later, in the superheated context of a coordinated and persistent national assault on academic freedom by the politically ascendant right, it prompted a rebuke of Churchill in a formal resolution passed by the Colorado House of Representatives and a call by the Colorado Governor for Churchill to resign from the university. This political attack on Churchill motivated a university investigation that concluded Churchill was operating within his right of free speech but also spurred another investigation to determine if he had misrepresented his Native-American ethnicity and plagiarized some of his writing. These latter issues presumably would not have arisen except in the context of a politically motivated attack on Churchill by right-wing critics who did not like the fact that he took exception to US foreign policy.

Attempting to suppress Churchill's voice for one politically motivated reason or another was a powerful maneuver by the surrogates of the governing discourse of war, whether or not they succeeded. The potential of the chilling effect on others in academia and society at large—by making an example of Churchill and putting him through a brutal regimen of intense public scrutiny—was obvious regardless of the outcome. Moreover, Churchill's rhetorical tack exposed him to the strength of the disciplining regime's strategy. His alienating style, although a legitimate exercise of academic freedom in the strictest sense of the term, was not a maneuver to evade entrapment and prevent the recapture of political and cultural legitimacy by the war regime through its surrogates. Instead of garnering cultural capital and gaining political ground, Churchill's overtly off-putting complaint may have diminished the perceived civic value of free inquiry and eroded public faith in the principle of academic freedom.

The full democratic benefit of academic freedom is not realized simply by promoting, exercising, and protecting free inquiry. That was only one-half of John Dewey's formulation. The other half was what Dewey called the artful communication of the products of free inquiry that enables a democratic public to come into its own. By the measure of artful communication, Ward Churchill failed to exercise academic freedom in a way that enriched democratic practice and society. His highly publicized, polarizing tactic simply reversed the ruling regime's strategic dichotomy of good and evil, rendering his position culturally absurd and exemplifying how antiwar dissent, even inadvertently, might diminish public receptivity to useful and unorthodox critiques of the war on terrorism, how that war was being conducted, the debilitating social policies authorized in its wake, the erosion of civil rights, and so on.

A deeply polarized people is a people at risk of losing their democratic sensibilities, especially when speaking one's mind against the orthodoxies of the time is considered tantamount to political treason and a just cause for stifling the expression of unwanted views. The state of political discourse is troubled when the democratic will to promote a constructive contestation of political opinions succumbs to the gravitational pull of polarizing demagoguery. Exercising academic freedom artfully in times of war and crisis is critical to enriching democratic culture and practice.

Democratic values are violated when those who are in the political ascendancy impose a test of political orthodoxy on those who dare to dissent. The ultraconservative attack on academic freedom aimed to do just that: to suppress dissent by equating it with political heresy and condemning it as unpatriotic. To achieve that end, it practiced and taunted others to mimic a form of political discourse that was demagogic and undemocratic, that strategically polarized debate and reduced public deliberation to an exercise in shouting at each other, that relegated opponents to mere caricatures of one another, and that therefore discouraged democratic dissent, which is the lifeblood of a free, fair, and progressive society.

John Dewey understood academic freedom was essential to cultivating an articulate public skilled in self-government. A democratic people could not become a "great community," he insisted, except through "freedom of social inquiry and...distribution of its conclusions."[74] Dewey maintained that the growth of political democracy depended on promoting intellectual freedom within academia and on communicating the results of scholarly inquiry to the public for public consumption and testing. An organized and articulate public must emerge for democracy to come into its own as a life of free and enriching communion, and such a public cannot come into existence without preserving free social inquiry and without practicing artful—that is, full and moving—communication.[75] Thus, the very function of the university is to enrich democratic community by exercising academic freedom, and the very character of academic freedom corresponds to the character of democracy itself in that both are dynamic and both, at their best, resist the oppression of orthodoxy.

The principle of academic freedom exists to promote unfettered scholarly inquiry, to protect it from institutional constraint, and to foster independent intellectual judgment, and it applies to a scholar's research, writing, and teaching. It is a long-established principle of promoting and protecting open and free investigation, speculation, imagination, and critical inquiry—of authorizing and legitimizing novel, pioneering, and iconoclastic inquiry. This is the kind of inquiry that can produce jarring results and that inevitably draws fire, in the form of charges of political or religious heresy advanced by the forces of orthodoxy. A democratic society would not need the principle of academic freedom to protect the right of unfettered scholarly inquiry, research, publication, and teaching unless innovative and iconoclastic thinking was controversial and subject to attack and suppression when it offends prevailing public sensibilities or the sensibilities of those who are in power.

Thus, a society that values free thinking and its essential contribution to a healthy democratic culture must remain true to the principle of academic freedom, especially when most tempted to compromise or abandon it—that is, when most off-put by the results of free and critical inquiry—because the function of open inquiry is, in Dewey's words, "to break through the crust of conventionalized and routine consciousness."[76] The principle is worthless unless it applies to the hard cases, including the specific instance of Ward Churchill. The hard cases define a society's level of commitment to constituting and sustaining a viable democratic public by supporting unfettered scholarly inquiry.

Controversy is at the heart of scholarship and teaching, no less than democracy exists in the expression of dissent and the contestation of ideas. This is what makes the exercise of academic freedom an exercise in democratic pragmatism. It is the source of constructive criticism of existing economic doctrine, social practice, and political truisms, the way of sorting through the complexities of the human condition without falling prey to specious dualisms or holding fast to doctrinaire positions. It is what keeps society dynamic and responsive to changing circumstances and competing perspectives. An attack on academic freedom is an assault on democracy itself, but the full democratic value of academic freedom cannot be realized except through the artful communication of dissenting opinion in ways that do not exacerbate the ritual of recrimination or fall prey to the polarizing demagoguery of the ruling forces of political orthodoxy.

Churchill's dissent illustrates how the democratic value of academic freedom and antiwar dissent can erode for lack of artful communication tactics. If Horowitz was a polarizing voice of the ruling neo-conservative forces in his attacks on academic freedom from the outside, Churchill was a polarizing voice within the professoriate who exercised academic freedom in a manner that risked weakening the perceived value of free inquiry to democracy. Churchill's right to free inquiry and to express freely his considered views in his teaching and publication was fully consistent with the principle of academic freedom. Moreover, his substantive concerns and criticisms of US foreign policy and the war on terrorism were shared by a number of other scholars, but Churchill made it much too easy for his critics (and the public) to conflate *what* he argued with *how* he argued his case—what he said with how he said it—so that right-wing Colorado Governor Bill Owens could somewhat plausibly denounce the content of Churchill's views as "simply anti-American" on the grounds that the expression of those views was "far outside the mainstream of civil discourse and useful academic work."[77]

Indeed, Professor Churchill was rhetorically insensitive when he explained the terrorist attacks of 9/11 as a consequence of previous American military actions by comparing them to the "Nazis" invading Russia and by labeling the financial workers, or "technocrats of empire," in the World Trade Center as "little Eichmanns." Moreover, he seemed to condone the violence of the terrorist "combat teams" as "medicinal" and "worth a try," as perhaps the best, most effective and befitting penalty Americans could be made to pay for their collective guilt.[78] Not only did this volatile language make it difficult to hear the merits of Churchill's basic point about "chickens coming home to roost" and to appreciate the need to reflect upon the citizenry's responsibility to resist their government's violations of international law and human rights, but it had the polarizing effect of simply reversing the order of guilt and blame. Instead of blaming the evil terrorists, Churchill would have Americans blame the guilty victims. Thus, his critique failed to move the democratic contestation of ideas productively forward.

Robert Jensen, a journalism professor at the University of Texas who was also highly critical of the administration's war on terror, affirmed Ward Churchill's right to speak out about 9/11 and agreed with the substance of Churchill's claim that the terrorism of 9/11 was in response to the depravity of US foreign policy. However, Jensen challenged Churchill's comparison of run-of-the-mill US stocktraders to Adolph Eichmann. Eichmann, more than just a technocrat, was a high-level Gestapo bureaucrat directly involved in planning the holocaust. "Collective responsibility," Jensen observed, "cannot mean all are responsible to exactly the same degree." Jensen also noted that Churchill's argument was "hard to read as anything other than an endorsement of the use of deadly force against all those involved" in callous US military operations and corporate capitalism "from the level of stocktraders and above."[79] How could such violence, Jensen asked, bring about a more just world? This was not a question to which Churchill's polarizing and blame-shifting discourse invited serious deliberation. He spoke more like a demagogue than a democrat, that is, more to provoke and inflame than to deliberate.

William Norwood Brigance made the point over fifty years ago that a healthy democracy, even in the backwash of war, finds ways to express and talk through its differences using what Dewey called the art of communication. Brigance's notion was to engage in peaceful persuasion instead of resorting to demagoguery. Healthy forms of public persuasion, Brigance observed, aim to improve bad human relations and to enrich democratic exchange by being intellectually honest, rendering significant ideas in ordinary language, and lifting the tone of discussion above the level of name-calling. Artful democratic speech avoids double-talk and deception, eschews the technique of repeating the big lie, does not engage in character assassination or resort to the hysterical approach, and does not use speech as a weapon of political assault and hate mongering.[80]

Articulating a productive relationship of consubstantial rivalry between war dissenters and a multifaceted democratic public in turbulent times is no small or easy rhetorical achievement. Dewey's criterion of artful communication is not one to be taken lightly, either for its importance in adding democratic value to the exercise of free intellectual inquiry or for the difficulty of meeting such a public standard for legitimizing unorthodox ideas that might otherwise be deemed heretical and disciplined accordingly. Communicating artfully the fruit of free intellectual inquiry amounts to speaking in the democratic idiom, and dissenting in the idiom of democracy means contesting opinions robustly but respectfully, that is, with respect for the diverse views and plural interests of a strong and inclusive—open and vital—democratic public. Dissenting in the democratic idiom is an attempt to bridge differences without effacing them or polarizing them. It means speaking clearly to the complexities of issues rather than caricaturing opponents and oversimplifying problems. It means speaking of an opponent or opposing idea as mistaken rather than evil and thus as subject to persuasion and correction rather than to coercion and destruction. It means crossing conceptual boundaries—making them permeable, flexible, and adaptive rather than rigid and brittle—in order to articulate common ground in a context of contested opinions. It means holding one's arguments accountable to differing perspectives and remaining open oneself to counter-persuasion. It includes pointing out similarities where others see only differences and underscoring differences when others treat mere similarities as if they are identical and exactly the same. This is what enables rivals also to remain sufficiently consubstantial with one another in a healthy state of ambivalence and that ultimately permits a diverse people to act collectively with a maximum degree of critical consciousness, which is to be much preferred over a condition of sheer polemics and utter confrontation between adversaries turned enemies, enemies who would fight over, rather than talk through, their differences only to condemn, excommunicate, and annihilate each other. Practicing a constructive rhetoric of metaphor and irony enables a people to bridge differences and cross boundaries that separate adversaries much too neatly and completely. A rhetoric of identification aims to compensate for a condition of social division to make cooperation between adversaries possible without resorting to rituals of vilification and victimization. It is an artful and democratic discourse—a pragmatic practice of speaking more humbly and less arrogantly.

There is much about US history, not all of it pleasant, that the American people should consider and confront as they try to sort through the complications of terror and determine the best course of action to support. Central to that history is the volatile question of culpability—the question of who is at fault in what way and to what degree for the death and destruction that was visited upon the US on 9/11, and what can be done to correct for the errors of the past that continue to haunt the present.

Ward Churchill is one academic voice, but certainly not the only such voice, that would open the nation's eyes to the consequences of exercising unmitigated power and righteous force. If people were to read his now infamous statement in its original and revised form without being too distracted or offended by the hard-hitting charge that the American citizenry is complicit in a history of war crimes and that the US got its just desserts on 9/11, that is, if people were to read enough of what Churchill wrote, they would be confronted with the millions of Native Americans, Filipinos, Indochinese, and others—men, women, and children, civilians more than soldiers—who have died in the wake of US progress and how far out of proportion those numbers are to American losses. For nearly 300 pages, Churchill details the violent and often lawless history of the US as a bellicose but peace-professing nation, arguing that it is the collective responsibility of the citizens of a modern democratic state to ensure that their government respects the rule of law domestically and internationally and offering the American citizenry some insight into how they earned so much resentment that has now come back at them in the form of what the CIA itself calls "blowback."[81]

The problem was not so much the basic point of Churchill's message but that his inflammatory language made the point too problematic to apply constructively. The tactic of shifting the blame, by depicting ordinary US citizens as evildoers and representing the 9/11 terrorists as innocent victims, discouraged collective reflection. Dispensing an overdose of pure polarizing polemics and alienating guilt can only bury a nation deeper in the abyss of denial and defensiveness. It was a tactic of disrespectful dissent that administered a sharp rebuke without offering a reassuring embrace and that assumed a position of radical difference devoid of compensating points of identification. It was nonconforming dissent without a gesture of solidarity. By exercising his right to speak out in this alienating way, Churchill abandoned the democratic purpose of academic freedom that Dewey had postulated and squandered the pragmatic value of innovative, unorthodox, and controversial ideas.

If America's universities are democracy's think-tanks, as Garrison Keillor has mused;[82] if democratic societies need unorthodox ideas and political dissent to make better decisions even in troubled times of war and crisis, as Cass Sunstein has argued;[83] if the democratic value of dissent is largely its resistance to social pressures to conform and to outmoded habits of thought, as Steven Shiffrin has insisted,[84] then attacks on academic freedom by the likes of David Horowitz, who would impose a government-mandated ideological litmus test on the professoriate, amount to an assault on democracy itself. Academic freedom exists to challenge debilitating dogma and to protect against the forces of political and religious orthodoxy. It is an ethic of open and free investigation and critical inquiry that produces novel and iconoclastic ideas with potentially jarring results. It can add vibrancy and value to democracy when those ideas are communicated artfully enough for public consumption and testing. Breaking through the crust of conventional and routine consciousness is tough under any circumstance, especially in turbulent times, but it is made all that much tougher by speaking in a manner that is the mirror image of a war regime's polarizing demagoguery.

The difficulty of overcoming a governing orthodoxy was clearly illustrated in Ward Churchill's dissent and its vulnerability to the stratagems of the war regime's surrogate forces. The surrogacy's relentless cultural war on academic freedom, especially after 9/11, was aimed at discrediting, intimidating, and disciplining alternative thinking about issues of war and peace—alternative thinking of the kind found in intellectual fields such as Peace Studies, Middle East Studies, Ethnic Studies, and the arts, humanities, and social sciences more generally. True to Horowitz's undemocratic dictum that politics is war by other means, the goal was to render critics of the war regime incapable of resistance. Churchill's negative tactics inverted and reproduced the cycle of recrimination instead of transcending or transforming it. Unlike the dissent of *Uncovered*, which adopted tactics of negation and inversion but within a double gesture of culturally affirming rationality, Churchill's dissent was defiantly offending and thus doubly problematic. Yet, neither *Uncovered* nor Churchill advanced a strategically unifying or synthesizing theme with which to gauge the tactics of dissent, and without the development of an alternative perspective, dissent was susceptible to being recaptured within a governing order of recrimination that dictated unrestricted warfare.

Thus, a lesson to draw from these two examples is that dissent from war must develop *ascending tactics of communication that strategically rise above and supersede the rhetoric of recrimination.* That is, a discourse of dissent needs to deploy systematically *tactics to (re)humanize* rivals instead of defaulting to framing tactics that reproduce the war regime's strategic dehumanization of adversaries. Absent communication that articulates a sense of shared humanity, the possibilities of reconciliation with a designated enemy of the state remain outside the prevailing framework of interpretation and beyond the citizenry's political imagination. Despite any reservations the people as a whole may have about war, they must be able to envision an alternative to the monster they have been taught to see and fear.[85] As Lakoff would say, people can think only of monsters if that is the sole frame available to them in the public discourse.[86]

WEB-WATCHING AND MEDIA OF DISSENT

Besides grounding nonconforming statements in culturally adept and resonant gestures of solidarity to bolster the credibility of a dissenting opinion, and beyond speaking in humanizing terms to envision options to warfare, the feasibility of dissent also depends on circulating its message as widely as possible. This third consideration brings into focus the media of dissent and how they figure into resisting a war regime's strategy of dehumanization. What are the resources of media for circulating information, images, and narratives that (re)humanize the parties in conflict? Which media are readily accessible to the citizenry for actively resisting war propaganda? What are the media of democratic dissent and their potential for promoting peace and justice?

These are important questions about the intersection of media and messages that dissenting citizens must ask and answer in particular circumstances. There are no universally valid answers when citizens operate in the realm of rhetorical invention to develop tactics of resistance. The art of maneuver requires adaptation to specific situations and shifting conditions. It is an exercise of wit, dexterity, and ingenuity—a matter of tricks, twists, and rhetorical turns to enrich the democratic imagination and evade the tyrannizing image of a dehumanized enemy. Thus, the question of media is a consideration of usage, that is, a matter of how a potential resource might be utilized in certain instances for express purposes by actual citizens or networks of dissenting citizens.

If the specific aim is to resist a war regime's dehumanizing propaganda, citizens operating in a media-saturated environment will encounter a confounding plethora of alternative resources on the internet alone. Moreover, dissent may be stymied or misdirected by the negative tactics of reverse recrimination, which dominate a multitude of dispersed sites of resistance. Even web sites founded on a principle of reconciliation and committed to the purpose of humanizing society can default to tactics of dissent that vilify the agents of war, thus rearticulating and recirculating the rhetoric of evil and perpetuating a forced choice between Us and Them that underpins the case for war. To ascend strategically beyond the discourse of evil and to see the face of humanity in a reputed enemy of the civilized world—that is, in Certeau's terms, to achieve a new understanding that resists recapture by the ruling discursive order—requires innovative uses of existing media resources.

Resourceful media usage by US citizens who would resist a debilitating war on terror means assembling information into humanizing perspectives on Islamic peoples, beliefs, cultures, and grievances, for instance, in coordinated acts of dissent from war propaganda. Given the consolidation of corporate control over mainstream media, dissent depends heavily on alternative media and thus must develop content from diverse and divergent sources, making coordination difficult and circulation of messages circuitous, reflecting multiple frames of reference, and increasing demand for artful rhetorical invention.[87] Under these circumstances, passive consumption of anti-war messages simply is not a viable alternative. Creative media usage is an absolute necessity for dissent to develop its tactical maneuvers into an alternative expression of human solidarity that is resistant to recapture by a governing authority seeking "information dominance" and thus to contribute over time to the formation of a culture of peace.[88]

Engaging media actively and imaginatively at the grassroots of dissent is feasible but challenging. A culture of peace can develop and exist only in a context of respect for human diversity, and achieving solidarity in a context of diversity is a function of communication. As such, solidarity is shaped or formed by communication adapted to particular audiences and circumstances. It must emerge from and, as Kenneth Burke underscored, contribute to an ongoing and unending conversation.[89] No single configuration of humanizing messages can serve as a universal standard of reconciliation appropriate to all media, audiences, and situations. Thus, a principal challenge of communicating dissent is devising messages that are configured to respond to specific contingencies of time but also are tailored to capitalize on the resources of media in order to enhance circulation and transcend strict limitations of space. In meeting this challenge, anti-war dissent can cultivate everyday tactics at the grassroots into a larger and more lasting strategy of peace.

Developing tactically adept messages for culturally strategic media usage is an exercise in what John Paul Lederach has called "the messiness of innovation."[90] Peacebuilding, he argues, is primarily a creative act, an exercise of "moral imagination," an innovative response in a context of human conflict and violence.[91] It is a grounded and reflective process of "constructive social change" rather than an exercise in rote technique.[92] It is a capacity to imagine something new that is responsive to existing conditions—to operate within the complexity of a situation and respond to the "actual messiness of ideas, processes, and change."[93] Imagination "must emerge from and speak to the hard realities of human affairs" if it is to facilitate peacebuilding by envisioning a "canvas" or "web" of human relationships that includes even our enemies.[94]

The pragmatic aesthetics of grounded innovation link intuition to observation and experience. They involve a focus on synthesizing images both in deep listening and creative expression. With a disciplined stillness in places of conflict, we can watch for images and listen to metaphors that infuse communication and shape experience. These images and metaphors comprise "a living museum of conflict resources" for developing a meaningful "voice" and participating in substantive conversations that restore, repair, or reconstitute broken narratives.[95] Lederach calls this a process of "web watching," of vigilantly observing and patiently locating the web of relationships that is in place before stepping into it to repair or remake it.[96]

When the innovative responses of moral imagination are grounded in the complexities of situations, they operate somewhat paradoxically as a form of constructive realism, which is "a type of imagination capable of transcending violence while engaging the immediate historical challenges that continue to produce [violence]."[97] It is a capacity to envision "relational interdependency" without ignoring complex history or reducing it simplistically to the "dualistic polarities" of one side being right and the other wrong, of one side the victim and the other the victimizer, and so forth. Instead of tunnel vision, it exercises peripheral vision. Simplicity and complexity converge in a unifying image, an image of human connectivity that emerges out of the discourse of violence, the few synthesizing words of an apt metaphor that capture the fullness of experience and constitute the art of peacemaking in a given situation.[98]

Dissent in a media-saturated environment builds toward and affirms peace by unconventional, artful means. The conventional, but less productive, mode of negative dissent is to articulate opposition to war and, in so doing, replicate an inverted version of the simplistic polarity of good versus evil, which largely alienates and demoralizes ordinary citizens, leaving them without an alternative vision of how to proceed constructively toward peace.[99] An uncommon emphasis on innovation in media usage is strategic, not only in its synthesizing and transcending capacity but also in its potential to connect people who can make a difference in different venues. It works strategically over time much like "social yeast" to activate a process of changed thinking when mixed with appropriate ingredients under the right conditions.[100]

Tapping into the strategic resource of creative media usage requires monitoring metaphors and images in situ, that is, observing closely the media of dissent. The challenge is to mix the yeast of unifying imagery into a negative tactical discourse so that it can rise above the stasis of recrimination. If relationships between warring peoples can be envisioned anew in ways that are indigenous to a given discourse of dissent, then key players in those venues can redirect their dissent toward articulating constructive social change, which is a mode of resistance more difficult for governing regimes to counter and discredit.

Any number of potentially synthesizing metaphors may emerge from web watching in alternative media. Not every metaphor, of course, possesses the same potential for rehumanizing degraded images of designated enemies. There are no guarantees of success in the domain of rhetorical invention, just as there are no universally valid responses to the contingencies of particular rhetorical situations. Innovation is an exercise in calculated risk taking, an attempt to create something new and beneficial but also recognizable and appropriate in circumstances of human conflict. It is a tactical exercise of practical wit in the sense that it is grounded in particular complexities and adaptive to certain constraints and exigencies. One should expect only modest innovations in their singularity. The strategic value of separate tactical tropes can develop over time only as they accumulate within, and propagate across, contexts into a collective antidote to demonizing imagery.[101] Envisioning the web of humanity can be achieved only one grounded metaphor at a time. This is the creative rhetorical process by which an idea of peace eventually might "move from the unimaginable to common sense."[102]

Citizens can undertake this creative exercise of the moral imagination by monitoring alternative media for latent, dormant, and/or underdeveloped rhetorical resources to supplant the hostile imagination with viable visions of constructive cooperation and respectful coexistence. They can look for incipient metaphors of a common humanity amid clashing differences. They can watch for potentially empathizing images to project onto otherwise estranged peoples across political barriers and to recast alienated identities despite cultural differences and divisions. They can search for seeds of commonality that might be nurtured and developed into expressions of identification and figures of solidarity. In sum, watchful citizens might locate in alternative media rudimentary rhetorical starting points, or emergent expressions of convergence, that enable them to begin seeing a reassuring likeness of themselves reflected in reconfigured images of others whom war propagandists have stereotyped as subhuman and threatening.

Using the alternative press and the internet, as Robert Jensen observes, "has to be part of any long-term media strategy" because, at their best, they are an independent and rare source of information, analysis, and communication that is "vital to activists."[103] Moreover, mainstream news media rarely carry stories that relate to articulating a culture of peace. Mainstream media, as Johan Galtung has underscored, exhibit a "perverse fascination with war and violence" and thus "neglect the peace forces at work," which undermines the emergence of a peace perspective.[104] Computers, however, are changing the way people access information and organize their lives. As the "centerpiece of the global information society," Elise Boulding argues, computers make available to ordinary citizens—not just to governments, the military, and corporations—a worldwide web of communication and thus open up "the possibility of widespread democratic participation in public policymaking." Thousands of web sites, she explains, "tell the stories of peacebuilding around the world that the media ignore"; these web sites are concerned with issues such as human rights, development, and the environment and with making visible "zones of peace unreported by the press."[105] Peace-building web sites range from online journals and electronic books to alternative news and commentary, internet radio news, discussion forums and blogs, protest organizing, and on-site reports by peace activists and peace journalists operating in war zones around the world. This is a tangled, decentralized, and transnational zone of information proliferation, alternative news, and contested opinions that is not controlled by government or commercial media and thus can be confusing to ordinary citizens, 80 percent of whom are accustomed to receiving their news mainly via television.[106] Computer citizenship is a challenge—a test of will—to use information and communication technology creatively as a resource for democratic peacemaking.[107]

The very notion of peace journalism is instructive in this regard. Even though little of it actually exists, the concept of what can and should be done by journalists to promote a peace perspective is indicative of what citizens who are actively engaged in web watching might hope to discover in alternative media. Galtung's model of peace journalism stresses, for example, that stories should be written to give voice to all parties in the conflict, to explain in a longer timeframe the multiple conditions out of which the conflict arose, to identify the variety of issues and goals at stake, to bring into focus the invisible damage to cultures and structures, to feature the suffering of people impacted by war, to be creative and solution oriented, highlighting peace initiatives, and so on.[108] Jake Lynch adds suggestions such as avoiding "stark distinctions between 'self' and 'other'"; "asking questions that may reveal areas of common ground" between the divided parties; avoiding disempowering and "'victimizing' language such as 'destitute,' 'devastated,' 'defenseless,' 'pathetic' and 'tragedy,' which only tells us what has been done to and could be done for a group of people"; similarly, "avoid demonizing adjectives like 'vicious,' 'cruel,' 'brutal' and 'barbaric'" or "'terrorist,' 'extremist,' 'fanatics and 'fundamentalist.'"[109] Tehranian emphasizes that peace journalism should "identify the views and interests of all parties to human conflicts" because there "is no single truth; there are many truths." Moreover, he cautions that peace journalists can become part of the problem if their reporting "exacerbates dualism and hatreds" instead of employing "creative tensions in any human conflict to seek common ground and nonviolent solutions."[110] To the extent that alternative media work toward such goals, citizens who are actively monitoring and creatively using the internet should be able to locate incipient metaphors for (re)humanizing adversaries.

What kind of humanizing metaphor might include even our enemies? How, as in the case of America's preemptive invasion and occupation of Iraq, might US citizens achieve some degree of empathy with an enemy that has been designated a terrorist? The challenge might seem overwhelming when a Manichaean rhetoric of good versus evil pervades the nation's political atmosphere. It is a terrifying expression of the hostile imagination that is historically rooted in American political culture and was readily extended in a post-9/11 world to defending freedom, democracy, and civilization from the forces of savagery.[111] A reader of Howard Zinn's telling essay on the living myth of American exceptionalism, published online in the *Boston Review* midway through 2005, would be reminded of how powerfully this myth constrains domestic criticism of divinely sanctioned warfare in the name of liberty, democracy, and civilization. As Zinn observes, even the editors of the liberal magazine, *The American Prospect*, argued that the US has the right and the obligation to strike preemptively and unilaterally because "Islamist terrorists with global reach pose the greatest immediate threat to our lives and liberties."[112] No one should expect a single metaphor to discredit and overthrow by itself such a tyrannizing image of the enemy.

More modest metaphors, however, may well prove feasible to find and articulate one by one until they accumulate over time into a somewhat less stereotyped take on terrorism. By weaving a few strands here and there into a growing web of human relations, the tactical potential and humanizing entailments of multiple metaphors might accumulate enough momentum eventually to move the issue of terrorism beyond the stasis of recrimination. An example of one such incipient metaphor appeared June 10, 2005 on the Antiwar.com web site in an article by Michael Scheuer.[113] Antiwar.com described itself as a libertarian site dedicated to the cause of noninterventionism and to advancing a patriotic peace movement. It aimed to publish "citizen experts" and to reach out to conservatives, independents, leftists, pacifists, and greens opposed to imperialism.[114] Scheuer, author of the book *Imperial Hubris*, wrote from the vantage point of a CIA officer concerned with why the US might lose the war on terror.[115] His essay in Antiwar.com featured the argument advanced in a new book by Robert Pape on the subject of "suicide terrorism."[116]

Pape, a public intellectual and political science professor at the University of Chicago, directed the Chicago Project on Suicide Terrorism. His book, Scheuer wrote, destroyed the argument advanced by neo-conservatives that "Islamist suicide attacks against America and other countries are launched by undereducated, unemployed, alienated, apocalyptic fanatics." Pape's data demonstrated that "there is little connection between suicide terrorism and Islamic fundamentalism, or any of the world's religions." Instead, terrorist attacks are motivated primarily by the secular and strategic goal of compelling a foreign occupying force to withdraw from their "homeland." Their aim is "victory, not mere destruction." The US "faces a logical, patient, and deliberate enemy" that "is attacking because he perceives his country, culture, and/or religion are under attack." He is revered by his people for defending their society from "a foreign threat," that is, from an occupier that would "conquer" and "transform Muslim societies" and thus devastate their "way of life." Thus, Scheuer observed, attempting to destroy Islamist "monsters" in order to "install democracy" may be well-intentioned, but it is a myopic course of action that courts "disaster."[117]

Jude Wanniski, who ran his own "supply-side investor" consulting practice and monitored Antiwar.com for arguments that he could use against recent US interventions that had been concocted by his "old neo-con allies," spotted a metaphor of interest to him in Scheuer's internet article about Pape's findings on suicide terrorism.[118] Are these secular suicide bombers, Wanniski asked, the equivalent of "freedom fighters"? "From the dawn of civilization," Wanniski observed, "the man of the house has been the protector of hearth and home from outside enemies." Aren't these so-called "insurgents" assuming "the role of the male in defending the 'home,' or the 'homeland'" from "American invaders and occupiers"?[119] Wanniski's commentary, with Scheuer's article attached, was picked up and republished on the internet the next day by LewRockwell.com, an "anti-state, anti-war, pro-market" web site.[120] It also reappeared on web sites such as The Conservative Voice and uruknet.info ("information from occupied Iraq") and was linked from the latter by the likes of williambowles.info, Iraq News Network, and Orb Standard world news.[121]

The metaphor in Wanniski's post that may have been potentially most suggestive to Americans was not the notion of terrorist as freedom fighter but rather the image of suicide bomber as homeland defender. Freedom fighter implied some kind of ideological equivalency between American and Islamist conceptions of liberty or liberal democracy—an unlikely equivalency that neither comports with common sense nor respects cultural differences but instead imposes the logic of an alien political system and way of life onto an occupied people. Thus, a predictable objection raised in internet posts was that insurgents in Iraq could not be considered freedom fighters because they opposed liberty and democracy and they killed civilians instead of, or in addition to, soldiers. There is no "moral equivalence between these animals and coalition soldiers," wrote "Greyhawk" on "The Mudville Gazette" blog. Referencing Pape's book, "Mountain Girl" retorted that "they are freedom fighters. There were never suicide bombers in Iraq until Bushitler invaded." Michael McLarney objected to Mountain Girl's take on Iraqi freedom fighters, insisting instead that:

> the terrorists (not insurgents!) are viscious [sic] criminals and sociopaths who desire killing as a fulfillment of some sick need. There is no military justification for these attacks. If they were insurrgents [sic] they would attack the army not the innocents. Many Iraqis have died during these last two years, but most of those dead were killed by Islamic terrorists not American bullets. To leave Iraq now would be to abandon the innocent to the rule of the minority.[122]

In short, terrorists could not be considered freedom fighters because they had no military purpose and no respect for life, liberty, or democracy.

The metaphor of homeland defender, however, suggested a comparison that did not presume suicide bombers were fighting for American notions of freedom and democracy or against Americans enjoying their own liberty and security. It invited instead the assumption that these Muslim fighters were protecting a way of life from foreign invaders, that they were the weaker party protecting their home from a stronger occupying force that would conquer and transform their country, that their targets included anyone who would cooperate with or support such an occupation, that they were defenders, not aggressors, and harbored no desire to impose their way of life on Americans, and that continued occupation would strengthen their resolve to resist the American occupation rather than quell the rebellion. This, more than an image of freedom fighters, was the metaphor lurking within Mountain Girl's online observation that "the terror has not abated" because "civilian Iraqi's who were not part of any terror group are now seeing terrorist tactics as their only way of survival against the Forces invading their country. When civilians feel this way we must be doing something wrong. . . . The war is simply feeding the fire and perpetuating terrorism."[123] As Robert Pape emphasized in an online interview with The American Conservative, "The central fact is that overwhelmingly suicide-terrorist attacks are not driven by religion as much as they are by a clear strategic objective: to compel modern democracies to withdraw military forces from the territory that the terrorists view as their homeland."[124]

As with any metaphor, this one could be challenged or even redirected, but it also offered American citizens an opportunity to grasp a basic point of identification with another people in a different land who, like Americans, would defend their home by whatever means available to them when they were invaded and occupied by an alien force, especially when that force threatened their basic way of life. It was a metaphor that suggested the Iraqi "insurgents" were in some degree rational, not merely irrational; that they were defenders more than aggressors; that they were resisting coercion rather than either exalting it or succumbing to it; that, in short, they were complex humans, not simplistic monsters. It was the kind of metaphor that might help Americans understand in some small measure the humanity of their enemy when, for example, *Chicago Tribune* columnist Steve Chapman wrote in the *Baltimore Sun* that "Americans have trouble imagining how the insurgents could hope to succeed without any positive vision of Iraq's future—and without any apparent agenda except slaughtering people. But the core of their appeal is the same as that of most other suicide bombing campaigns: nationalistic opposition to a foreign military presence."[125] It was a metaphor that could even catch the eye of some members of the US Congress, eighteen of whom attended a briefing by Professor Pape. According to the *Washington Post*:

Several of the 18 legislators at Pape's Capitol Hill briefing last month found his ideas interesting. Sen. Richard G. Lugar (R-Ind.) "was impressed with the analysis," his spokesman, Andy Fisher, says. And Sen. Craig Thomas (R-Wyo.) says he found it plausible. "Apparently his findings are that these folks want to get everyone out of the Middle East who aren't native to it," Thomas says, and although he does not regard the U.S. military presence as an occupation, "I could see how they would use that" word.[126]

Moreover, it was an image that did not require Americans to invalidate themselves in order to empathize with an enemy. As Scheuer observed, people were not attacked by suicide car bombs because of who they were or what they believed but because they were occupying someone's homeland.[127] This was the kind of metaphor that could help citizens to conclude, as did blogger Darrell Udlehoven, that "invading Iraq was a gigantic mistake."[128]

My purpose is not to examine definitively the metaphor of terrorist as homeland defender or to develop it fully, along with other humanizing imagery, as it eventually would have to be developed in order to achieve the symbolic form and rhetorical force of a full-blown peacebuilding ritual or drama. Peacebuilding, as Schirch underscores, must be no less dramatic than the conflict it attempts to resolve if it hopes "to capture people's imagination and interest." Thus, "peacebuilders are the choreographers, directors, and set designers of a drama" on "a stage that must be constructed and set in a way that draws people to observe and take part in the peacebuilding drama." For this "peacebuilding stage," themes must be articulated, scripts developed, and movements choreographed to develop meaningful messages that "engage people's emotions, senses, and passions" enough to transform their "worldviews, identities, and relationships."[129] As Bleiker has demonstrated in the case of popular dissent that ended eventually in the fall of the Berlin Wall, such change does not occur quickly or through simple cause-and-effect calculations but is the outcome of collective agency, diverse articulations, and multiple symbolic practices.[130] My immediate and more limited goal is to indicate the promise and potential of creative media usage—specifically, of web watching on the worldwide web—to contribute to this overall process of peacebuilding.

Watching the internet for metaphors to articulate into peacebuilding images can help a democratic public resist war by empathizing or identifying with others, even enemies, who have been dehumanized in war propaganda. By itself, the metaphor of homeland defender is a modest construction, as it must be for immediate tactical uses, but it is the kind of trope that, together with other (re)humanizing figures, might contribute strategically over time to an alternative image of human solidarity that transcends the rhetoric of retribution and constrains the hostile imagination of ruling elites. As we can see from this single instance, bridging metaphors do travel about on new and old media and between alternative and mainstream venues, enabling citizens with different ideological orientations to interact with one another and even to interface with experts and political elites. Accordingly, it would seem that the feasibility of dissenting from war constructively can be enhanced by the democratic prospects of internet web watching and thus that citizens might reasonably expect to formulate and communicate many more peacebuilding figures of human solidarity by engaging alternative media artfully.

The peacebuilding metaphors produced by dissenting citizens exercising their moral imagination in a media-saturated state of ongoing warfare are ultimately the strategic source of an alternative vision of human relations. More immediately, they are also a tactical resource or thematic ingredient for structuring healthy political relations of consubstantial rivalry in the constructive double-gesture of nonconforming solidarity. Communicating dissent is made most feasible for everyday citizens and tactical maneuvers become less vulnerable to strategic countermoves when metaphors, such as homeland defense, become available to reconfirm and reconfigure—rather than disconfirm and denigrate—the cultural capital of an embattled nation. Without such metaphors to establish links between contesting parties, dissent defaults to negative tactics and fails to rise above a self-perpetuating and polarizing rhetoric of recrimination, as illustrated by the culture wars generally and the specific struggle over academic freedom between the likes of David Horowitz and Ward Churchill. Without constructive dissent that resists demonizing domestic political rivals and alienating the general public, antiwar discourse remains at the tactical disadvantage of operating within a controlling framework of reciprocal recrimination with little chance of developing a strategic alternative to the war regime's dehumanizing constructions of foreign foes.

Creative media usage is vital to achieving a world communication order that is more democratic and a world that is less violent. Democratic dissent from war becomes increasingly constructive as its tactics develop strategic vision to transcend fearful stereotypes and build toward a culture of peace based on relations of consubstantial rivalry and configured in the double gesture of nonconforming solidarity. A culture of peace, as Boulding explains, exists "when groups of humans hold the need for bonding and autonomy in balance—nurturing one another, engaging in many cooperative activities, and also giving each other space." Peacebuilding is a dynamic process, not a static end state. It actively promotes "peaceable diversity" and requires a "willingness to venture into the unknown."[131] It is a creative process of web watching and metaphor-making. It is a messy, grounded, and intensive exercise in innovation with no guaranteed outcomes.

Media, especially alternative media, are rich resources for just this kind of web-watching ingenuity. They make the articulation and circulation of constructive dissent feasible, but not inevitable. Anti-war dissent in the form of cyber-activism can draw on new information and communication technologies as a resource for progressive change but not as a panacea.[132] The digital world must be actively engaged by citizens to realize its potential, and even then it can be utilized to promote narrow interests rather than peace and social justice. As Bruce Gronbeck notes, surfing the net for political purposes is definitely on the rise, but the search processes utilized by citizens influence the messages they produce and consume.[133] Dissent configured for peacebuilding messages—for transforming a warrior culture into a dynamic peace culture—deploys humanizing metaphors drawn creatively from and grounded deeply in the internet and other media to transcend the cycle of reciprocal recrimination. In this critical sense, dissent from war is a question of communicating a web of human relations that bonds people with their political adversaries and even their enemies under circumstances of continuing rivalry and contestation. There are many possible answers to this question of communicating constructive dissent and articulating human solidarity in the midst of conflict and division, but they can be found only one modest metaphor at a time by media-spanning cyber-citizens exercising their democratic imagination individually and collectively in an ongoing practice of web watching.

NOTES

1. Jonathan Schell, *The Unconquerable World: Power, Nonviolence, and the Will of the People* (New York: Henry Holt and Company, 2003), 3.

2. See, for example, the chapter on "Fighting Terror" in Robert L. Ivie, *Democracy and America's War on Terror* (Tuscaloosa: University of Alabama Press, 2005), 123–47.

3. Sean MacBride, et al., *Many Voices, One World: Towards a New, More Just, and More Efficient World Information and Communication Order* (1980; Lanham, MD: Rowman & Littlefield Publishers, 2004).

4. Andrew Calabrese, "Foreword to the R&L Edition," in MacBride, *Many Voices, One World*, xiii.

5. Amadou-Mahtar M'Bow, "Foreword," in MacBride, *Many Voices, One World*, xvii–xix.

6. Sean MacBride, "Preface," in *Many Voices, One World*, xxi.

7. MacBride, *Many Voices, One World*, 13, 166.

8. MacBride, *Many Voices, One World*, 265. Emphasis in original.

9. MacBride, *Many Voices, One World*, 172, 179. Emphasis in original.

10. See Elise Boulding, *Cultures of Peace: The Hidden Side of History* (Syracuse, NY: Syracuse University Press, 2000), 213–14; Colleen Roach, "Information and Culture in War and Peace: Overview," in *Communication and Culture in War and Peace*, ed. Colleen Roach (Newbury Park, CA: Sage Publications, 1993), 29–32; Vincent Mosco, "Communication and Information Technology for War and Peace," in Roach, *Communication and Culture*, 54–55.

11. MacBride, *Many Voices, One World*, 254.

12. MacBride, *Many Voices, One World*, 205.

13. Mosco, "Communication and Information," 59–69.

14. MacBride, *Many Voices, One World*, 14.

15. I am referring here to the kind of distinction in cultural studies that is often made between media institutions and media texts, economic structures and discursive articulations, political economy and discursive analysis, and so forth. See, for instance, Graeme Turner, *British Cultural Studies: An Introduction*, 2nd ed. (New York: Routledge, 1990), 174–81. A variation on this same distinction is evident in Colleen Roach's discussion of communication and culture as an approach to the study of war and peace. For her, communication is a matter of mass media that can be separated from the "distinct area" of human communication. See Colleen Roach, "Introduction," in Roach, *Communication and Culture*, xx.

16. Michel de Certeau, *The Practice of Everyday Life*, trans. Steven Rendall (Berkeley: University of California Press, 1984), 35–36, 38.

17. Certeau, *Everyday Life*, 37, 38. Emphasis in original.

18. Michel de Certeau, *The Capture of Speech and Other Political Writings*, ed. Luce Giard and trans. Tom Conley (Minneapolis: University of Minnesota Press, 1997), 30; Certeau, *Everyday Life*, 39.

19. Certeau, *Everyday Life*, 39.

20. Certeau, *Everyday Life*, 40.

21. Certeau, *Capture of Speech*, 29, 32, 39.

22. Lisa Schirch, *Ritual and Symbol in Peacebuilding* (Bloomfield, Connecticut: Kumarian Press, 2005), 41, 49–51.

23. Robert L. Ivie, "Savagery in Democracy's Empire," *Third World Quarterly* 26: 1 (November 2005): 55–65.

24. On this point, see Chantal Mouffe, *The Return of the Political* (London: Verso, 1993), 1–8.

25. Kenneth Burke, *Attitudes toward History*, 3rd ed. (Berkeley: University of California Press, 1984), 41–42.

26. Kenneth Burke, *A Rhetoric of Motives* (1950; Berkeley: University of California Press, 1969), 20–23.

27. On the notion of consubstantial rivalry, see Ivie, *Democracy and America's War on Terror*, 169–87.

28. On this point, see Sam Keen, *Faces of the Enemy: Reflections of the Hostile Imagination* (San Francisco: Harper and Row, 1986).

29. Burke, *Rhetoric of Motives*, 179.

30. Michael Walzer, *Interpretation and Social Criticism* (Cambridge, Massachusetts: Harvard University Press, 1987), 39.

31. Anthony Kaufman, "Docs Populi: Raging Against the Republican Machine," *The Village Voice*, 11 May 2004, available online; Robert Greenwald, "The Director's Introduction," July 2004, available online.

32. Cinema Libre Distribution, "About the Film," available online.

33. Jean Oppenheimer, "Uncovered: The War on Iraq," *Screen Daily.com*, 20 May 2004, available online. Another reviewer, Ann Hornaday, referred to the film version of *Uncovered* as "prose, not poetry" that is "quick, efficient polemic, the cinematic equivalent of a good op-ed piece" featuring "impeccably credentialed witnesses to debunk the case made for going to war." It presents a "convincing and

well-organized . . . case . . . systematically breaking down the administration's arguments regarding WMC and terrorism, as well as the use of dubious informants, manipulated intelligence, intimidation and a supine media and Congress." The film's experts "provide quietly persuasive arguments" that "quietly deconstruct" the administration's "political theater." In short, "it's smart, engaging discourse." See Ann Hornaday, "'Uncovered' Makes Strong Case Against Iraq Invasion," *Washington Post*, reprinted in *The Herald-Times* (Bloomington, Indiana), October 1, 2004, C7.

34. A transcript of the film, *Uncovered: The War on Iraq*, is available online.

35. *Uncovered*, 7.

36. *Uncovered*, 22.

37. *Uncovered*, 22, 18, 19.

38. *Uncovered*, 21, 26, 21, 23, 39.

39. *Uncovered*, 16, 25, 35, 9, 36, 12, 17.

40. *Uncovered*, 29.

41. Gregg Toppo, "Education Dept. Paid Commentator to Promote Law," *USA Today*, January 7, 2005.

42. George Lakoff, *Moral Politics: How Liberals and Conservatives Think*, 2nd ed. (Chicago: The University of Chicago Press, 2002), 222.

43. James Davison Hunter, *Culture Wars: The Struggle to Define America* (New York: Basic Books, 1991).

44. Accuracy in Academia, which is available online, also sponsors Campus Report Online. Other immediate forerunners of the right-wing attack on academic freedom include, for example, Dinesh D'Souza, *Illiberal Education: The Politics of Race and Sex on Campus* (New York: Free Press, 1991); Roger Kimball, *Tenured Radicals: How Politics Has Corrupted Our Higher Education* (New York: Harper and Row, 1990); and Alan Bloom, *Closing of the American Mind* (New York: Simon and Schuster, 1988). Quotation from "Our History," American Council of Trustees and Alumni, available online. Clarke refers to Lynne Cheney, like her husband, as "a right-wing ideologue." Richard A. Clarke, *Against All Enemies: Inside America's War on Terror* (New York: Free Press, 2004) 18.

45. "Academic Freedom," American Council of Trustees and Alumni, available online.

46. Information about the report is available online from American Council of Trustees and Alumni. Consistent with ACTA's post-9/11 call to save civilization from academics in the face of terrorism's threat, the pressure on the professoriate was intensified. As Kenton Bird and Elizabeth Barker Brandt observed a year after 9/11, "College and university faculty members who have spoken out against US foreign policy, particularly after the terrorist attacks on September 11, 2001, have been reprimanded, disciplined, harassed and, in one case, threatened with dismissal from a tenured position." Academic criticism of US foreign policy "has been denounced as counterproductive and even seditious." In this time of national crisis, public support for academic freedom is eroding in a context where constitutional and court support is tenuous and "ambiguous at best." Thus, the "foundation of academic freedom" will be "worn away" as a "bulwark of intellectual inquiry" should universities fail "to vigorously protect it." Kenton R. Bird and Elizabeth Barker, "Academic Freedom and 9/11: How the War on Terrorism Threatens Free Speech on Campus," *Communication Law and Policy* 7 (Autumn 2002): 431–60.

47. Henry A. Giroux, *Fugitive Cultures: Race, Violence, and Youth* (New York: Routledge, 1996), Chapter 6. Giroux's argument reminds me of a comment made by an undergraduate student in my course on democracy and dissent when we were discussing the efforts of ACTA, Campus Watch, No.Indoctrination.org, and Students for Academic Freedom to protect students from being indoctrinated by their professors. Her assessment of these self-proclaimed protectors was that "they don't give students much credit" for thinking critically and exercising judgment in a context of what Giroux calls critical learning.

48. "About Campus Watch," Campus Watch, available online.

49. Jonathan Calt Harris, "The New McCarthyism?" *National Review Online*, May 21, 2003, 25. Also available on the Campus Watch website.

50. I am drawing details about Campus Watch and Daniel Pipes from Kristine McNeil, "The War on Academic Freedom," *The Nation*, November 11, 2002. For more information on legislative efforts to transform Title VI, control curriculum, and turn Middle East studies into an instrument of US foreign policy, see Bruce Craig, "The Battle Continues: Advisory Boards and the Title VI Higher Education Act," *Perspectives Online* 42:4 (April 2004); "Education Subcommittee Approves Hoekstra Measure to Strengthen International Studies in Higher Education, Ensure Programs Fulfill National Security Needs," *News from the [House] Committee on Education and the Workforce*, John Boehner, Chairman, September 17, 2003, available online; Stanley Kurtz, "Studying Title VI: Criticism of Middle East Studies Get A Congressional Hearing," *National Review Online*, June 16, 2003, 27; Stanley Kurtz, "Reforming the Campus: Congress Targets Title VI," *National Review Online*, October 14, 2003; Jennifer Jacobson, "The Clash Over Middle East Studies," *The Chronicle of Higher Education*, February 2, 2004: 8. Pipes and Kurtz seem to have gotten a strong hearing within the administration itself, as evidenced in a line from George W. Bush's speech of June 2, 2004 defending his policy in Iraq and the Middle East. In his words to the graduating class of the US Air Force Academy, "America will need a generation of Arab linguists and experts on Middle Eastern history and culture" in order "to prevail" and to bring "greater freedom to the nations of the Middle East." George W. Bush, "Transcript: Bush Casts War on Terrorism in Historic Terms," *The Washington Post*, June 2, 2004.

51. "About Us," NoIndoctrination.org.

52. Stanley Kurtz, "Students Fight Back: Introducing NoIndoctrination.org," *National Review Online* December 2, 2002. Wright's charge of "PC oppression" puts me in mind, ironically, of a story told to me when I was a faculty member at Texas A&M University in College Station, a conservative institution with a military ethos and, at least at that time in the late 1980s and early 1990s, a predominantly white male faculty. A new African American assistant professor in our department taught a compelling course on the discourse of the Black civil rights movement, which our predominantly white students found especially engaging and enlightening. When one of those students returned from a Thanksgiving break in the fall semester, she reported to her professor that she had shared her enthusiasm for his course on the civil rights movement with her parents only to be told by her father that he had sent her to Texas A&M so that she wouldn't have to deal with that sort of thing.

53. Daniel P. Denvir, "Reluctant Foot Soldiers: America's Undergraduates Rebuff Opponents of Academic Freedom," *Academe* 89 (May/June 2003): 36–39.

54. Sara Hebel, "Patrolling Professors' Politics," *The Chronicle of Higher Education*, February 13, 2004, 29 March 2004, available online; "The Center's Mission," *Center for the Study of Popular Culture*, available online.

55. Available online.

56. "About Us," Students for Academic Freedom, available online.

57. Hebel, "Patrolling."

58. David Horowitz, "The Professors' Orwellian Case," *FrontPageMagazine.com*, December 5, 2003.

59. Kurtz, "Studying Title VI."

60. David Horowitz and Eli Lehrer, "Political Bias in the Administrations and Faculties of 32 Elite Colleges and Universities," available online.

61. For a detailed critical analysis of Horowitz's arguments and evidence and Hamilton's position, see Robert L. Ivie, "A Presumption of Academic Freedom," *The Review of Education, Pedagogy, and Cultural Studies* 27 (January-March 2005): 63–68, 73–76.

62. David Horowitz, "The Campus Blacklist," *FrontPageMagazine.com*, April 18, 2003.

63. John Stauber and Sheldon Rampton, "The War at Home," CommonDreams, May 17, 2004 available online.

64. Even Horowitz acknowledged that "the evidence regarding its [that is, the systematic exclusion of conservatives from academia] mode of operation and the extent of its impact is anecdotal or confined to research that is incomplete. Nevertheless," he continued, "its reality is undeniable." David Horowitz, "The Campus Blacklist."

65. "Academic Bills of Rights," American Association of University Professors, December 3, 2003, available online.

66. "Controversy in the Classroom," American Association of University Professors, February 3, 2004, available online.

67. "Academic Freedom and National Security in a Time of Crisis," American Association of University Professors, available online.

68. Scott Jaschik, "A Win for 'Academic Bill of Rights,'" *Inside Higher Ed News*, July 7, 2005, available online.

69. Jo Ann Gora, "Ball State's Critics Ignore Facts, Policies," *Muncie Star Press*, December 15, 2004.

70. Sara Dogan, "Open Letter to Indiana Legislators," December 7, 2004, available online.

71. Quoted in Gora, "Ball State's Critics."

72. Press release by Students for Academic Freedom, "Despite Criticism, Ball State Continues Using Taxpayer Dollars to Fund Liberal Agenda," January 24, 2005, was posted online at their web site.

73. My account of Horowitz's speech is based on my observation of his presentation that night and a story the following day in the Bloomington daily newspaper. See Steve Hinnefeld, "Protesters Disrupt Speech: Horowitz Blasts Leftists as Menace to Humanity, *The Herald-Times*, April 8, 2005.

74. John Dewey, *The Public and Its Problems* (1927; Athens, Ohio: Swallow Press/Ohio University Press, 1991), 157, 166.

75. Dewey, *The Public*, 184, 176–77.

76. Dewey, *The Public*, 183.

77. For a copy of Governor Bill Owens letter, see "Gov. Owens Letter Calls for Churchill to Step Down," *TheDenverChannel.Com*, February 1, 2005, available online. It was also posted by Ward Churchill on his web site.

78. A copy of Ward Churchill's controversial commentary following the events of 9/11 was posted by him on his web site: Ward Churchill, "'Some People Push Back': On the Justice of Roosting Chickens."

79. Robert Jensen, "Ward Churchill: Right to Speak Out; Right About 9/11," *Counterpunch*, February 14, 2005, available online.

80. W. Norwood Brigance, "The Backwash of War," *Vital Speeches of the Day*, December 1, 1945, 107; William Norwood Brigance, "Demagogues, 'Good' People, and Teachers of Speech," *The Speech Teacher* 1 (September 1952): 160–62; W. Norwood Brigance, "Security is an Illusion," *Vital Speeches*, July 15, 1951, 596; William Norwood Brigance, *Speech: Its Techniques and Disciplines in a Free Society* (New York: Appleton-Century-Crofts, Inc., 1952), 432–33, 460–61, 531.

81. The revised version of the original statement now appears as the opening chapter of a book by Ward Churchill, *On the Justice of Roosting Chickens: Reflections on the Consequences of U.S. Imperial Arrogance and Criminality* (Oakland, California: AK Press, 2003). On the subject of blowback, see for example, Chalmers Johnson, *Blowback: The Costs and Consequences of American Empire* (New York: Henry Holt and Co., 2000).

82. Garrison Keillor, *Homegrown Democrat: A Few Plain Thoughts from the Heart of America* (New York: Viking, 2004), 26.

83. Cass R. Sunstein, *Why Societies Need Dissent* (Cambridge, Massachusetts: Harvard University Press, 2003).

84. Steven H. Shiffrin, *The First Amendment, Democracy, and Romance* (Cambridge, Massachusetts: Harvard University Press, 1990), 77–78, 85, 91–99.

85. Edward Ingebretsen, *At Stake: Monsters and the Rhetoric of Fear in Public Culture* (Chicago: University of Chicago Press, 2003).

86. George Lakoff, *Don't Think of an Elephant!* (White River Junction, Vermont: Chelsea Green Publishing, 2004), 3–4.

87. For a discussion of mainstream media consolidation, see Ben H. Bagdikian, *The New Media Monopoly*, rev. ed. (Boston: Beacon Press, 2004), and Robert W. McChesney, *The Problem of the Media: U.S. Communication Politics in the 21st Century* (New York: Monthly Review Press, 2004).

88. The US military doctrine of "information dominance" explicitly aims at capturing and neutralizing dissent that interferes with its plans. There is reason to suspect that independent media and critics are being increasingly targeted when they are perceived to be challenging US information dominance. This is a program of "weaponized information." See David Miller, "Information Dominance: The Philosophy of Total Propaganda Control?" in *War, Media, and Propaganda: A Global Perspective*, ed. Yahya R. Kamalipour and Nancy Snow (Lanham, Maryland: Rowman and Littlefield Publishers, 2004), 9–10, 12, 14.

89. Kenneth Burke, *The Philosophy of Literary Form*, 3rd ed. (Berkeley: University of California Press, 1973), 110–11.

90. John Paul Lederach, *The Moral Imagination: The Art and Soul of Building Peace* (New York: Oxford University Press, 2005), viii.

91. Lederach, *Moral Imagination*, 29, 52, 171–72.

92. Lederach, *Moral Imagination*, x, 42–43, 52, 58–59, 175.

93. Lederach, *Moral Imagination*, ix–x, 29, 55–58.

94. Lederach, *Moral Imagination*, x, 5.

95. Lederach, *Moral Imagination*, 72, 56–57, 146–47; see also 69, 70–71, 105–06.

96. Lederach, *Moral Imagination*, 34–35, 111.

97. Lederach, *Moral Imagination*, 58–59.

98. Lederach, *Moral Imagination*, 35–36, 115, 66–70.

99. Lederach, *Moral Imagination*, 87–88.

100. Lederach, *Moral Imagination*, 91–92.

101. For a useful discussion of how sustained and decentralized popular dissent expressed in distinct forms can accumulate rhetorical force over time, see Roland Bleiker, *Popular Dissent, Human Agency and Global Politics* (Cambridge: Cambridge University Press, 2000).

102. T. V. Reed, *The Art of Protest: Culture and Activism from the Civil Rights Movement to the Streets of Seattle* (Minneapolis: University of Minnesota Press, 2005), 76.

103. Robert Jensen, *Writing Dissent: Taking Radical Ideas from the Margins to the Mainstream* (New York: Peter Lang, 2001), 131–32, 141.

104. Johan Galtung, "Preface," *Communication and Culture in War and Peace*, ed. Colleen Roach (Newbury Park, California: Sage Publications, 1993), xi–xii.

105. Boulding, *Cultures of Peace*, 219, 221.

106. Majid Tehranian, "War, Media, and Propaganda: An Epilogue," in Kamalipour and Snow, *War, Media, and Propaganda*, 239.

107. Mosco, "Communication and Information Technology," 68–69.

108. Galtung's chart of criteria is reproduced in Jake Lynch and Annabel McGoldrick, "Peace Journalism: A Global Dialog for Democracy and Democratic Media," in *Democratizing Global Media: One World, Many Struggles*, ed. Robert A. Hackett and Yuezhi Zhao (Lanham, Maryland: Rowman and Littlefield Publishers, 2005), 271.

109. Jake Lynch, "17 Tips: What a Peace Journalist Would Try to Do," media channel.org, available online.

110. Tehranian, "Epilogue," 241–42.

111. Ivie, "Savagery in Democracy's Empire," 55–65.

112. Howard Zinn, "The Power and the Glory: Myths of American Exceptionalism," *Boston Review*, available online.

113. Michael Scheuer, "Throwing America a Life Preserver," Antiwar.com, June 10, 2005.

114. Antiwar.com, "About Us."

115. Anonymous [Michael Scheuer], *Imperial Hubris: Why the West is Losing the War on Terror* (Washington, D.C.: Brassey's, Inc., 2004).

116. Robert Pape, *Dying to Win: The Strategic Logic of Suicide Terrorism* (New York: Random House, 2005).

117. Schueur, "Throwing America a Life Preserver."

118. Jude Wanniski, "Check Out Antiwar.com," available online.

119. Jude Wanniski, "Suicide Bombers as Freedom Fighters?" June 27, 2005.

120. LewRockwell.com, June 28, 2005, available online.

121. Theconservativevoice.com; uruknet.info; iraq-news.de; orbstandard.com, available online.

122. This exchange on "The Mudville Gazette" occurred July 13, 14, and 15, 2005, respectively, on mudvillegazette.com, available online. Mountain Girl's reference to Pape's book sent the reader to her own blog (thinkingwomanslife) for details: "Life Is a Comedy for Those Who Think...Counterpoint," July 13, 2005.

123. Mountain Girl, "Life is a Comedy."

124. Interview with Robert Pape, "The Logic of Suicide Terrorism: It's the Occupation, Not the Fundamentalism," *The American Conservative*, July 18, 2005, available online.

125. Steve Chapman, "To Stop Suicide Bombings, Bring Troops Home," *Baltimore Sun*, June 6, 2005.

126. Caryle Murphy, "A Scholarly Look at Terror Sees Bootprints in the Sand," Washingtonpost.com, July 10, 2005, available online.

127. Michael Scheuer cited in Murphy, "A Scholarly Look."

128. Darrell Uderhoven posting on Bredan Nyhan: The Art and Science of Politics, July 17, 2005, available online.

129. Schirch, *Ritual and Symbol*, 1, 17.

130. Bleiker, *Popular Dissent*.

131. Boulding, *Cultures of Peace*, 1–2.

132. For a discussion of cyberpolitics, see Martha McCaughey and Michael D. Ayers, *Cyberactivism: Online Activism in Theory and Practice* (New York: Routledge, 2003), and Vim van de Donk, Brian D. Loader, Paul G. Nixon, and Dieter Rucht, ed., *Cyberprotest: New Media, Citizens and Social Movements* (London: Routledge, 2004).

133. Bruce E. Gronbeck, "Citizen Voices in Cyberpolitical Culture," in *Rhetorical Democracy: Discursive Practices of Civic Engagement*, ed. Gerard A. Hauser and Amy Grim (Mahway, New Jersey: Lawrence Erlbaum Associates, 2004), 28.

5

A Question of Citizenship

Peacebuilding dissent, as an exercise in democratic citizenship and an expression of human solidarity, is an ongoing process of cultural change and renewal. It operates creatively and constructively (that is, tactically and strategically) within the constraints of existing political culture even as it works to transform the prevailing war culture. It encompasses street protests and mass marches as an exercise in political pressure, dramatically rallying the people to build a demonstrable public opinion against an impending or ongoing war, but it includes much more than protests and rallies—much more, indeed, that impacts our everyday way of thinking and living.

As a progressive movement to build a culture of peace, democratic dissent from war involves overcoming a condition of "warism," the term philosopher Duane L. Cady uses to describe "the view that war is both morally justifiable in principle and often morally justified in fact," that is, "that alternatives to war may be entertained only insofar as they promise distinct advantages over war options."[1] A culture predisposed to peace, in contrast, would consider war a moral defeat and would strive to find alternative ways of managing human conflict wherever possible. Warism so normalizes violence, as Cady observes, that "it even seems natural to try to prevent war by threatening it."[2] This prevailing presumption that peace is a by-product of violence and of coercion is reinforced in so-called value-free school curricula, which feature war histories and military heroics while downplaying or discrediting peace advocates, ethics, and models as unrealistic. It is the basic assumption rehearsed regularly for general consumption in television programming and other dominant forms of cultural reproduction.[3]

In contrast, peacebuilding citizenship involves occupying a "shared space of humanity" that gives "ongoing presence" to "activities of conciliation," in the words of peace scholar and practitioner John Paul Lederach. It is a continuing, long-term commitment, he maintains, to "cultivating" relationships "across the lines of conflict over time" and keeping the focus "on people, realities of histories and perceptions as the source that generates and regenerates cycles of deadly conflict."[4] The citizen's dissent, like that of Pope John Paul II, is to continue to say "NO TO WAR! War is not always inevitable. It is always a defeat for humanity."[5] There are better ways to manage conflict than brutal warfare. So strong a dissent from war as this, such a powerful exercise of citizenship and firm resistance to warism by ordinary folk as well as secular and religious leaders can be made commonplace and considered common sense only when it reflects and is premised on a broad array of humanizing practices of reconciliation that comprise a healthy democratic culture of constructive political contestation.

Yet, dissent was rendered antithetical to democracy in America after 9/11 under the foreboding sign of a timeless war on global terror. As a form of political activism, dissent was placed strategically by the rulers of the security state on a continuum of lawlessness leading to terrorism, a continuum in which protest was perceived as disloyal, as the unpatriotic act of the enemy within, as a threat to the safety of the polity—in short, as anti-democratic. The police, authorized by secret courts, might spy on, harass, and incarcerate dissenters on behalf of a state that would curtail civil liberties while prosecuting a war in the hallowed, but hollowed, name of freedom and democracy. In the words of US Attorney General John Ashcroft, speaking to the Senate Judiciary Committee just three months after 9/11, "those who scare peace-loving people with phantoms of lost liberty" while criticizing the administration's methods of fighting terrorism at home and abroad provide "ammunition to America's enemies" and "aid [to] terrorists."[6] By this twisted, Orwellian logic, dissent terrorizes democracy whereas political quiescence and submission to a condition of warism promotes peace and security.

Such logic not only confounds democratic politics but also rationalizes state terror in response to a state of terror. State terror is legitimized as counter-terror and antiterrorism rather than condemned as terrorism redux and reduplicated. Jude McCulloch has observed this fallacy from his Australian vantage point as a lecturer in police studies at Deakin University. "The history of state terror," he notes, "illustrates that counter-terrorism is used to punish, intimidate and disappear politically inconvenient citizens. In the 'war on terrorism' politically inconvenient citizens will include peace and anti-war activists. . . . [A]nti-terrorism is the new McCarthyism."[7] This is the degraded condition of official political discourse practiced in the United States and by its "democratic" allies to exploit popular fear and mute criticism of a crusade against evil rather than address the root causes of terror, including a misguided US foreign policy.

Configuring democracy and dissent as oxymoronic—a contradiction of terms and thus a political incongruity—is rhetorically strategic to dividing the world inextricably between good and evil—us versus them—in a deadly dual for global domination. Not since the Cold War has an American administration articulated an apocalyptic vision backed by such a massive commitment of military might, huge expenditure of economic resources, and wanton sacrifice of human life. By presidential decree, everyone must decide whether they are allies or enemies of the United States in a global war to eradicate terrorism. No shades of grey, no differences of perspective, no room for dissent can be abided if freedom is to endure and democracy is to prevail. The boundary must be drawn fast and firm between righteous truth and wicked persuasion. Thus, the domestic dissenter symbolizes democracy's foreign threat, its enemy Other, a traitor to the people and their cause, or so an empowered elite would have the public believe rather than suffer even a modicum of democratic debate.

Accordingly, one might conclude that unmaking the oxymoron of democratic dissent would be tantamount to striking at the rhetorical Achilles heel of a discourse that suppresses the actual practice of politics in the very realm of the political. The political, as Chantal Mouffe and Ernesto Laclau emphasize, is the realm of managing antagonism that is endemic to human relations and of contesting opinions on matters that are beyond perfect decidability.[8] Politics is the process of articulating positions and making contingent decisions in a context of irreducible difference, conflict, and division through "persuasive redescriptions of the world."[9] Metaphors can help us to redescribe, revise, and repair troubled social relations enough to achieve partial and provisional, but sufficient, agreement without insisting on total consensus or imposing a single worldview.[10] Indeed, social divisions cannot be reconciled entirely or finally; they are inherent to pluralistic democratic politics, which requires a lively dynamic between consensus and dissent.[11] Politics, Mouffe stresses, is an "ensemble of practices, discourses and institutions which seek to establish a certain order and organize human coexistence in conditions that are always potentially conflictual."[12] The central question of democratic politics, therefore, is how to tame and diffuse antagonism in human relations, not eliminate it—how to articulate a practical but partial unity in a pluralistic context of conflict and diversity by transforming sheer enemies into legitimate adversaries.[13]

This vision of constructive contestation, or agonistic pluralism, makes dissent not only compatible with democracy but also represents it as a practice of persuasion common to democratic culture, a resource for addressing antagonism productively on the shifting terrain of conflicted political relations. Yet it is a vision seemingly in remission, a radical notion of democratic practice difficult to grasp and trust in America, perhaps no more than a mere fantasy for many, or even most Americans. What, we might ask, are the contours of this resistance to democratic dissent in the United States and the cultural resources for rehabilitating its good name? How might we understand better the obstacles to accessing dissent's democratic properties and potential? What are the challenges to overcome and the opportunities to affirm dissent within the *sensus communis* in order to enrich democracy? These are the questions we must begin to answer if we wish to resist the militarization of global politics. The answers to such important questions are difficult to learn and never easy to remember, however, not even when the hard lessons of experience would seem to mark them indelibly on our collective memory.

DEMOCRATIC DISSENT IN WAR AND CRISIS

Democratic dissent in a period of war or crisis is as alarming to the purveyors of prevailing opinion as it is critical to a nation's political welfare. This is especially the case when the democratic nation in question is as powerful as the US and so prone to denigrating anti-war dissent as unpatriotic and disloyal. The most common complaints about critics and protesters alike throughout US history include accusations that they abuse the very freedom the nation is fighting to preserve, that they undermine public morale and political authority when it is most required, that they put the lives of American soldiers at further risk, that their criticism of political leaders aids and abets the enemy, and that their resistance ultimately prolongs the war. Often dissenters are accused of being enemy agents and sympathizers, dismissed as dangerously unrealistic isolationists and naïve pacifists, or characterized as irresponsible agitators exposing the country to the twin perils of chaos and tyranny. None of these delegitimating themes amounts to an affirmation of democracy or, more specifically, to an expression of confidence in democracy's stamina, its genius for managing divisive political relations, or its dependency on dissent for continuing vitality. Fighting wars in the name of democracy is one thing; practicing it in times of crisis is altogether another. Resistance to dissent, even relegating dissenters to the political margins while curtailing civil liberties on the whole, functions to defer the nation's democratic impulse into perpetuity, that is, until that mythical moment of universal peace and total security finally arrives but which always remains just beyond the limit of living history (catch-22).

In the periods between wars, Americans have often reflected on the lessons to be learned from the excesses of the preceding war, including the cost of suppressing democratic dissent and violating civil liberties. After World War I, in particular, the cause of protecting political rights received a significant boost in the public's consciousness as a result of some of the most egregious violations of civil liberties perpetrated during and immediately following the war, including an espionage act that allowed the Postmaster General to ban from the mail any seditious materials that encouraged insubordination or otherwise impugned the government, a sedition act that criminalized any disloyal or abusive language about the nation's form of government, its constitution, and its institutions, the American Protective League and a number of other vigilante organizations encouraged by the government to inform on citizens, and the infamous Palmer raids on suspected radicals during a Red Scare in the US triggered by Russia's Bolshevik revolution. Not only were German books burned and banned during the war, German teachers and musicians fired, German ideas suppressed, and speaking the German language punished, but in the sheer absurdity of war fever even sauerkraut was renamed "liberty cabbage."

Out of this onslaught on the Bill of Rights grew the American Civil Liberties Union and an emergent precedent of Supreme Court dissenting opinions that evolved into a majority position of the 1950s and 1960s, which tenuously bolstered civil liberties. Yet each war or crisis has brought with it renewed violations of civil rights and displacements of democratic practices, including the internment of Japanese Americans during World War II, Cold War blacklisting and political intimidation during the McCarthy era of guilt by association, and exclusion of the press from direct reporting on US military action in Grenada, Panama, Kuwait, and Kosovo followed by the strategic embedding of reporters in the second war on Iraq. Indeed, threats to civil liberties and the curtailment of political dissent after 9/11 may yet develop into the most damaging, systemic assault on democratic values since the founding of the republic, reducing American citizenship to the consumption of "freedom fries" while their government reads citizens' e-mail and tortures suspected terrorists with little or no legal constraint or accountability.

The lesson Americans find most difficult to master is that vigorous dissent and debate are especially critical in times of national crisis in order to keep ambitious governments honest. Without open debate, governments tend to exaggerate the danger to the nation, target unpopular groups for vilification and repression, enact preexisting political agendas under the cover of national security, and generally spawn a culture of secrecy and suppression that fosters poor decision-making with regrettable consequences. Already under the prolonged and pervasive emergency of fighting global terrorism, the Bush administration has taken several dangerous steps to shore up the purported vulnerabilities of an open society. The USA Patriot Act may be the most invasive legislation passed or contemplated since World War I. The legislation creating the Homeland Security Department increased information gathering on citizens and decreased citizen access to government information previously provided by the Freedom of Information Act. A TIPS program would muster citizens into a national self-surveillance corps, just as the administration's Total Information Awareness program would integrate private-sector and government data bases into a unified monitoring system. A policy of preemptive wars to maintain global military dominance was initiated with the invasion of Iraq. All of this emerged from a condition of limited debate and marginalized dissent and with the broad-based approval of a public uninformed of the negative consequences of these untoward initiatives because of an overly quiescent press and remarkably subdued opposition party.[14]

The risk facing a democratic nation sans a strong ethic and robust practice of dissent is extraordinary in an open-ended condition of crisis and a prolonged war on terrorism that could institutionalize allegedly temporary encroachments on freedom. A permanent diminishment of liberty and democratic vigor could be the ultimate legacy of a largely uncontested political agenda that would increase government secrecy, unfetter law enforcement, and deploy military power actively in support of an aggressive policy of unilateralism and preemption. The strongest and smartest government, on the contrary, is that which is made transparent by democratic dissent. In the appropriately partisan words of Republican Senator Robert A. Taft, spoken just after Japan's surprise attack on Pearl Harbor, "criticism in time of war is essential to the maintenance of any kind of democratic government" and to the prevention of "mistakes which might otherwise occur."[15] Why has this proved to be so difficult a lesson to remember?

Perhaps the difficulty of assimilating the lesson of fettered dissent is a function of how Americans routinely speak and think of politics as problematically irrational and perplexingly rhetorical, presuming instead that politics can and should be clearly, cleanly, efficiently, and reliably rational and thus by implication entrusted to qualified elites rather than to ordinary folk. Perhaps this old habit of mind about the discourse of politics fixes expectations so firmly, dichotomizes choices so definitively, and diminishes faith so profoundly in the public's capacity for practical reason that censorship and conformity just seem more prudent in moments of perceived crisis than risking an unruly cacophony of voices. Maybe the myth of privileged rationality overpowers the public's memory of, and imagination for, collective self-rule. Possibly this very myth can and should be debunked to bolster our democratic resolve.

If it is the case, as Nancy Chang and others insist, that strengthening "our commitment to the First Amendment and the democratic values it embodies becomes all the more essential" when the nation's security is threatened (which is precisely the point at which government and society at large are most inclined to curtail freedom of speech), then it is especially important to understand what is at stake when democratic dissent is curbed and to explore how the agonistic edge of vigorous dissent can be sharpened to address more effectively the present crisis of terrorism under prevailing conditions of division and diversity.[16] This is a task that benefits considerably from reexamining the confluence of politics and communication.

A politics of dissent constituted in a discourse of identification may be the purest expression of the democratic idiom and the most constructive vehicle for managing troubled relations among rivals. By specifying similarities within differences, we might expect to gain added purchase on overdrawn and threatening images of domestic adversaries and foreign enemies—those propagandizing caricatures that stifle dissent by associating difference with deviance and malevolence and that demand political consensus and quiescence as a mark of allegiance, loyalty, and virtue. We might construct more flexible attitudes that enable dissent to perform the crucial function of holding delimited perspectives accountable to one another, which is far more conducive to managing the human divide constructively than a rigid rhetoric of good versus evil, but is the American body politic a viable candidate for such a transplant, for replacing the rhetoric of evil with an idiom of humanizing identification in order to strengthen democracy by dissent?

Political dissent outside of a democratic culture is generally considered destabilizing, subversive, and even revolutionary. In an undemocratic context it functions as an illegitimate expression of power contrary to the will of prevailing political authority and thus is routinely suppressed as a threat to order, security, and the general well-being of the people and the state. Within a thin or relatively weak democratic context, dissent is more or less tolerated, depending on circumstances, but is treated essentially as an outlet or luxury rather than a necessity of good government and as something therefore that should be curtailed during dangerous periods of national crisis.[17] Within a strong democracy, however, dissent would be privileged even in circumstances of war.

Strong democracy remains an unrealized ideal of our time. A deep suspicion of collective self-rule has troubled the American republic from its founding. As Robert Dahl observes, "A substantial number of the Framers believed that they must erect constitutional barriers to popular rule because the people would prove to be an unruly mob, a standing danger to law, to orderly government, and to property rights." As Dahl also notes, the American citizenry throughout its history has supported orderly government over the temptation of demagoguery, contrary to the Framers' pessimistic expectations and their elitist fear of democratic distemper.[18] Experience aside, this legacy of demophobia still haunts the nation's collective psyche and continues to foster a deep distrust of dissent. The presumption of a critically deficient and inherently irrational citizenry requires elites to deliberate among themselves on behalf of the people and in the spirit of universal reason. More democracy in the form of popular dissent would only exacerbate the inherently fragile condition of an easily confused public.

To the extent that dissent specifically and democratic politics generally operate within the realm of public persuasion instead of in a rarified world of privileged rationality, they are deemed a danger to public health by political elites who, from their own necessarily delimited and self-interested perspective, would transcend persuasion in the service of universal reason. Their conceit aside, no political discourse is nonrhetorical, and no particular construction of rationality is universal despite pretensions to the contrary. The political is by definition the arena of contested aims and opinions, and persuasion is by default the discourse of this realm of contingencies through which relations of power are articulated, judgments fashioned, decisions derived, and actions taken.[19] Nevertheless, political elites profess to deliberate rationally on behalf of and in place of the people, masking their own rhetoric even from themselves.[20] Within America's weak democratic culture, persuasion operates covertly among elites in the guise of rationality rather than overtly among the people as a viable mode of political deliberation and judgment. This clearly is a strong constraint against endorsing a democratic practice as robust as popular dissent.

Yet, if dissent thrives it "makes room for a more tolerant politics" by recognizing "that a society is oppressive and closed if all major questions either have an answer or are considered irrational, absurd, taboo."[21] Tolerance and its ugly converse, repression, are indicative of the political problem revealed in the presence or absence of democratic dissent. The heart of the matter is achieving a lively politics of contestation and identification in a context of difference and division. Conflict, rather than something to overcome and contain, is a continuing circumstance of divisive social relations that gives politics purpose but that defaults to antagonism, vilification, and victimization unless it is addressed productively. A well-functioning and strong democracy requires a contestation of differences and vigorous debate over real alternatives, a healthy mix of division and identification.

Promoting constructive dissent would serve a purpose far greater than the diffusion of pent-up political pressure. Rather than being just a way to let off steam, dissent can articulate alternatives to prevailing policies and points of view. It can work against tendencies of political alienation and victimization in a given political order by resisting problematic reifications and by providing degrees of flexibility for adapting to changing circumstances. It can sustain the productive tension that liberal democracy requires in order to meet the exigency of pluralism in a global information age. Yet, when dissent occurs, as it did worldwide in massive demonstrations against America's impending invasion of Iraq, it is all too easily reduced by ruling elites to a political irrelevancy. George W. Bush imperially dismissed such dissent by diminishing it to mere confirmation that "democracy is a beautiful thing" in which "people are allowed to express their opinion" short of influencing his presidential decisions.[22]

INCENTIVE TO DISSENT

Although the body politic as currently constituted seems disinclined toward raising its democratic consciousness, tensions exist that nevertheless are increasingly difficult for political elites to manage under the pretense of universal reason. Even conventional political wisdom, as articulated by Cass Sunstein, dictates that society needs dissent. Dissent, he argues by mustering evidence primarily from studies in social psychology, helps to avoid the unchecked inflation of blind, ideological thinking, extremism, and polarization that ruins good decision-making. Groups make better decisions when they encounter dissent than when they succumb to conformity. Extremism and poor decisions are the bitter products of minority voices being silenced, even self-censored, and of dissenters withdrawing from active participation in the business of the polity.[23] Moreover, as Roland Bleiker observes, "no political system, no matter how authoritarian, is ever able to dominate all aspects of society" just as "no form of dissent, no matter how radical, is ever entirely autonomous from the political practices it seeks to engage or distance itself from." Dissent, he continues, necessarily arises out of "existing webs of power and discourse," and thus must be considered as part and parcel of everyday democratic politics.[24] Thus, it would seem plausible, even though difficult, to transform America's weak democratic tradition into a more robust culture of constructive dissent. How might such a transformation occur over time?

The incentive for converting America's weak democratic culture of public quiescence into a stronger practice of popular dissent may already exist following the emergence of the presidential republic, which should goad any democratically-inclined people to resist the establishment of a permanent regime of executive governance by crisis. This is a watershed development that ultimately will diminish or enrich democracy in the United States depending on how the nation responds.

What historians refer to as the rhetorical presidency evolved in the US throughout the twentieth century, expanding executive authority into a full-fledged presidential republic.[25] As one student of this phenomenon, Gary Gregg, observed in 1997, "We have gone far toward creating a presidential republic. Many have seen the president as a white knight doing battle with the forces of evil, both domestically and internationally, in the name of the American people and their values and beliefs." Even as others warned against "investing too much in 'Caesar' and becoming too reliant on executive benevolence, the general trend over the last century [was] in the opposite direction."[26] The ultimate risk to democratic culture was made palpable on 9/11 when crisis became the ubiquitous shadow of presidential rule and terror was articulated by executive fiat into a permanent and pervasive state of warfare that penetrated all walks of life and tainted every political issue, domestic and foreign.

Yet, the very transformation of the rhetorical presidency into a presidential republic occurred in the context of an evolving rhetorical republic, thus providing a wider context that may well prove to be a resource for combating the perversion of post-9/11 presidential rule. Frederick Dolan and Thomas Dumm argued in 1993 that the United States by then already had become not just the feared rhetorical presidency but even more radically "a republic of words" wherein the problem of governing amounted to the problem of governing representations, "of reinterpreting the phantasmagoric mix of images and tonalities, claims and counterclaims, that shape political discourse in the United States today." In such a republic, they argued, there is no "master discourse unquestioningly shared or respected by all." Even "national security" is a trope, an image of vulnerability and sign of national identity that would convince Americans to believe, in the words of David Campbell, that they "are always at risk in a dangerous world." Danger, Campbell emphasized, is an effect of interpretation, not an objective, knowable condition; not all risks are interpreted as dangers, but "the ability to represent things as alien, subversive, dirty, or sick has been pivotal in the articulation of danger in the American experience."[27]

We may be inclined to attribute the emergence of this potentially decentralized and phantasmagoric rhetorical republic largely to the profusion of electronic media. We may even wish to speak instead of the existence of a digital or electronic republic and its impact on democracy in the information age.[28] Political persuasion, nevertheless, is practiced more overtly and acknowledged more readily in such a republic where the choice is between better and worse kinds of persuasion, not between mere rhetoric and sheer rationality, and where in principle it can be more difficult to close off debate with an authoritative declaration of truth. This potential for openness and accountability amounts to an opportunity, not a guarantee, to strengthen democracy by practicing dissent.

As a case in point, the rhetoric of George W. Bush's presidency is a rigid discourse of good versus evil in a world marked by radical divisions, a world interconnected by electronic media and by a global economy in which serious differences can no longer be easily ignored or readily suppressed. Bush's rigid rhetoric confronts Americans with the clear choice of conforming to or dissenting from his call to arms as the solution to terrorism. For many Americans, the terrorism of 9/11 presented a rare and meaningful opportunity for a people that bowled and shopped alone to come together as one nation in opposition to an evil adversary. That, at least, was an initial impulse that the president's apocalyptic rhetoric promoted. It is a rhetoric that personifies evil in the image of nineteen hijackers, Osama bin Laden, and Saddam Hussein. It is a discourse so hyperbolized that it cannot mask its own rhetorical character even as it demands assent and defies dissent, and it is a rhetoric that cannot be ignored as such, a rhetoric operating within a rhetorical republic in which the people either may succumb to propaganda and demagoguery or may choose to speak up and listen to alterative points of view. In short, Bush's blatant rhetoric may, but not necessarily will, prod the nation to choose a richer, more democratic politics of dissent.

CONTESTING THE DEMONIZING LANGUAGE OF WAR

Censorship, silence, and submission to presidential governance by terror and by the threat of terror are stark alternatives to democratic dissent in a thoroughly rhetorical republic. Thus, if a political incentive already exists for adopting stronger democratic practices and for developing a more democratic republic, we should consider how such a cultural shift can be facilitated by concrete acts of citizenship. One such act of citizenship is to finesse a course correction through constructive language critiques, that is, to revisit the reified metaphors and denigrating myths that tyrannize our collective outlook on a troubled world. The purpose of this exercise in critical thinking is to contest the dehumanizing language that justifies war and thus to pierce the stifling shroud of silence that now envelops America's languishing democracy.

The challenge of enriching US political culture and revitalizing peacebuilding democratic practices, as a project of critique from within the existing culture, must be addressed in the broadest terms and understood at the most fundamental level as a constructive exercise in enhancing liberal democracy by balancing two competing languages or discourses. It requires correcting the present and persistent imbalance between a dominant discourse of liberalism and individualism and a subordinate discourse of democracy and community. This power imbalance between liberal and democratic discourses, as Russell Hanson explains, has marked and marred the American republic throughout its history.[29] Peacebuilding dissent seeks a better balance between liberalism's emphasis on freedom and rights and democracy's stress on inclusion and equality. It integrates the two political impulses, requiring the protection of civil liberties and individual rights from governmental encroachment in order to promote equality and collective self-rule and thereby engender a democratizing influence on liberalism. As a progressive political movement, dissent from war enriches citizenship by drawing on an existing but underdeveloped democratic ethic of participation in public life, respect for others, and celebration of human decency.[30]

Peacebuilding democratic citizenship is therefore largely about changing national images of alienation between "us" and "them," images common to a war system nurtured in a war culture. In Paul Joseph's view, it is about articulating an alternative vision of positive peace that redefines national security instead of defaulting to the political orthodoxy of militarism. It means exercising our capacity "to recognize the common humanity in people who seem to be different from ourselves" rather than focusing primarily on the human "capacity to do evil." It involves nurturing a political culture that endorses nonviolent conflict resolution. These are long-term, continuing commitments to cultural transformation, Joseph insists, not short-term, immediate-impact goals. Peace movements that measure their success by the criteria of unambiguous impact, political victory in the near term, and immediate policy change are doomed to failure. To leave a living legacy of positive change, a peace movement's demonstrations, protests, lobbying efforts, educational initiatives, electioneering, and other dissenting practices must "build a culture of peace, not only by advancing a critique of policy, but also in opposing more generally the use of war, militarism, and the threat of organized violence to settle international disputes."[31] Crucial to this long-term process of dissenting from warism is overcoming a negative notion of citizenship that amounts to an exercise of individual rights, separates individuals from the larger community and social responsibility, and alienates the nation from humanity at large in all its global diversity.[32]

Strengthening democracy through peacebuilding citizenship requires, in the first instance, attention to language critique as a way of thinking imaginatively, freshly, or somehow differently about troublesome, but reified constructions in the discourse of the war culture—those literalized, naturalized, conventionalized, or otherwise privileged ways of speaking belligerently that are deeply embedded in the political culture and life world. This amounts to a process of metaphorically redescribing relations of hostility.[33] Through language critique, Roland Bleiker explains, discourse can be turned "from a system of exclusion to a practice of inclusion, from a method of domination to an instrument of resistance." This crucial turn is achieved by revising troublesome concepts and even, on occasion, by creating new concepts.[34]

The rearticulation of troublesome or otherwise unserviceable categories of speech and thought involves, in the second instance, an analysis and critique of specific terminologies that operate in particular contexts to diminish peaceful motives and undermine democratic practices. For instance, the Bush administration's discourse of "preemptive" war on terror, supposedly in defense of freedom and civilization, is based largely on an opposition between Islamism and democracy. Accordingly, coerced democratization of rogue states is represented favorably as the key to national security and world peace.

Susan Buck-Morss, however, would have us think past the self-perpetuating cycle of terror and counter-terror by critically engaging such a hard and fast opposition between "the discursive field of 'Islamism'" and an indigenous discourse of democracy. Toward that end, she critiques the reduction of Islamism to terrorism, arguing that Islamism is itself a multifaceted critical discourse rather than a monolithic ideology of militant violence. Like the discourse of liberalism, she maintains, "Islamism frames social and political debates without preempting their content." As a framing discourse, Islamism "is the politicization of Islam in a postcolonial context, a contemporary discourse of opposition and debate, dealing with issues of social justice, legitimate power, and ethical life in a way that challenges the hegemony of Western political and cultural norms." Again like Western liberalism, Islamism can and has been appropriated across the political spectrum "from terrorist networks, to right-wing authoritarianism, to neo-liberal centrism, to left-radicalism, to secular-state egalitarianism, to guerrilla warfare. The political impact of Islamism, far from being monolithic, has been reactionary, conservative, democratic, revolutionary, conspiratorial," depending on its specific contexts of interpretation. These "political variations and historical complexities," however, are effaced by stereotypically opposing an evil Islam to everything Western, good, and modern.[35]

Specifically, Buck-Morss finds within Islamist discourse the resources of a political language that can support goals of "global peace, economic justice, legal equality, democratic participation, individual freedom, [and] mutual respect." Moreover, she argues, this is a discursive field that can with effort be translated and extended creatively to enrich a truncated Western imaginary and exercise the otherwise rigidified conceptual frame of globalization that overlooks disastrous environmental and social consequences of free trade and economic interdependence. Her dissent from the cultural confrontation presumed by a triumphal discourse of good versus evil and its "insensate scenario of unlimited warfare" aims to "imagine alternative forms" by exposing Western hegemonic discourse to nonfundamentalist Islamic principles of "socio-economic justice and essential human egalitarianism." The West might learn to appreciate the work of Islamist feminists operating within contemporary Iran, for instance. Drawing on an Islamist discourse that articulates respect for women (in contrast to the Western commodification of women as sex objects), Iranian women are advocating "legal equality, divorce reform, reproductive rights, equality in the workforce, and social recognition as political advocates, members of parliament, professionals, and producers of culture and the arts." These women are the avant-garde voices of a progressive, reformist Islamism. They are struggling to rearticulate political culture from within in an attempt to dissociate Islam from an oppressive patriarchy.[36]

"Terrorism will disappear," Buck-Morss concludes (perhaps too absolutely), "because nonviolent ways of communication and debate are possible" within and between cultures, not because democracy is imposed by a military invasion based on the simple mentality that "you are with us or against us." "By attempting to silence Islam as a political discourse, by reducing it to a religious practice," Buck-Morss observes, "Bush is in effect closing off public discussion of how the many varieties of Islamism are challenging and extending the discursive field of political resistance." At bottom, to treat criticism of either/or, friend/enemy, good/evil dichotomies as unpatriotic is to make democratic debate impossible and to retreat into a hardened and hopeless opposition of fundamentalisms.[37]

Similarly, the dichotomous language of good versus evil can be critiqued usefully for the way it has deterred dissent and debate over the character of terrorism and, by extension, reinforced the unexamined presumption that freedom and democracy are at issue. As Michael Mann notes, it became nearly impossible after 9/11 for Americans to raise questions about or "to distinguish between different types of terrorism" because "terrorism was evil, period." Yet, making a distinction between two types of terrorism is critical, Mann argues, to enhancing American security.

While all terrorists share the strategy of attacking civilian targets, the vast majority of terrorists are national terrorists who see themselves as attempting to liberate their land from "alien oppressive rule." Relatively few terrorists resort to attacking abroad those whom they perceive to be "allies of their local enemy." Accordingly, US efforts should be aimed at international terrorists rather than national liberation movements because, as Mann observes, international terrorists are the ones attacking Americans, because they are fewer in number and much weaker than national terrorists who can fight effectively as guerrilla forces on their own home territories, and because fighting national terrorists, which diverts and defuses American resources, works counterproductively to spawn additional international terrorists from the ranks of homeland defenders who become increasingly convinced that America's indiscriminant war on terror amounts to an attack on Muslims and the nation of Islam.

International terrorists, Mann insists, do not strike the US because they hate American culture, democracy, or wealth but instead because they hate an American foreign policy that targets Muslims. As long as Americans continue to conflate distinct forms of terrorism, they will remain linguistically imprisoned in the false dilemma of either abandoning their culture, democracy, and wealth or killing terrorists indiscriminately. Ironically, this amounts to a dichotomization of choices that sacrifices freedom and democracy immediately while producing future international terrorists at an even faster rate than before the US declared war on terror.

Following Mann's critique of the language of terrorism (even after observing that Muslims who hate US foreign policy logically could also despise the excesses of US culture), it is easier to see that American freedom is not necessarily at stake and that transplanting democracy is not a sure solution to terror or a reliable means for achieving peace. Instead, enhanced national security would seem to require a refocusing of US foreign policy to concentrate on defeating a relatively vulnerable al Qaeda (which "consists of Arab exiles too weak to take on their own states") and other international terrorist organizations actually targeting Americans. This does not imply that the US should continue to ignore underlying conditions of terrorism, only that it should recraft its current foreign policy so as not to further exacerbate the problem. Such a recrafting could also reinforce a more balanced and less paranoid perspective on terrorism that respects American civil liberties, including dissent, by "demonstrating that democracy can subject violence to the rule of law."[38]

Yet, as a "linguistic marker of American culture," Carol Winkler observes, terrorism functions in contemporary presidential rhetoric more and more like an ideograph strongly influencing how the nation defines and governs itself. It is a dangerous marker that "demarcates the unacceptable" in the embodiment of a barbaric and unholy evil, an ambiguous but palpable malevolence that must be destroyed for the nation to cleanse itself. Its associations with images of the enemy's stealth and speed, for example, with deadly consequences for innocent civilians and unsuspecting soldiers, have reinforced a regime of executive authority that erodes civil liberties and undercuts the separation of governing powers and that increasingly eschews diplomacy, all in the name of responding rapidly and forcefully to ubiquitous terrorist threats. As a term that emphasizes civilian victims, terrorism also deflects attention from economic targets and from the ruling elite's special interest in protecting the profit margins of global enterprises. Moreover, "presidents have highlighted terrorism attacks happening in the Middle East," Winkler notes, even though "the bulk of actual terrorist incidents involving the United States" since the 1970s "have happened outside of the Middle East" in Latin America, Europe, and Asia.[39]

Not only does this calculated use of terrorism as a politically efficacious term distort national identity and disguise untoward interests, it also stifles public deliberation of terrorist motives. Terrorist goals and purposes are reduced in presidential war propaganda to attacks on freedom, democracy, and other "foundational American values," Winkler points out, thus minimizing "questions about how earlier US actions might have contributed to such acts of violence." The obvious symbolism of striking at the twin towers of the World Trade Center in New York and at the Pentagon in Washington, DC— sites of empire and globalization that represent economic exploitation backed by the military might of the world's only superpower—is seemingly lost on Americans as a clear indication of the motivations and aims of terrorists who have been reduced by administration propaganda to demonic enemies of civilization. Stripped of any purpose and strapped with the sole burden of culpability for terror, America's enemies are thoroughly dehumanized and thus deserving of righteous retribution. Like world communism in the Cold War narrative that remains a working analogue for legitimizing an aggressive US foreign policy, international terrorism is a term that seeks to provide "a simple public explanation for the diverse range of violent actors around the globe." As such, it mischaracterizes and exacerbates threats issued by the likes of Osama bin Laden, which were made against any country occupying Middle Eastern holy lands. Such warnings are relegated to a single diabolical ambition to attack all democratic countries and to destroy freedom itself.[40]

Such a dehumanizing ideograph—a reified metaphor of absolute evil made to rule the national conscience in a phantasmagoric presidential republic—cannot go unchallenged without undermining democratic governance and perpetuating an ascendant war culture. Since 9/11, the Bush administration has instigated massive increases in the military budget, major reorganizations of the federal government, significant decreases in human services, huge transfers of wealth to the nation's economic elites, and serious curtailments of civil liberties "all in the name of a necessary response to a new terrorist threat."[41]

Holy terror—a terrorizing war on terror—is a failure of citizenship no less than a consequence of poor leadership, a rhetorical malfunction that prods the nation, in Terry Eagleton's phrase, to displace "its own deformities on to a vilified other" so that it might "rid itself magically of its defects" without recognizing in the scapegoat a "horrific double" and thus acknowledging America's own "collective disfigurement." The evil terrorist is the all too convenient and comprehensive scapegoat that "marks the place where this dehumanization is most purely distilled."[42] When terrorists are rendered as dehumanized scapegoats, as "inanimate bombs, psychologically damaged, diseased, and subhuman—in all cases portraying them as acting without forethought, provocation, or reason," in the words of Stephen Hartnett and Laura Stengrim, "it clouds our abilities to think about the historical, political, economic, and cultural causes of violence."[43]

Hartnett and Stengrim are particularly concerned with contesting the political discourse of a war on terrorism that is an instrument of globalization and empire—a discourse consisting of propagandizing language, images, and arguments that dragged Americans into "a needless war in Iraq over mythical weapons of mass destruction and equally mythical Iraq/al Qaeda connections." They offer their readers sustained examples of language critique aimed at promoting rhetorical integrity, bolstering the fading habits of democracy, and resisting the creeping practices of totalitarianism in America. Their way of resisting "the rhetoric of patriotic provincialism" and its "warmongering spells" and of advancing informed dissent through critical thinking case by case is to place the stories, visual images, metaphors, assumptions, and evidence of propagandists in tension with the counterclaims of critics who can be found among political activists, journalists, and scholars and with "the best available empirical evidence provided by experts."[44]

They are able to penetrate the Bush administration's war rhetoric, for example, to challenge its stark linguistic opposition between good and evil, which imagines an enemy that hates America for what it is rather than what it does. Drawing on multiple scholarly and empirical sources, Hartnett and Stengrim make the case that a war rhetoric of good versus evil, which degrades public deliberation while providing rhetorical cover for a foreign policy of imperial globalization and preemptive warfare, "inflames already rising anger toward the United States"—anger as measured, for example, in a July 2004 survey of public opinion in Morocco, Saudi Arabia, Jordan, Lebanon, and the United Arab Emirates, anger that is directed at the actual policies rather than the basic values of an intrusive international colossus, policies of brutal disregard for another culture, policies that humiliate and thus enrage the Arab world. The Bush administration's so-called "Coalition of the Willing" is shown empirically to be a "patchwork of reluctant and sometimes even unaware partners," indeed, a "dwindling coalition" and "rogue's gallery of authoritarian regimes" such as Albania, Azerbaijan, Colombia, Eritrea, Ethiopia, Georgia, Macedonia, Nicaragua, Turkey, and Uzbekistan, all of which are notorious for their use of torture and extrajudicial killings. Dissent from stupefying imperial "chants of freedom and democracy" is, in Hartnett and Stengrim's terms, a rhetorical struggle "to control the meaning of language itself."[45]

Archibald MacLeish, himself a minister of government propaganda during World War II, knew that dissent and democracy rely on the capacity of citizens to exercise critical thought. The democratic dissenter, in his view, is nothing less than "every human being at those moments of his life when he resigns momentarily from the herd and thinks for himself."[46] These moments of linguistic resistance by the citizenry to presidential war propaganda can be perilous, as Lewis Lapham notes, because "unlicensed forms of speech come to be confused with treason and registered as crimes."[47] They would be recorded as thought crimes in George Orwell's undemocratic *1984*.

Language is vital to contesting and transforming a war culture. Many of the same words of American supremacy Lapham remembers hearing at the end of World War II, that is, at the beginning of the so-called American Century, were deployed in the Bush administration's rhetorical war on terrorism.

These words spin a narrative of American innocence, entitlement, and sancti-
fication that threatens to ruin the nation's democratic enterprise, no matter
how good its intentions. It is a narrative that confuses power and wealth with
liberty and justice, and it sacrifices the "virtues of citizenship" in an "increasingly dangerous world" by questing incessantly after profit. Has the republic
become an empire unmindful of its dehumanizing demeanor? Can the
momentum of decline be slowed, stopped, and even reversed? The more the
world's "hostages to fortune" can be recognized as fully human, Lapham
insists, "the less seductive the voices prophesying war" become.

Dissent, then, is a matter of unmasking an imperial discourse of American
innocence and its demonizing caricatures of the enemy. We must always
remain suspicious of rhetorical practices that invoke the sign of evil.

FOSTERING A HUMANIZING LANGUAGE
OF CITIZENSHIP

Is there an alternative incantation that beckons us not to evil but instead to
abide by our better inclinations? Is it possible, as Danielle Allen argues, to
practice democratic citizenship in a manner that bridges positions of mutual
disdain and repairs distrustful talk between strangers who operate from different perspectives and experiences and with competing interests and aspirations? Political friendship of this kind is not easily won, she acknowledges,
"nor is democracy," even within a given polity, but the question is worth careful consideration as an alternative to a politics of evil, distrust, hate, and civil
war.[48] Similarly, developing habits of citizenship to bridge trouble *between*
polities, not just within a given polity or nation, entails the cultivation of
humanizing talk among strangers who are foreign to one another, that is,
among adversaries who may or already have become enemies to one another.
Besides contesting the alienating language of a war culture, then, dissent promotes a peacebuilding culture by developing the language of democratic citizenship into a humanizing idiom.

Citizenship, as an act of peacebuilding dissent, is a quintessential expression
of what little remains of democratic politics in an undemocratic age—an era of
superpower imperialism, globalizing capitalism, and open-ended warfare on
terrorism, "a general climate of fear and suspicion," a state of "inverted totalitarianism" with the false pretense of freedom that is a caricature of democracy. Democracy, argues Sheldon Wolin, has been relegated to the status of a
fugitive. With an alienated citizenry depoliticized, society politically demobilized, and the individual thoroughly privatized, institutionalized propaganda
in the mainstream media of a "corporatist" superpower sans dissident voices

sustains a decidedly elitist agenda. Unlike the classic fascist totalitarian regime in which organized capitalism is subordinated to state control, the inverted totalitarianism of the superpower corporatist state elevates corporate power so that it might dictate state policy to and through the political establishment.[49]

This same inverted totalitarian state demobilized the citizenry after 9/11, exhorting Americans to consume rather than to act politically, encouraging them to inform on their neighbors and co-workers, and conditioning them to cower under a regimen of color-coded threat levels, violations of civil liberties, mistreatment (including torture) of captured and suspected enemies, brutal downsizing, outsourcing, and downgrading of jobs with diminishing benefits, and systematic reductions in social services. In this manufactured climate of fear and suspicion, Wolin observes, "a nervous subject has displaced the citizen." Furthermore, one of the two major political parties has become "fervently doctrinal, zealous, ruthless, opportunistically populist, pro-corporate, and successful in winning a popular majority, sometimes by dubious methods" while the other has conceded to the ideological strictures of these new polarizing politics and abandoned the role of an opposition party that offers the electorate "a genuine alternative."[50]

This "evisceration of democracy," Wolin argues, renders the people unfit for self-governance. They have devolved into a collection of self-interested, fearful, and distracted individuals indifferent to egalitarian politics and the common good. America's transition to superpower imperialism makes even its shallow claim to democracy hypocritical. Governance has become hierarchical, elitist, and bureaucratized, "in short, anti-democratic."[51]

Under such dismal conditions but from a less negative or hopeless and yet pragmatic perspective, the democratic function of citizenship is not to govern but instead to dissent. Fugitive democracy is not collective self-rule but rather an array of localized activities and ongoing, episodic, circumstantial practices with a cumulative potential for transforming the war culture over time. In this more limited but very important sense, the dissenting demos under conditions of empire and executive rule signifies a recalcitrant citizenry that opposes structures of domination, exploitation, and state violence and is thus the carrier and caretaker of "everyday cultural traditions."[52] Such is a democratic citizenry that would practice dissent as a humanizing expression of political friendship toward strangers and foreigners who otherwise are portrayed by ruling elites as diabolical enemies.

Political friendship must be rescued, Allen contends, if democracy is to be revitalized or at least not entirely lost to a cynical age of political alienation. Democratic citizenship recovered and regenerated is an egalitarian politics of friendship based on respect.[53] "The cultivation of a cultural orientation" of political friendship based on respect and equity involves "first, recovery of the idea that self-interest comes in a variety of forms; second, recognition that preserving the political bond is in every citizen's interest; and third, an understanding that only equitable forms of self-interest can sustain the political bond, or any form of social bond."[54] Transforming unrestrained self-interest into equitable self-interest, Allen argues, is more a matter of habit than affect, of political practices than intimacy, of technique than (or even instead of) feelings of love and goodwill, of acting like political friends beyond (or even in the absence of) any "sentiment of fellow-feeling." Practicing techniques of political friendship is the way "to transform our daily habits and so our political culture."[55]

Humanizing techniques of political friendship are necessarily rhetorical, and thus they are instruments of democratic citizenship well suited to resisting the demonic phantasms of the imperial republic. To persuade rather than coerce, Aristotle taught and Allen extrapolates, we must address ourselves to one another more like friends and equals who come from diverse, even alien backgrounds. We must acquire the habit of talking to strangers and antagonists in an idiom like that of friendship if we hope to dispel distrust and overcome hostility, to develop a sufficient degree of goodwill, and to prove that we are not sheer enemies.[56]

The rhetorical idiom of friendship enables us to talk ourselves down from anger, for instance, by showing that no slight was intended, none occurred, or at least that it was involuntary, not as egregious or harmful as it appeared, and/or that the perpetrator of the slight is honorable and apologetic. As Aristotle explains, anger can be defined as a response to the perception (that is, to a construal) of being slighted conspicuously without justification, whether the slight is understood as an expression of contempt, spite, or insolence. We are particularly prone to anger when we feel weak, vulnerable, deprived, and the like, and we become angry at those whom we believe are mocking or otherwise injuring us, especially if we consider them to be our inferiors.[57] Similarly, fear—which Aristotle defines as an image of impending harm or destruction by a powerful force or terrible adversary—can be reduced by giving presence to confidence-building safeguards and by making what appears terrible and immediately threatening appear more remote.[58]

Proving goodwill and trustworthiness—two additional elements of a humanizing language of citizenship understood as an expression of political friendship—is also a rhetorical practice that citizens who dissent from war can develop into peacebuilding habits of the political culture. It is a practice of speaking of points of identification between adversaries, such as similar pleasures and pains, overlapping aspirations and frustrations, shared histories, adversities experienced in common, convergences of values, analogous habits of living and traits of character, and other points of intersection. Identification is also expressed as respect for another, praise for their good qualities, including those qualities they may be less confident of possessing, and admiration for their achievements. By contrast, feeling shamed and dishonored are cause for alienation and motivation for redemption by vicarious sacrifice. Acts of kindness and generosity to another in need, undertaken without ulterior purpose or for reasons of self-interest, with no expectation of repayment, and not even at the request of the beneficiary, are gestures of identification, respect, and political friendship. Pity is yet another potential point of identification when we speak of some undeserving harm that has befallen an adversary and that could befall us as well. In Aristotle's words, "What we fear for ourselves excites our pity when it happens to others."[59]

Allen draws on Aristotle's insight to underscore that expressions of political friendship are not the same as achieving intimacy with one's adversary. They are instead ways of speaking to and about strangers, protagonists, adversaries, and enemies more like they are friends than foes so that relations can be established, sustained, and even returned to the realm of the political instead of degenerating into violence. To achieve a relationship of political friendship requires addressing others as protagonists, as humanized adversaries, rather than as demons. It requires speaking to and about them in a manner that habitually takes into account their perspective, holding one's narratives of reality accountable to an adversary's judgment, not just privileging one's own point of view.[60]

This humanizing language of citizenship is no short-term panacea for overcoming the alienation that motivates war. It is instead a way of being with and toward strangers, a habit culturally ingrained over time, a matter of regular and reliable practice, a living history of repeated transactions to establish a positive baseline or minimal presumption of trust and to develop a more durable predisposition toward peacebuilding. Eventually, such habits of character establish an attitude and ethos of reconciliation.

When clouds of hostility loom, a vital question to ask is how citizens might dissent from war by speaking of their so-called evil enemy in friendlier, less hateful and fearful ways. For a habit of this kind to be formed, we must begin somewhere, sometime, at a point of impending crisis, to speak more heedfully of foreign adversaries. What can be said in a particular circumstance (1) to mitigate an allegation of willful slight or actual harm, (2) to defuse a contention of vulnerability and focus attention on existing or potential safeguards, (3) to articulate points of identification with an allegedly unworthy foe, and (4) to express goodwill by taking an alien point of view into consideration? How, for instance, might these general considerations of cultivating political friendship have applied to the war on terrorism and the battle for democracy in the particular case of Islamic Iran at the specific moment the Bush administration located it rhetorically on an axis of evil?

As distinguished historian Ervand Abrahamian at the City University of New York pointed out in 2004, "The United States is on a collision course with Iran. The main casualty could well be the democratic movement in Iran." Since the Islamic revolution of 1979, and especially after President Bush placed Iran along with Iraq and North Korea on his "axis of evil" in 2002, Iran has been perceived in the US as "an intractable foe threatening to export revolution throughout the Middle East." This image of Islamic Iran obscured an internal tension between Iranian reformers striving "to extend the republic's democratic features" and conservatives "determined to preserve its theocratic features." Instead of facilitating reform, the administration's rhetoric of evil created a perception of imminent danger within Iraq that bolstered conservatives and jeopardized the progress made by reformers prior to 2002.[61] What are the lines of argument Abrahamian advanced to dissent from the Bush administration's provocation and to speak of Iranians more heedfully, that is, to assuage accusations of Iranian slights and contentions of US vulnerability and to articulate points of identification and opportunities for goodwill?

There was no slight, no harm done to America, actual or imminent, by Iran. The "axis of evil" accusation of 2002, in Abrahamian's words, "came as a bolt out of the blue sky," without provocation. In fact, Iraq's relations with Europe and even the US had been on the incline over the last five years. The President of Iran, Muhammad Khatemi, elected in 1997, had praised American civilization and expressed a desire for dialogue. He had even suggested that the notorious sacking of the US embassy and holding scores of US citizens hostage for 444 days at the time of the 1979 Iranian revolution was excessive and tragic. The Clinton administration had reciprocated by no longer referring to Iran as a rogue or pariah state and by finally admitting the US had orchestrated the unfortunate coup that overthrew the popular Iranian Prime Minister Mohammad Mossadeq in 1953. After the terrorist attacks of September 11, Iran had assisted the US in Afghanistan against the Taliban and helped Hamid Karzai become Afghanistan's president, consistent with US wishes. Iran's involvement in international terrorism following the revolution of 1979 had "diminished in the late 1980s and ended entirely after President Khatami's election in 1997." Even Iran's human rights record substantially improved, beginning in 1989 and especially after Khatami's election to the presidency, and its hard stand on the Israeli-Palestinian impasse softened "to accept any agreement palatable to the Palestinians—even the two-state solution with its implicit recognition of Israel."[62]

There were safeguards, which could be reinforced rather than undermined, to curtail Iran's resort to nuclear weapons. Contrary to the Bush administration's assertion that Iran is developing nuclear weapons to assist international terrorists, Abrahamian notes that any nation's nuclear intentions are likely to be "shrouded in mystery." Moreover, one cannot distinguish "until late in the day" between strictly civilian nuclear programs and those that ultimately become militarized. Whereas US hostility and threatening gestures provided Iran with an incentive to militarize its nuclear program, the European Union preferred diplomacy, inspections, and trade incentives to keep Iran's nuclear program on the civilian track. Iran already lived in a tough neighborhood, its rivals such as Pakistan and Israel armed with nuclear weapons. Surrounding Iran with American military bases in neighboring countries while calling for a regime change undermined rather than strengthened nuclear constraints internal to Iranian politics. Abrahamian reports that members of the US State Department and CIA, as opposed to the neo-conservatives dominating the Defense Department, recognized that "Iran is not an imminent danger to the United States." Its missiles could not reach the US; it would take years to develop a nuclear bomb; inspections could delay the development of a bomb even longer; the European Union and the United Nations could help the US to influence Iran's intentions positively through means other than confrontation; and the Iranian Islamic regime was not readily subject to collapse from negative US pressure.[63]

Americans might readily identify with and should respect the developing democratic inclinations of Iranian politics. As Abrahamian explains, the constitution of the Islamic Republic of Iran, written under Ayatollah Khomeini's supervision and amended after his death, "tried to synthesize theocracy with democracy...clerical authority with popular sovereignty." Possibilities for grassroots democracy were expressed, for instance, in the election of provincial, city, district, and village councils that would oversee regional officials, such as governors, mayors, and village headmen, and would supervise educational, social, and cultural programs at the local level. The constitution pledged to protect its citizens' rights of liberty, property, and security, freedom of speech and worship, and freedom to organize into trade unions, professional organizations, and political parties. It guaranteed due process of law and proscribed the use of torture and other forms of coercion, but the Ayatollah's constitution also provided for the work of the elected president and ministers to be overseen by religious authorities. The president, elected to a four-year term and limited to two terms in office, would head the executive branch with a substantial grant of authority, and the majles, also elected to four-year terms, would constitute a 290-seat national parliament, but the country's ultimate authority rested constitutionally in the Leader, that is, a cleric of the highest rank who would insure that governance of the state accorded with the shariah—the body of Islamic law.[64]

With the Iraqi war's termination in 1988 and Khomeini's death in 1989, Iran's political environment began to gravitate toward a somewhat more secularized, less theocratic form of governance. The language of revolution, martyrdom, crusade, and so forth, which had set the tenor of the Islamic Republic in the 1980s, gave way increasingly in the 1990s to a new emphasis on the democratic language of pluralism, freedom, equality, modernity, civil society, human rights, dialogue, and citizenship. This shift toward democratic aspirations was as significant a cultural change, Abrahamian argues, as the revolution of 1979, which had produced the Islamic Republic. Candidates for political office campaigning on themes such as the rule of law and women's rights received overwhelming public support at the polls. Democratic reformers were ascending as religious conservatives began to lose their firm grip on the nation. By 2002, reformers controlled the legislative and executive offices of the country, while conservatives retained control of the judiciary and influence over the military and intelligence establishments. Conservatives still had power to veto reform bills and to control public media, but they were placed on the defensive. As progressive forces gained momentum, Iran was transformed in the 1990s from "one of the world's most inhospitable places for foreign investors" to being rated in 2002 as "safe" for investment by Europeans and Japanese, even receiving "high marks" in economic growth and fiscal reforms that same year from the International Monetary Fund. Significant improvements in education, health care, and the country's overall infrastructure had also been registered by the turn of the century. The momentum of progressive change was broken, though, after Bush's "axis of evil" speech, which rendered democratic reforms moot and national security and homeland defense preeminent given the threat of a preventative US strike.[65]

The US could have demonstrated goodwill and understanding by letting Iran's political culture evolve toward democracy without outside interference. Abrahamian observes that Iran "has struggled for a hundred years to gain full independence from colonial powers." It perceived the US as just such a power. That perception was reinforced by Bush administration neo-conservatives professing their desire to undo the 1979 Iranian revolution, their antipathy to the very inception of the Islamic Republic of Iran, and their determination to effect no accommodation with the Iranian government but instead to engineer the demise of an Islamic Republic that they insisted was "anathema" to US interests.[66]

Rather than attempt to overthrow the government of Iran or even to influence it directly, the US might have extended a peacebuilding gesture of standing down and letting the tensions between theocracy and democracy internal to Iran work themselves out gradually through peaceful reform rather than "through drastic externally driven forces." Labeling Islamic Iran evil and avowing support for its democratic reformers was counterproductive in the extreme and most likely reinforced reactionary forces who would build a nuclear bomb. Working diplomatically through third parties, such as the United Nations, the European Union, Japan, and Russia, to secure Iran's consent to nuclear inspections was a better way to slow its nuclear weapons program and to facilitate change indirectly by easing the pressure on its democratic reformers. A gesture of standing down out of regard for the point of view of progressive voices within Iran and inviting Iranians to judge the sincerity of a peacebuilding initiative was a small sacrifice to make with little risk to the United States. Moreover, the magnitude of this modest hands-off gesture would have been considerably amplified in an otherwise corrosive context of neo-conservative hostility toward the Islamic Republic of Iran.[67]

Here, then, we have an example, an indication of practical options, a suggestion of reasonable alternatives for managing a tense relationship more constructively, not a full account or a comprehensive history with a definitive outcome. It is an example that illustrates a pragmatic way of speaking of an adversary as a protagonist, the possibility and plausibility of speaking in an idiom that is more like (but not identical to) befriending a stranger or foreigner and less like alienating a terrifying antagonist. It points to an idiom that is more respectful or heedful of another protagonist's humanity, an idiom that dissents from the vilifying language of war by cultivating a discourse of political relations—a humanizing idiom of democratic citizenship extended to foreign affairs.

TRANSCENDING THE VIEWPOINT OF WAR

Peacebuilding acts of citizenship extend to creative and contemplative uses of language and symbols in order to achieve a level of mindfulness that sees beyond rhetorical blinders and "cultural predispositions to warism." For a peace movement to amount to more than just an antiwar protest it needs, as Cady points out, a *positive* vision or conception of peace. Such a vision must be *created* in order to *make* a world in which people might habitually live more peacefully. This is a challenge that calls for citizens to stretch their collective powers of imagination enough to envision a unity of humanity sufficiently strong to compensate for persistent tensions, conflicting loyalties, and chronic divisiveness.[68]

Cady characterizes positive peace in its "highest ideal" as "the widening of one's moral vision, and with it the widening of one's sense of community, beyond the immediate and familiar." In the wider vision of peacebuilders, people are inclined "to see every human as a kindred being, [and] to see nature itself as a home to live in, not as conditions to conquer." With this broader vision, people look to pursue self-interest "within a consciousness of the whole."

A raised consciousness fosters a "sense of global community" and of "inter-relatedness among peoples, institutions, religions, races, and nations," and it resists a "preoccupation with and polarization of differences." It is a vision of an ideal of "tolerance and respect where differences are seen as enhancing, broadening, and deepening the possibilities for human experience rather than as threats that must be destroyed or dominated."[69] Such is the highest ideal of positive peace, which requires peacebuilding citizens to envision a strong sense of their common humanity within and across political barriers.

Seeing above and beyond the conventional wisdom and narrow perspective of ruling authorities is the particular purview of "artists in times of war," according to Howard Zinn. The artist in these circumstances is "a citizen and a human being" who creates works to "transcend" the immediate "madness" of a world of terrorism and war. Toward this end of showing us "what the world should be like," the artist "thinks, acts, performs music, and writes outside the framework that society has created." The artist's role, Zinn stresses, is to "transcend conventional wisdom, to transcend the orthodoxy, to go beyond and escape what is handed down by the government or what is said in the media," that is, to "think outside the boundaries of permissible thought and dare to say things that no one else will say." Transcending and criticizing government's narrow perspective as an act of dissent in a time of war is "the highest act of patriotism."[70]

Thinking outside the boundaries of conventional wisdom to recover a common humanity among protagonists involves not only resistance to the dehumanizing images of war propaganda and cultivation of a humanizing language of political friendship but also, as Zinn notes, looking at our own country "honestly and clearly" enough "to bring ourselves down a peg, to the level of other nations in the world." Our arrogance—thinking of America as the strongest world power, and therefore the best, freest, and most democratic country, and thus the most deserving nation in the world that others attack out of hateful envy and sheer spite—prompts us to demonize adversaries, blinds us to our own culpability and responsibilities, and keeps us from asking the right questions about terrorism, that is, from thinking "carefully about what we have to do to end terrorism.... Because war is terrorism."[71]

Arrogance inhibits clarity and honesty of vision and therefore impedes self-assessment. To transcend arrogance and bring ourselves down a peg is the work of artists, for "artists can be sly. They can point to things that take you outside traditional thinking because you can get away with it in fiction." Thus, Zinn concludes, "art moves away from reality and invents something that may be ultimately more accurate about the world than what a photograph can depict." Writers can "use fiction to say things that could not easily be said in nonfiction."[72] Once revealed, envisioned, invented, and expressed artistically and thus made available to us for raising our collective conscience, these transcending images of unconventional wisdom can become vehicles of a new or revised perspective, positioning us better to grasp the common humanity of rivals.

Joseph Heller, one of those perspective-altering writers of fiction about real war, has allowed readers to see combat anew through the eyes of his somewhat autobiographical and allegedly crazy *Catch-22* bombardier Yossarian, who had seen all he wanted of the "sanity" of armed hostilities through a bombsite trained on undefended cities targeted for destruction and civilian communities marked for obliteration.[73] Kurt Vonnegut's *Slaughterhouse-Five*, another fictional narrative of war's insane logic based on the storyteller's direct experience but viewed from the ground instead of through a bombsite, revealed "the horror of Dresden" where as many as 100,000 civilians died from American and British firebombing.[74] Other novels that can be read as a genre transcending modern war's sanctioned inhumanity include Erich Maria Remarque's classic *All Quiet on the Western Front*, John dos Passos' *Three Soldiers*, and more recently Pat Barker's *Regeneration*, Nick Arvin's *Articles of War* or even Charles Frazier's best-seller, *Cold Mountain*. Some readers may find John Updike's flawed but popular novel, *Terrorist*, a vehicle for becoming more mindful of America's foibles as seen through the youthful, albeit wooden eyes of an estranged American Muslim.[75] Moreover, films such as *Dr. Strangelove, Apocalypse Now, Platoon, Gallipoli, Stalingrad*, and *Jarhead* critique the romance and sanity of war.

Seeing the insanity of warfare and the corrosive reflection of armed hostility on the American character gains us some purchase on the problem at hand but fails to transcend warism's cultural presumption enough to grasp Cady's moral vision of a positive peace. Like Goya's great pictorial essay on the disaster of war, such lurid and catastrophic imagery leaves us mired in despair with no epiphanic or transcendent notion of a plausible or likely alternative.[76] It proffers no standpoint above the fray, provides no unobstructed line of sight or viewpoint higher than the plane surface of seemingly endless killing fields, affords no vantage point beyond the ironic negation of war from which to glimpse an affirmation of peace.

A positive *for-peace* perspective foresees and promotes ways to transform the culture of war, which is to create a new paradigm of respect for humanity. It would make peacebuilding the daily work of democratic citizenship. This is the paradigm of the "peace on earth movement," which represents peacemaking as a state of mind, a way of life, an ongoing process, an integrating focus and enduring priority of everyday living with others, a realization of the interconnectedness of life and a transformation of attitudes and culture through democratic practices of talking and listening to others in search of common ground and with respect for differences of perspective. This "realization for peace" by the People for Peace Project achieves its new paradigm, its vision of an evolving consciousness for a better world and an active process of peacemaking, by taking for granted that such a movement already exists and has been reawakened by the current exigency of terrorism. It is a visualization meant to inspire and encourage an existing dream so that peace might become a reality. There are no membership fees to join a movement that is presumed already to exist, no ideologies to which members must subscribe, and no particular organizations or formal membership requirements. It is the ongoing community of "every person who has ever envisioned a better world," a movement comprised "of caring, compassionate people of the past, the present and the future." No matter one's age, occupation, place of residence, ethnicity, gender, or religion, anyone with a wish for peace and a concern for the children and for the future of the world is automatically "a part of the Peace on Earth Movement."[77]

This war-transcending perspective is originated and legitimated in the very recognition of an enduring desire shared by humankind across time and space, a common realization of the interconnectedness of humanity and life, and by transforming peace into an activity, a way of thinking and acting in everyday life that can count for something, that is, that can become ingrained in culture and embedded in "our collective consciousness" like a "natural reflex." The for-peace perspective is conceived as a movement that simply will grow to fruition through each person's regular efforts at peacemaking in his or her daily life and own way. These ways of peacebuilding are various, multitudinous, and cumulative. "When each of us takes every moment of our lives as an opportunity to build bonds of friendship, community, and peace, there will be peace on earth." Moreover, it is a way for patriots of peace to enact the democratic values of "fairness, justice, and equality" and to hold governments accountable to those values. It is a way to contribute to and coordinate with other peacebuilding initiatives consistent with one's own inclinations and opportunities. It is the way of an inclusive but loose and informal network of ordinary citizens working individually and together to transcend the viewpoint of war and thereby "to create a culture of peace" over time.[78]

This evolving consciousness of peace in the community of humanity can be achieved by each peacebuilding citizen striving to find "inner peace—a sense of calmness, security, joy and love" that can come from prayer, meditation, relaxation, and "a life of balance." It can involve developing positive peacebuilding habits through such activities as keeping a peace journal and initiating or joining small or large peace communities within a family, among friends and neighbors, at one's place of worship or other places where people encounter and befriend one another. It can extend to writing letters to the editors of local newspapers and to elected officials as well as marching, picketing, protesting, and lobbying for peace, supporting peace resolutions and proclamations, participating in teach-ins and sit-ins, wearing peace symbols, contributing to and/or compiling a body of literature, art, and music that celebrates peace, teaching a peace curriculum, linking into the internet for additional peacebuilding resources and opportunities, and more.[79]

Pro-peace activities of mindfulness are especially productive of peace culture in the degree to which they sustain a focus on humanizing images and themes. However, transcending the perspective of war through humanizing imagery requires of citizens a mindfulness of symbolism, a devotion to contemplating expressions of the spirit common to humankind, which is the ultimate source of reconciliation. Achieving a sense of communion with humanity through contemplation is crucial to securing a focus on the basic premise of peacemaking, especially in times of peril and throughout the ceaseless swirl of threatening news reports. It requires a practice of mindfulness that helps to acquire a more positive and reasonable viewpoint, "a certain mental attitude and awareness about peace," as the Dalai Lama says, that is important for "the general public to achieve" as a check on violent people who become leaders even in "a democratic society."[80]

Thomas Merton observes, too, that the noise and distractions of daily life—the "ceaseless motion" and the "crude hunger for results, for visible and tangible success"—fragments society and self and thus disconnects humanity. To remain human, it is necessary "to live in communion" and within community and thus to prepare for a "genuine dialogue with others" through a contemplative discipline that teaches us to share some of the joys, sufferings, ideas, needs, and desires of others, even if these others are foreign to us, of a different class, profession, race, culture, or nation, even if they are of groups "that are regarded as hostile." Rather than a withdrawal from "the miseries of life," contemplation is a continuous struggle for a "reunion" of divided humanity sufficient to the ends of peacebuilding.[81]

Hell, Merton observes, is the condition in which the only thing we hold in common with others is alienation from and hatred for one another, which has been "the social and political history of modern man." We quickly assume that our enemy is a "savage," he continues, even as our enemy thinks we are the savage to be feared and hated. Contemplation is a necessary corrective, a slowing of the socially ingrained reflex, a way to seek a healthy degree of humility and a positive regard for human equality. It is a quest for dialogue amidst difference and diversity. Through contemplation we mortals attempt to transcend "the devil's theology," that is to overcome a hateful mindset that exaggerates all distinctions between people who think they are in the right and those they deem to be in the wrong. Peace wanes when the devil's theology prevails because when "the important thing is to be absolutely right and to prove that everybody else is absolutely wrong," we have to "punish and eliminate those who are wrong" in order to prove our own "rightness."[82]

As Scott Hunt attests, after traveling the world to interview leading dissenters from war, the great contemporary peacemakers, such as Aung San Suu Kyi, the Dalai Lama, Thich Quang Do and others, share the belief that peacebuilding is "the quest to awaken the compassionate spirit in each of us," the "practice of tolerance and forbearance."[83] When they contemplate peace, they seek a vision with which to establish the "right motivation within" that "cannot be defeated by external circumstances." Meditation, as Suu Kyi told Hunt, "is a form of cultivating inner strength...and inner strength means inner peace." It musters the patience needed for persevering. Peace itself the Dalai Lama believes to be "an expression of compassion, a sense of caring" developed in an imperfect society through "the level of higher consciousness" that can be achieved in meditation.[84]

Contemplation, as an undertaking to experience the higher, humanizing consciousness of reconciliation, is mediated by language and symbols. Transcending war culture through art and other means of reflection—seeking to achieve greater insight and to sustain increased awareness over mind-numbing rituals of victimization—are acts of peacebuilding citizenship that involve mindfulness of symbolism. Art, alone and without a receptive audience, cannot depict, portray, or otherwise represent an actual experience of humanizing consciousness in which one feels a palpable connection that overcomes the estrangement of adversaries. It is instead a suggestive vehicle, not unlike a sacrament, that can stimulate interpretation and mediate an apprehension or raised sensibility of identification; it is a channel through which one strives to encounter and to grasp the spirit of shared humanity, with continuing respect for cultural diversity. Such an encounter with the common spirit of humanity, when it occurs, is a profound experience of transcendence that exists through but also beyond language; it is an experience that cannot be communicated exactly, easily, immediately, clearly, efficiently, mechanically, or unambiguously.

Art, as a medium of transcendence, cannot be reduced to a literal expression; it is instead necessarily symbolic and, as such, requires active interpretation to fulfill its promise. To literalize art is to destroy its credibility as an expression of insight or vision. Attentiveness to the suggestive symbolism of humanizing art is, therefore, a vital act of citizenship that can evoke a transforming awareness and renewed motivation to resist the otherwise mesmerizing logic of a relentless call to arms.

By way of example of the suggestive quality of art, muralist Juana Alicia, expressing her sense of art's key role in stimulating a peacemaking conscience, writes of working for peace "with pigment" and "images from dreams" while hearing the voices of ancestors and feeling the "private struggles of the heart." Through the "sensual glide of the paint" from her brush to the wall, she "bears witness to the conflicts we are living through." Like the soulful music of blues and jazz, her visual art presents an empathizing narrative of the pain and sacrifice of oppressed peoples. Her murals—which appear in public places such as the San Francisco International Airport, the Destiny Arts Center in Oakland, California, and the World College West's Commons Building in Petaluma, California—portray "little-seen histories of women and of people of color that run counter to the mainstream images and stereotypes." Producing such art, she feels, evokes a "sureness of purpose." Her art is a "calling" that serves as an "act of peacemaking," a "striving" that promotes a "dialogue between members of diverse communities," a "hope" that people will be energized "to know each other and to act for peace."[85]

Alicia even collaborates with other muralists so that she might "think and see from other minds and eyes" and stretch her "emotional capacities and communication skills."[86] Thus, her public murals, including "Bridge of Peace" and "Ceasefire," illustrate a visual language of change, what Leticia Hernandez calls "a medium for communicating a critical perspective, a revised interpretation" of what the artist sees. Alicia paints communal art that "belongs to everyone," art that invites the citizenry to become actively engaged in contemplating its significance as an expression of human dignity and interconnectedness.[87]

Similarly, Judith Francisca Baca's mural art is intended to foster civic dialogue and to promote social change. She seeks as a citizen artist to raise consciousness of a collective identity through a visual language and participatory process that strives to overcome a history that marginalizes minorities. Her murals are visual narratives that bridge ethnic differences to portray racial equality. Her half-mile long "Great Wall of Los Angeles," for example, was produced collectively over five summers by approximately 700 people, divided into working teams, with diverse ethnic, cultural, economic, and educational backgrounds, including gang youth, scholars, artists, and other community members. Their collaboration produced a running narrative of civil rights activists, Japanese immigrants, Chicanos, and other ethnic people making California and national history.[88]

Baca's "World Wall: A Vision of the Future without Fear," which was produced in cooperation with 45 international artists, is a portable display of 10' x 30' mural panels. The World Wall's various panels visually express themes of war, peace, cooperation, interdependence, and transformation. The display imagines peace as an active concept. "Triumph of the Hearts," for instance, is a panel that symbolizes the spiritual beginning of a movement toward peace by individuals from various races choosing to act together with a common faith in the promise of nonviolence. The vessel-shaped pupils of four tearful and hopeful female faces are symbolic of the heart of peace; a young black male figure, who casts the shadow of Mahatma Gandhi, moves with his candlelight of hope in hand toward the dark winds of war. The panel titled "Nonviolent Resistance" depicts men and women with arms interlinked pushing back against the industrial and mechanized instruments of deadly warfare to bury them under a green carpet of earth. The "Balance" panel visualizes in vivid acrylic colors an intertwining of moon and sun, sky and earth, blue water and green gardens, mountains and valley, and male and female to suggest the ideal of life's healthy balance. "Triumph of the Hands" portrays a "material transformation that must accompany the spiritual transformation" and triumph of the heart. The collective power of hands is shown to be sufficient to break the mechanical grip that unfettered capitalism has on the soul of humanity. Other panels express further themes, such as "New World Systems," and national perspectives, including Finnish, Russian, Mexican, and Israeli panels, with the expectation of future additions.[89]

Together, the bold panels of Baca's colorful World Wall mural give viewers an opportunity to ponder suggestive symbols of a positive peace beyond the dark horizon of war, but citizens dissenting from war, in the midst of alienating war propaganda and under the press of institutionalized violence, must choose to ponder the symbolism of art such as this if they are to grasp and remain sufficiently mindful of the spirit of humanity. One must linger and concentrate on artistic vehicles of transcendence enough to be moved above the madding fray. Whereas the pervasive propaganda of war culture would blunt thought and reduce people to unthinking, materialistic automatons of frenzied consumption, the art of transcendence must stimulate a thoughtful, reflective response—a mindfulness of symbolism—in order to achieve its liberating purpose.

Knowing and affirming the higher spirit of shared humanity is not, however, the same as sanctioning the homogenizing image of a melting pot. It is not a reductive principle of uniformity or idyllic model of oneness that effaces the separate identities of friends and enemies, treats difference as deviance, and molds diversity to a tyrannizing ideal such as the standard of whiteness. Rather than being repelled and threatened by human differences, a peacebuilding citizenry savors variation and is attracted to diversity. Moreover, a peacebuilding attitude is a bridgebuilding outlook where competing interests and deep divisions already exist. It recognizes that human relations are agonistic to the core and understands that finding points of identification and commonality compensates for and moderates, rather than removes or neutralizes, abiding divisions and discordant purposes.

The drama of human relations is always intense, one way or another. Whether organizing for violence or building bridges of reconciliation, whether glorifying war or imagining peace, the characters in the narrative are dramatically aligned with and against one another in some degree of tension. They are never unaligned, equivalent, or fully reconciled. In a transcendent state of mindfulness, these tensions of identification and division are balanced in some degree, but they are never fully resolved. Differences are cultivated rather than suppressed and points of commonality are established to compensate for chronic conditions of discord.

In an ongoing process of dissenting from the presumption and imminence of war, a peacebuilder's grueling struggle to stay the course and to realize the promise of cultural transformation requires patience and perseverance. Fortunately, the sorely tested morale of a peacemaker working under discouraging conditions can be nurtured by a contemplative discipline that brings inner peace. To draw from the Buddhist perspective of Thich Nhat Hanh, inner peace is a matter of connecting oneself to the larger web or infinite "chain of interbeing" by meditation, which involves "focused breathing, mindful walking, and careful attention to...natural objects." This meditation focuses the mind on meeting the demands of the moment and engaging fully in the task or activity at hand rather than looking anxiously ahead toward its completion. The mindfulness of taking "small, steady steps" yields a sense of satisfaction that can protect war dissenters from burnout, demoralization, and cynicism by keeping them alert and attentive to the present moment, despite inevitable setbacks.[90]

Just as Thây Nhat Hahn (Thây being the form of address for a Vietnamese monk who is a "teacher") would have peace workers slow their pace to become more mindful of the world they inhabit and receptive of the world that is within them, the impact of his teaching on willing learners increases through unhurried absorption. Over time, one learns to become grounded in the moment and is made increasingly conscious of what Nhat Hahn calls "being peace." Peaceful rites of mindfulness constitute an integrative practice, "not a discursive reflection" or a "philosophy" that separates the subject from the object of knowledge.[91] To integrate subject with object, Thây offers a short poem for recitation "from time to time, while breathing and smiling":

> Breathing in, I calm my body.
> Breathing out, I smile.
> Dwelling in the present moment
> I know this is a wonderful moment.[92]

"Mindfulness," Nhat Hahn writes, "makes it possible to live fully each minute of life." Without it, "no matter how urgent" their work, peace builders will quickly lose themselves and become useless "in a life full of worry and action."[93] Worrying, as they must, about the troubled state of the world, dissenters from war are subject to feelings of helplessness, to despair over widespread injustice, and even to the temptation of panic. Mediation helps them at such moments "to remain calm, to see clearly." Meditation is an "awakening," a way "to see deeply into things, to see how we can change, how we can transform our situation. To transform our situation is also to transform our minds. To transform our minds is also to transform our situation." One must be peaceful in order to contribute to the movement for peace. "Peace work means, first of all, being peace."[94] When peacebuilders lack peace for lack of a daily practice of mindfulness, their determination and patience dissipates.[95]

A peacebuilder's contemplation of interdependence and compassion is a way to broaden an otherwise narrow, isolated, and frightful view of life. As one becomes more conscious of his or her body, feelings, perceptions, physical surroundings, and mental functioning, particulars become connected to the larger whole. "When you touch one thing with deep awareness," Nhat Hahn observes, "you touch everything." As one contemplates more deeply and frequently, she or he touches the "ultimate dimension" and thus sees more "globally" with "a more profound view of happiness and life." The practice of mindfulness, of "conscious breathing," puts one in touch with a refreshing, healing, and transforming peace that is all around and within us in our immediate place of being and at the very moment.[96]

When deepened awareness of the particular produces a wider and more profound view of the whole, war dissenters and peacebuilders are better prepared to understand the suffering and perspective of parties on both sides of a conflict and thus better prepared for undertaking the important task of reconciliation. Nhat Hahn observes that the peace movement is fraught with too much "anger, frustration, and misunderstanding." It knows how to write protest letters better than how to speak in a language of friendship and respect that does not "turn people off." Practicing meditation is Thây's way of overcoming anger and fear well enough to overcome the language of alienation and to speak of reconciliation—the teacher's way of peaceworkers being mindful of being peace.[97]

APPREHENDING THE ADVERSARY'S PERSPECTIVE

In addition to resisting demonizing rhetoric, fostering a humanizing language of political friendship, and transcending the dehumanizing viewpoint of war, a fourth dimension of language critique as a concrete act of dissent and peacebuilding citizenship is to apprehend the adversary's perspective. War propaganda pursues its objective by depicting an enemy in caricature. What is perhaps less apparent, though, is that these crude renderings diminish all parties to a conflict, not just the designated enemy. To invoke the image of a demon foe is to summon the corresponding and equally simplistic persona of an innocent victim or heroic savior. Americans, taken as the blameless victims of evil Islamic terrorists and chosen redeemers of the sacred order, are stripped of any nuance of character, reduced to a thin veneer of virtue, and divested of the full measure of their versatile identity. To impute circuitously the degraded status of mere victim to the US citizenry effaces an otherwise resourceful people, thus misrepresenting them as feeble (that is, too weak and vulnerable to shoulder their country's fair share of responsibility for the rift) and inept (that is, too dim, inert, and foolish to cope with more complex adversarial relationships). To ascribe obliquely and even blatantly a divine mission for the United States is arrogance and effrontery compensating for self-induced paroxysms of self-doubt.

The war dissenter's constructive alternative to the propagandist's demeaning caricatures is to learn more about the worldview and circumstances of America's adversaries. Rounding out the character, situation, and perspective of an adversary creates opportunities to engage divisive issues thoughtfully and productively. Just as war propaganda impoverishes the nation's conception of nonviolent alternatives, increased knowledge of a foreign people can reduce the distance separating an "us" from a "them," facilitate the search for common ground and appreciation of potentially enriching differences, and help to manage conflicted interests justly without resort to force of arms. Garnering specific knowledge of otherwise threatening aliens can activate a people's cultural wherewithal for increased tolerance, empathy, compassion, and justice, for more determined diplomacy, and for creative problem solving.

Grasping a foreign perspective is a way of advancing the central aim of resisting war and of seeking nonviolent solutions to conflict. It is not inherent to the basic motive or intent of peacebuilding, for knowing one's enemy is also a main premise of successful warfare. A warrior can read a foe's history and study an enemy's ways in order to gauge tendencies and identify vulnerabilities for the purpose of outmaneuvering and ultimately defeating him. A peacebuilder is equally strategic but is guided by a higher goal. Looking and listening for the other side's presuppositions of fact and value, interpretations of events and understanding of history, perceptions of threat and opportunity, conceptions of self and other, expressions of aims and purposes, underlying images of social, political, and spiritual realities, sense of place in time and space, mannerisms of everyday living, predispositions to act one way or another, and so on, especially as they relate to the dispute at hand, helps to develop a working sensibility of another lifeworld, an alternative worldview on the other side of a human divide, and thus a richer comprehension of relevant differences and plausible points of contact. It is a matter of gaining perspective on another's perspective so that peacebuilders might better look at the parties in conflict through human eyes to spot possibilities of compromise, resolution, and reconciliation where otherwise the dehumanizing lens of war propaganda insists on the necessity of violence and coercion.

The process of getting better acquainted with how the other side sees a given conflict can take many forms. Women activists for peace in Israel and Palestine, for instance, have been meeting with one another for years, secretly when they must and openly when they can, to debate, discuss, and negotiate painfully divisive issues in order to locate crucial points of agreement in support of a just resolution and to put an end to the suffering. They have taken what they have learned about and from one another back to their own people to educate them "about the validity of both claims" to a disputed territory. They are "mothers, teachers, nurses, and social workers" in their respective societies who "serve up politics with dinner and teach lessons of nonviolence" to children in their classrooms, patients in their care, clients they advise, and youngsters they rear. This is their way of overcoming ignorance of one another and thus of refusing to give in to the violence by refusing to be enemies.[98] These are truly inspired acts of everyday citizenship.

Another face-to-face act of citizenship aimed at overcoming ignorance of an alien perspective is exemplified by a "pilgrimage for peace" undertaken by Americans Rabial Elizabeth Roberts and her husband Elias Amidon along with thirteen others from six Western countries. Their journey to Syria was a dual exercise in "citizen diplomacy" and "spiritual diplomacy" aimed at breaking through "our fears of the 'other.'" Toward that end, they met with ordinary Syrian men and women, young and old, students, teachers, business people, social workers, architects, sheikhs, and others. They met in mosques, churches, schools, offices, and homes to talk and listen so that they might understand better the fears, suspicions, anger, dreams, and beliefs of a Muslim people who "feel misunderstood," who believe Westerners in general and Americans in particular "don't understand our religions, our family ways, our history, or our politics" but "think we're terrorists." As one elderly human rights worker in Damascus joked, Americans think Syrians "eat foreigners." Roberts and Amidon believe in the value of "citizens reaching across borders" and "dream of communities of people coming together to send pilgrims . . . to places of conflict to extend friendship, humility, and openhearted listening." It proved a gift of perspective for them, a break through a wall of ignorance and fear, "a crash course in human trust," and an opportunity to speak on Syrian soil of their respect for Syrian culture, religious integrity, kindness and hospitality. They are convinced that their visit planted a "seed of understanding" in "rocky soil."[99]

Indeed, the responsibilities of democratic citizenship include the exercise of informed judgment on matters of such import as war and peace. To assess the possibility of resolving a dangerous conflict prudently and nonviolently, conscientious citizenship mandates a better understanding of those we have confronted, the kind of understanding that comes from apprehending our adversary's self-perception and perspective as a protagonist and reflecting back on ourselves as antagonists from that point of view. The persona of an adversary viewed as a protagonist is that of a central character acting with high purpose to overcome the resistance of an opposing force. A protagonist has elevated aims, layers and subtleties of character, a propensity to over-reach, and is the focal point of a tragic narrative. The protagonist is the character through whose eyes we see the scene, means, and purpose of dramatic action. The protagonist's role is to establish a dominant framework of meaning, a perspective on reality, a motivation for action with which we might identify, and then to put that attitude to a dramatic test by teaching the hazards of arrogance, of overextending any necessarily delimited perspective, of failing to recognize or heed the warning signs of error, which are misperceived as the evildoing of a demonic antagonist.

Reversing roles so that we may understand ourselves as the antagonist to our adversary's protagonist is an empathic act of citizenship that can yield useful insights. Seeing the meaningfulness of an opposing perspective and viewing our recalcitrance to it as a measure of our adversary's distended mind-set, helps us as peacebuilders to discern the points at which each side is over-reaching and where correctives need to be made and lessons might be learned. It is an exercise in taking the role of the other seriously enough to hold competing perspectives accountable to one another, to let each shed light on the other, and to draw insight from the constructive tension created. Juxtaposing one's own perspective against another is an opportunity to learn more about unexamined assumptions that might profit from further reflection.

The act of speaking of one's adversary as the protagonist is exemplified in the oldest surviving play from ancient Greece. Aeschylus's tragedy, *The Persians* (472 BCE), reflects on the defeat suffered by the invading Xerxes at the Battle of Salamis in 480. Aeschylus, himself a soldier who fought against the Persians in 490 at Marathon and again in 480 at Salamis, wrote his play to be performed for an Athenian audience, most of which had participated in the fighting or were touched by it. Rather than pander to Athenian pride, mock a beaten foe, or propagandize a decisive Greek victory over the numerically superior Persian forces of Xerxes' great empire, Aeschylus tells a cautionary tale with "a poet's vision."[100] The moral of his play—a warning addressed to Greeks and barbarians alike—is that the pride of tyranny and oppression and the hubris of empire inevitably suffer a divine reckoning. The gods, not the

Greeks, punished Xerxes' hubris with defeat at Salamis. Xerxes, the subject of Aeschylus' story, is the tragic hero; Susa, the Persian capital, is the site of the dramatic action. From an alien point of view—the perspective of an over-reaching foreign protagonist—Athenians were prompted to learn and apply to themselves an ennobling lesson of humility.

Aeschylus could not write about the Persians or speak from their viewpoint other than as a Greek. He did not attempt to achieve total authenticity or objectivity and even allowed himself to invent the names of Persians and project Greek gods and rituals onto the scene in Susa. He was addressing Athenians in a manner of perspective-taking designed to promote empathy and deepen understanding for the better learning of a crucial lesson about the pride of nations, a lesson that might transcend time and place. Accordingly, his characters were more textured than alien enemies commonly appear when cast as mere antagonists to an indwelling protagonist. This twist of perspective produced a dramatic tension conducive to sustained reflection.

What lessons might one draw from reflecting on such a perspective-gaining drama as this ancient story of imperial warfare and woe? The first lesson of the play is a reminder of war's anguish, the personal despair suffered by all concerned. It is not portrayed as a faceless affair. The horde of perhaps 200,000 Persian invaders amassed against a much smaller force of Greek defenders loses its anonymity as a chorus of Persian elders, anticipating news of the fate of Xerxes' embattled troops, opens the play asking by name after great chieftains and inquiring of warriors who have endured the painful march on foot as well as those mounted on proud steeds, bold warriors known for their manly strength and those trained to the stout oar, warriors from the forest inlands and those from the distant sea, those with lance, those with bow:

> This
>   is the flower of Persian earth
> the men now gone
> and Asia's land that held their roots
> groans out loud,
>   aflame with yearning,
> Parents, wives in cold beds
> Count the days.
>   Time stretches thin.
> They wait and shiver. (81–90)[101]

These were Persia's sons charged by fate with a holy task of waging "tower-splitting war" (127), absent sons fighting far away in foreign fields, flesh-and-blood sons for whom Persia now sighed and worried on end. None before had been able to withstand these "men in ceaseless stream" (117) or resist "Persia's armed flood and the war-joy that crests in her sons" (120–121). Nervously, though, the elders fretted aloud that "Blind Folly fawns a man into her net, nor can he hope to work loose and escape unhurt" (145–148). While tearful wives were left behind "bereft of love" (181), Xerxes' mother Atossa dreamed ominously that her kingly son, "gone to Greece, bent on making it Persian" (274–275), would be made himself to fall by stubborn Greeks from his imperial chariot (310–311).

When "bitter news" (422) arrives by distraught messenger, who is compelled to speak "Cruel cruelest evil newmade" and thus cause those "who hear this pain" to weep (426–429), the chanting chorus of elders wails a death howl for "DEAD MEN shrouded in sea-drowned cloaks" (450–451). Atossa asks to know by name who has fallen and who has survived the lost battle. Xerxes lives, she is told, but "Artembares, commander of ten thousand horses, is hammered along Sileniai's raw coast" (494–496), a fate similar to that of the great Dadakes, the brave Tenagon, Lilaios, Arsames, Argestes, Arkteus, Adeues, Matallos, and many more of Persia's illustrious leaders, each mentioned by name, who now lie prostrate "on that harsh ground" (525). Alas, "the young men, our sons are all of them gone" (1074–1075).

The second lesson, drawn from the anguish of defeat and terrible loss of loved ones, is that providence punishes the arrogance of imperial aggression and oppression. Something "monstrous" had "twisted" Xerxes' "good sense" (1181). With "his ignorance, his reckless youth" spurred on by "Consort with evil-minded men" (1238), vain and presumptuous Xerxes set out to prove his mettle and avenge his father's previous defeat at Marathon, only to waste Persia's brave sons and haul in "countless cruelties upon himself and us" (773–774), while leaving Persia itself exposed and mighty Susa easy prey. "Mere man that he is, he thought, but not on good advice, he'd overrule all gods" (1226–1228), the Ghost of Darius affirmed.

To temper a soul fraught with ambition, pride, and greed, Xerxes must learn to listen to wise counsel. The prudence that mitigates arrogance, moderates empire, and restrains tyranny is to come from public deliberation, from "deep-debated thoughts" (187) and pondering over the events of war. It is to arise from the faithful advice of experienced confidants and rendered palatable to a tortured and now humbled king with "kind words" spoken "in a calming voice" by the "aged mother whom Xerxes loves" (1372, 1365). Independence from imperial rule was the cause for which the Greeks had fought, the heart of their victorious battle cry:

> Sons of Greece, go!
> Free fatherland,
> free children, wives,
> shrines of our father's gods,

tombs where our forefathers lie.
Fight for all we have!
Now!

The hard lesson of Xerxes' ignoble defeat was driven home forthrightly by the ghost of prudent Darius as a warning that mortals "not overreach themselves" (1346).

Zeus the Pruning Shear of arrogance run wild
is set over you, a grim accountant.
Because events have prophesied
    That my son learn to know himself,
teach him in gentle admonitions
to stop
    wounding gods with young reckless pride. (1357–1363)

Thus, Aeschylus helps us to see through the eyes of his Persian characters that Xerxes was wrong, indeed, grievously wrong, but subject to learning from the error of his arrogant ways and to correcting his mistakes with the benefit of wise counsel. The issue was not one of overthrowing his rule. It was instead a matter of how to govern better the tragic impulse to war. With Xerxes' uninhibited will and power broken, those who lived "under empire's commanding grip" no longer would "fling themselves earthward in awe of kingship" (949–951). The defeated ruler was redeemed in human terms, humbled but not reduced to a demon tyrant, overthrown, and destroyed. The tragic lesson he was taught was a warning for Athenians to ponder so that they might not also suffer the wrath of Jove, advice they did not take well enough to heart during their own subsequent empire-building years.

How might an analogous shift of perspective on contemporary Iran—that is, thinking of the modern Persia as a troubled protagonist rather than merely as an evil antagonist to freedom's virtue—gain us some useful insight into the folly of an imperial war on Islamic terrorism? How might we see better the error of vengeance's counsel, the wages of arrogance, and the consequences of imperial overreach? What lessons can we draw by crafting an adversary's perspective from which to contemplate a constructive course correction?

The trenchant voice of Shirin Ebadi—Iranian judge, jailed human-rights activist, and first Muslim woman recipient of the Nobel Peace Prize, awarded in 2003—speaks to these questions from a position of insight within Iran. Her words can set the cornerstone of practical wisdom for attentive listeners in the US. Democracy and human rights, she avers, are needs common to all cultures, Muslim as well as Western. Rather than listen to those in power (and the media that amplify their voices) repeatedly advance the charge of "Islamic terrorism," we must learn "to separate the crimes of individuals from their religious affiliations." Just as the misdeeds in Bosnia should not be pinned on Christianity or Israel's disregard for a United Nations resolution attributed to Judaism, the misdeeds of misguided Islamic individuals should not be charged against Islam. Like Judaism and Christianity, Islam is a faith of peace and justice. Thus, her first premise is that "the Western world should not vilify Islam."[102]

Her second premise—that peace must be based on respect for, and behavior consistent with, the two pillars of democracy and justice—identifies a point of potential cooperation among civilizations that would inhibit war between them. Democracy, she muses, is a long and perpetual struggle for freedom, "not something that occurs overnight" nor a valid pretext for a powerful country to attack a weaker state. Democracy cannot be exported with weapons. Even well-intentioned military attacks "harm democracy as society degenerates into violence." The way "the sapling of democracy will bear the flower of freedom" is for sincerely concerned outsiders to render nonviolent support patiently to those struggling on the inside against dictatorial rule.[103]

Words are her "peaceful weapons" and, she believes, the "most powerful tool" for protecting human rights and transforming reality. She and other Iranian women dissent through words—not in the Western stereotype of docile, forlorn, female Muslim creatures—but in recognition of the reality that "change comes to the Islamic Republic in slow and subtle ways." A continuing "exchange of ideas" between the US and Iran is imperative to gain greater access to each side's culture and attitudes beyond offensive ideology, official rhetoric, and mutual suspicion. The "language of force" and of "bellicosity and brinkmanship" are the "ingrained habits for both sides," bad habits that work against peaceful transition toward democratic governance in Iran.[104]

Patient diplomacy and keeping a spotlight on Iran's human rights record are the best ways to support Iranian women agitating for their rights and to facilitate a democratic transformation of the Islamic Republic. Threatening regime change by military force "endangers nearly all of the efforts democracy-minded Iranians have made in these recent years." It provides a pretext to crack down on dissent and undermines a "nascent civil society that is slowly taking shape" in Iran. Moreover, the threat of military force motivates Iranians to set aside their resentment of the ruling regime because their first priority as patriots is to protect their country.[105]

The tension between democratization and state building in Iran has been a defining consideration over the last century, according to Ali Gheissari and Vali Nasr—the former a visiting scholar of religious studies at Brown University who was educated at Tehran University as well as at Oxford, and the latter a professor of Middle East Politics at the US Naval Postgraduate School. Gheissari and Nasr look at the evolving history of modern Iran from an interior angle to explain the complexities of contemporary Iranian politics and the ongoing movement toward democratic reform. From the vantage point of what is likely a "new perspective" for most Americans and thus contrary to stereotype, democracy is indigenous to an evolving Iranian political culture despite the anti-democratic ideology of the Islamic revolution of 1979. In the last twenty-five years, Gheissari and Nasr argue, the Iranian citizenry have embraced "the fundamental logic of democracy and the laws that govern its practice." The Iranian people have become familiar with "the mechanics of democratic practice" even though they have yet to realize a democratic state, and this democratic ethos has emerged from the bottom up, as a complex "grassroots phenomenon," not as a Western import or a top-down project of the state.[106]

The presidential election of 2005, which resulted in the selection of a non-clerical, hard-line conservative over democratic-reformist and pragmatic-conservative alternatives, was a highly contested campaign with a strong voter turnout that reflected the increasing "importance of competitive politics, public debates, and elections" in Iran. Although half or more of the votes cast in the first round of the two-round election were in support of reform of one kind or another, the main beneficiaries of those votes were pragmatic conservatives who promised not democracy but instead "economic growth, better living standards, accountable and strong government, and engagement with the outside world with a strong appeal to Iranian nationalism." Reform, in this sense, meant better government rather than more democracy. Democratic reformists, failing to recognize the importance of economic issues, neglected the principal interest of lower-class voters and thus fell out of the competition for office after the first round of balloting, while the victorious conservative hard-liners fashioned their winning campaign around a decidedly populist appeal. The moral of electoral defeat for democratic reformers was to link future demands for democratic change to socioeconomic grievances, that is, "to build bridges between the middle and lower classes."[107]

Making internal adjustments calibrated to a changing scene in a political process looks more hopefully like the advance of politics and less stereotypically like a theocratic state mired hopelessly in the absolute rule of mad mullahs. A political movement toward democracy is afoot under the "theocratic edifice and authoritarian power structure," Gheissari and Nasr contend. Democracy, which was not the "declared goal of the Islamic Revolution," is an "unintended consequence" of the revolution's unfolding.[108] From this point of view, American impatience with the complexities of an evolving Iranian state is likely to undermine rather than advance a developing democratic movement in a proud country still smarting from a long history of European and US attempts to control its politics and direct its economy. America's counterproductive impatience is based largely on the clichéd image of an evil Iran completely under the sway of an irrational, emotionally unstable regime of revolutionaries and religious fanatics.

The legacy of Ayatollah Khomeini looms large in the basic American attitude and official government orientation toward contemporary Iran. Khomeini died in 1989, but the humiliation and frustration of the 1979–1981 hostage crisis (the US embassy overrun and 52 Americans held hostage in revolutionary Iran for 444 days to revenge the CIA's 1953 coup against the popular Iranian Prime Minister Mohammad Mosaddeq, a coup that returned the Shah to power) "has left a terrible scar on the American psyche," Kenneth Pollack observes. It is an "underlying grievance" that has colored American perceptions and US policymaking and that has magnified American outrage at Iranian actions ever since.[109] Khomeini's oft-expressed hatred of the US—the "Great Satan" against which he railed relentlessly throughout the decade of the 1980s, claiming it was the source of Iran's troubles—defined the Islamic revolution as a "cleansing of American influence from Iran, including America's puppet, the shah."[110] The satanic US, insisted the revolution's "founding father," was "the source of all evil in the world."[111]

Khomeini's legacy of hostility not only has cast a dark shadow on America's image of Iran but also has had a "profound impact" on Iranians who continue to "struggle with his legacy."[112] Thus, it is difficult for either side to see the other except as an antagonist. Yet, viewing post-Khomeini Iran as a protagonist in an unfolding drama of troubled relations with the US and internal struggle for political reform can be instructive for Americans.[113] In assuming such a perspective, America might heed the moral of Xerxes' lesson of revenge and imperial overreach, thus adopting a more prudent attitude than preventative military strikes against the so-called axis of evil.

Trying to understand the complexities of the "Persian puzzle" in an act of perspective-taking, American analyst Kenneth Pollack cautioned against an aggressive policy of confrontation, including military invasion. A declaration of war on Iran "figuratively or literally," he argued, presented "the greatest danger" with the least chance of a positive outcome.[114] An invasion would be a "daunting task," much more difficult and costly than the invasion of Iraq because Iran is four times the size of Iraq and has a population three times larger, and Iran's mountainous terrain presents "formidable barriers."[115] Moreover, the threat to the US posed by Iran "probably does not justify" a costly military invasion. Iran's worrisome involvement in international terrorism did not constitute "an overriding threat to the United States." Even the threat of Iran acquiring nuclear weapons "probably [did] not rise to the level of justifying what would be an extremely costly and risky invasion." The current Iranian leadership did not have a record of "reckless behavior," he observed, nor was there persuasive evidence that they wanted nuclear weapons to support an aggressive foreign policy. Finally, in Pollack's judgment, "Iran's human rights abuses [did] not rise to the level that demands extreme forms of intervention by the United States."[116]

Not only were there inadequate grounds for what would be a costly, bloody invasion of Iran, Pollack also argued that any attempt to force a regime change was most likely a "lost cause" that would leave the US "worse off." Moreover, a preventative strike against Iran's nuclear facilities would probably incite Iranian retaliation by terrorist attacks on the US and trouble-making in neighboring Afghanistan and Iraq. It also would undermine the reform movement inside Iran and would sour US relations with other Muslim countries throughout the Middle East.[117] Accordingly, US policy toward Iran should be flexible, ready to negotiate long and hard with the Iranian leadership when they are ready to work out their differences with the US, should include the development of a set of positive and negative incentives for progress on terrorism and nuclear issues, and should avoid inflammatory rhetoric (such as the infamous "axis of evil" phrase) while advocating human rights and democracy by way of our own good example and as a matter of indirect assistance to an indigenous reform movement rather than direct intervention in Iranian affairs.[118]

Perceived from the vantage point of a protagonist, Iran becomes a more complicated, more conflicted character in an adversarial relationship with the US, a dramatic, agonistic relationship to be sure but one that cannot be reduced so easily to a simple confrontation between good and evil or resolved merely by force of arms. Patience and flexibility would appear to be the more prudent attitude on which to base a constructive US foreign policy aimed at reducing hostility and enhancing security. Proceeding otherwise amounts to a decision to remain locked in the tragic role of Iran's antagonist, playing the Great Satan even as we reassure ourselves that we are the victim and our motives are pure. This, at least, is a lesson we might choose to draw from an exercise in perspective-taking, a lesson that argues for peacebuilding remedies over war-making measures.

JOINING THE PEACEBUILDING COMMUNITY

Apprehending the adversary's perspective, along with other exercises in language critique to resist demonizing rhetoric, to foster a humanizing language of political friendship, and to transcend the dehumanizing viewpoint of war, constitutes a crucial act of citizenship that works to establish a basic foundation for dissenting from war and to sustain the vital attitude of building toward a culture of peace. Its potential impact is magnified within the facilitating and reinforcing context of the peacebuilding community. Participation in the peacebuilding community is an amplifying act of citizenship and a conditioning exercise in democratic dissent. It brings similarly motivated individuals into closer contact with one another and promotes greater coordination among them. It can be a transforming exercise in fellowship, partnership, and solidarity among otherwise diverse citizens.

One can join the peacebuilding community in many different, large and small ways and with various degrees of involvement at any given point in time. The multiple points of contact existing within the sphere of civil society include, for example, local peace societies that are secular in orientation as well as peace-and-justice initiatives organized by various, sometimes coordinated, religious institutions.

Where I live and work, for instance, the Bloomington Peace Action Coalition coordinates nonviolent dissent from war. It is "dedicated to educating, encouraging, and empowering everyone to participate in activities that promote Peace and Justice for all."[119] In an effort to promote tolerance and compassion as anti-war, peacebuilding activists, its members facilitate involvement at the local, regional, and national levels in rallies, marches, and demonstrations; they organize "peace vigils; anti-war and counter-recruiting demonstrations, marches, and rallies; pledge and petition drives; letter writing and Congressional lobbying campaigns; film presentation series...and lecture and public forum presentations."[120] They maintain a web site with multiple links to relevant information and news sources and to state and national peace groups, and they conduct face-to-face business meetings regularly at the local public library.

The Presbyterian Church (USA) is one among many religious groups that maintains an organized peacebuilding project. The "Presbyterian Peacemaking Program" develops and promulgates peacebuilding resources, reaches out to church members within local congregations, and coordinates with corresponding religious and secular organizations, including the United Nations (where the church maintains a permanently staffed office) and the National Council of Churches.[121] Its calendar of events includes hosting peacemaking seminars at its "Ghost Ranch" education and retreat center in New Mexico. It compiles relevant information on current peace-and-justice issues such as torture awareness, illicit trade in small arms, the war in Iraq, and the Israeli/Palestinian conflict. Its several listservs and publications include occasional advocacy alerts as well as news and resource updates.

These are just two examples of how citizens can become directly connected to the peacebuilding community where they live and/or worship. Citizens with access to the internet can readily monitor and variously participate in a wide range of anti-war and peacemaking web sites. "United for Peace and Justice" is a coalition of over 1,300 local and national groups in the US resisting the war culture. It provides information on ongoing peace campaigns, directories to activist groups and to grassroots actions, and much more. Nonviolence.org is an independent peace activist web site that features articles written from a nonviolent perspective. Pax Christi USA is the internet home of the National Catholic peace movement. Waging Peace is the web site of the Nuclear Age Peace Foundation, which supports worldwide efforts to abolish nuclear weapons. Antiwar.com is a libertarian site that features news, viewpoints, and activities in support of noninterventionism and opposed to US imperialism. These five web sites are a small sample of the resources available to citizens interested in participating in the peacebuilding community.

War monuments are everywhere in America's small towns and large cities, but peacebuilding anti-war activists rarely have access to a peace memorial. On the internet, though, they can visit a site such as the Peace Museum located in Chicago's Gold Dome Building, "a museum dedicated to peace through the arts."[122]

> The unique and valuable collection consists of more than 10,000 artifacts including original paintings, sculptures, drawings, ribbon banners, posters, buttons, and lithographs. Exhibits focus on individual peacemakers and artists, the horrors of war, Central America, domestic violence, human rights, prisons, and women's leadership.[123]

Its "Peace 2005 & Beyond" Peace Crane Installation is a permanent installation of participatory art designed "to unite citizens of the world for a wish for peace." As donated paper peace cranes accumulate, they are fashioned into colorful displays of 1,000 each that are then sent "to a region suffering from political violence, war or protracted conflict."[124] Besides serving those who can visit Chicago, the Peace Museum also makes traveling exhibits available to universities, churches, and cultural organizations in the US and other countries.

Individual citizens can contribute to the larger peacebuilding community according to their own inclinations. Mural art, as previously illustrated in the works of Juana Alicia and Judith Francisca Baca, can bring people together in the very process of creating images that would transcend war culture. In a similar act of war-dissenting citizenship through artistic expression, Merridee LaMantia used fabric scraps found by her husband at a local recycling center and a $1,000 grant for materials from the Indiana Arts Commission to craft, during the winter of 2006, a multipaneled fabric installation piece entitled, "Illuminating Peace: A Global Perspective." Her creation was displayed in the atrium of Bloomington City Hall during the month of July. Her aim was to produce a "counterforce" to war talk that would "stimulate discussion" and "honor" the spirit of peace that "is present within us, and in our interaction with others." As a Bloomington resident, she wanted to create something that made other members of the community feel as though they are in the "presence of peace." Toward that end, the word peace appears in 168 languages along with a culturally diverse array of peace images and symbols and the sentence, "May peace prevail on Earth," written in 50 languages in hand-painted gold letters on the large fabric panels. My experience in viewing the display, consistent with the artist's stated intention, was that it moves and breathes with you to create a sense of inner peace. LaMantia's commitment to "stand up for peace," as a citizen artist, extends to making "Illuminating Peace" available to others as a traveling exhibit.[125]

Citizens enrich the culture of peace by their participation in public expressions of a humanizing conscience. Visiting public displays of peace art, viewing public screenings of anti-war documentaries, attending meetings of peace activist organizations, participating in nonviolent marches for peace and in peaceful demonstrations against war, attending educational retreats sponsored by religious or secular peacemaking organizations, signing petitions, speaking up at peace rallies, monitoring and contributing to anti-war blogs—these are the daily and concrete acts of citizens dissenting from warism and contributing to the development of a culture of peace. They are opportunities to embed and spread constructive practices of language critique into the collective conscience of communities. They are democratic practices of dissent from war that restructure daily life to give peacebuilding a higher priority and a greater degree of legitimacy in our economic, social, political, and spiritual transactions with one another. They are opportunities to witness, express, learn, and affirm humanity's enriching diversity. They are, in short, public performances and rituals of peacebuilding citizenship that bring a collective conscience to bear and civic mindfulness into being.

One such collective-consciousness-raising opportunity to participate locally in a transnational expression of the humanizing attitudes that nurture peace culture is to celebrate annually on September 21, the International Day of Peace. As a vehicle of the United Nation's Culture of Peace Initiative, the International Day of Peace designates a date to be shared worldwide by individuals and groups organizing practical acts of peace. Since 1982, people have been nurturing the global peace culture from within their local communities. They engage in prayer and meditation and join people worldwide in a minute of silence. They plan local events in schools, libraries, parks, municipal buildings, and places of worship. They ask city councils to pass proclamations affirming the International Day of Peace. They ring bells and light candles for peace at their places of worship. They write peace letters to the editors of their local newspapers, take the peace pledge, hold peace parties and vigils, make peace bracelets, watch peace films together, and organize peace-day parades, among many other activities and events.

Over 1,000 organizations in more than 100 countries sponsor "humanity's first global holiday." In the US all fifty states plus Washington, DC, maintain Peace Day web pages. Peace Day in Indiana, for example, publicizes "community-uniting and peace-inspiring events" such as the "Pinwheels for Peace" project for elementary schoolchildren undertaken in several Indiana cities and towns and the planning for prayer services by the congregation of the Spencer Presbyterian Church and by the Sisters of St. Francis in Oldenburg. Other sites, such as Peace Day New York, feature an array of additional activities, including peace concerts, peace festivals, interfaith peace processions, the planting of peace poles, peace walks, peace flag ceremonies, and peace speeches. Resources for planning these kinds of events, including videos, posters, and local contacts also can be found on the web site.

September 21 is a day for citizens to act together on the pledge of peace. As they observe a holiday from violence, affirming their commitment to a global ceasefire and a day of nonviolence, they make a public gesture to the "vision of world peace" as "humanity's guiding inspiration" and participate in a collective acknowledgment that "global crises impel all citizens to work toward converting humanity's noblest aspirations for world peace into a practical reality for future generations."[126] When such a gesture takes the form of an official state proclamation it adds presence and bestows gravitas on peacebuilding as an alternative to war; it recognizes, as in the case of the State of Indiana's Peace Day Proclamation signed by Governor Frank O'Bannon on May 22, 2003, that there is "growing support in our state" to observe a day of peace as an affirmation of the "vision" of a world at peace and as a commitment to foster "cooperation between individuals, organizations and nations" in the midst of global crises.[127] Proclaiming and celebrating an international holiday for peace is a way of making the dream a publicly affirmed, legitimate, and realistic aspiration for progressive, humanizing political relations within and across national boundaries. It is a way to exercise democratic citizenship on behalf of making war difficult instead of easy.

NOTES

1. Duane L. Cady, *From Warism to Pacifism: A Moral Continuum* (Philadelphia: Temple University Press, 1989), 3–4.

2. Cady, *Warism*, 6. To make this point, Cady draws on Iredell Jenkins, "The Conditions of Peace," *The Monist* 57 (October 1973): 508.

3. Cady, *Warism*, 6–7.

4. John Paul Lederach, "Cultivating Peace: A Practitioner's View of Deadly Conflict and Negotiation," in *Contemporary Peacemaking: Conflict, Violence and Peace Processes*, ed. John Darby and Roger MacGinty (New York: Palgrave Macmillan, 2003), 34–37.

5. Pope John Paul II, "Why I Say No to War," *London Times*, February 12, 2003, reprinted in *The Antiwar Movement*, ed. Randy Scherer (Farmington Hill, Michigan: Greenhaven Press, 2004), 175.

6. Quoted in Neil A. Lewis, "Ashcroft Defends Antiterror Plan and Says Criticism May Aid Foes," *The New York Times*, December 7, 2001.

7. Jude McCulloch, "'Either You Are with Us or You Are with the Terrorists': The War's Home Front," in *Beyond September 11: An Anthology of Dissent*, ed. Phil Scranton (London: Pluto Press, 2002), 59.

8. Ernesto Laclau and Chantal Mouffe, *Hegemony and Socialist Strategy: Towards a Radical Democratic Politics*, 2nd ed. (London: Verso, 2001), xi.

9. Jacob Torfing, *New Theories of Discourse: Laclau, Mouffe and Žižek* (Oxford: Blackwell, 1999), 302.

10. Chantal Mouffe, *The Return of the Political* (London: Verso, 1993), 57; Torfing, *New Theories*, 101, 116.

11. Laclau and Mouffe, *Hegemony*, xvii, xiv; Chantal Mouffe, "Deconstruction, Pragmatism and the Politics of Democracy," in *Deconstruction and Pragmatism*, ed. Chantal Mouffe (London: Routledge, 1996), 8.

12. Chantal Mouffe, *The Democratic Paradox* (London: Verso, 2000), 101.

13. Mouffe, *Democratic Paradox*, 103, 101.

14. For an efficient summary of the Bush administration's post-9/11 assault on civil liberties and stifling of antiwar dissent, see Geoffrey R. Stone, *Perilous Times: Free Speech in Wartime, From the Sedition Act of 1798 to the War on Terrorism* (New York: W. W. Norton & Company, 2004), 552–57. An extended critique of the structural dimensions of the failure of the fourth estate to meet its reportorial responsibilities is available in Robert W. McChesney, *The Problem of the Media: U.S. Communication Politics in the 21st Century* (New York: Monthly Review Press, 2004). Also see Douglas Kellner, "The Media and the Crisis of Democracy in the Age of Bush-2," *Communication and Critical/Cultural Studies* 1 (2004): 29–58.

15. Quoted by Richard C. Leone, "The Quiet Republic: The Missing Debate About Civil Liberties After 9/11," in *The War on Our Freedoms: Civil Liberties in an Age of Terrorism*, ed. Richard C. Leone and Greg Anrig, Jr. (New York: Public Affairs, 2003), 18.

16. Nancy Chang, *Silencing Dissent* (New York: Seven Stories Press, 2002), 92.

17. For a now classic distinction between thin, or weak, democracy and strong democracy, see Benjamin Barber, *Strong Democracy: Participatory Politics for a New Age* (Berkeley: University of California Press, 1984).

18. Robert A. Dahl, *How Democratic Is the American Constitution?* (New Haven: Yale University Press, 2001), 24–25.

19. Thomas B. Farrell, *Norms of Rhetorical Culture* (New Haven: Yale University Press, 1993), 39, 48, 76, 99, 142, 146. In Farrell's words, "rhetoric has always been . . . the worst fear of idealized reason and the best hope for whatever remains of civic life" (p. 1).

20. For an example of one elitist realist masking his own rhetoric in the name of reason, see Robert L. Ivie, "George Kennan's Political Rhetoric: Realism Masking Fear," in *Post-Realism: The Rhetorical Turn in International Relations*, ed. Francis A. Beer and Robert Hariman (East Lansing: Michigan State University Press, 1996), 55–74.

21. Roland Bleiker, *Popular Dissent, Human Agency and Global Politics* (Cambridge: Cambridge University Press, 2000), 45.

22. David Stout, "Bush Says Worldwide Protests Won't Change Approach to Iraq," *New York Times,* February 18, 2003.

23. Cass R. Sunstein, *Why Societies Need Dissent* (Cambridge, Massachusetts: Harvard University Press, 2003).

24. Bleiker, *Popular Dissent,* 39, 269.

25. For a discussion of the concept and emergence of a rhetorical presidency, see Jeffrey K. Tulis, *The Rhetorical Presidency* (Princeton, New Jersey: Princeton University Press, 1987).

26. Gary L. Gregg II, *The Presidential Republic: Executive Representation and Deliberative Democracy* (Lanham, Maryland: Rowman and Littlefield Publishers, 1997), 1.

27. Quoted in Robert L. Ivie, "Tragic Fear and the Rhetorical Presidency: Combating Evil in the Persian Gulf," in *Beyond the Rhetorical Presidency*, ed. Martin J. Medhurst (College Station: Texas A&M University Press, 1996), 166–68. See also Frederick M. Dolan and Thomas L. Dumm, eds., *Rhetorical Republic: Governing Representations in American Politics* (Amherst: The University of Massachusetts Press, 1993), including David Campbell's chapter, "Cold Wars: Securing Identity, Identifying Danger."

28. See, for instance, Lawrence K. Grossman, *The Electronic Republic: Reshaping Democracy in the Information Age* (New York: Viking, 1995).

29. Russell L. Hanson, *The Democratic Imagination in America: Conversations with Our Past* (Princeton, New Jersey: Princeton University Press, 1985).

30. Paul Joseph, *Peace Politics: The United States Between the Old and New World Orders* (Philadelphia: Temple University Press, 1993), 243.

31. Joseph, *Peace Politics,* 141–42, 147, 158, 167, 171, 176–77.

32. Joseph, *Peace Politics,* 244, 247.

33. Laclau and Mouffe, *Hegemony,* 105; Torfing, 98; Mouffe, *Return of the Political,* 57.

34. Bleiker, *Popular Dissent,* 46, 225, 229–32.

35. Susan Buck-Morss, *Thinking Past Terror: Islamism and Critical Theory on the Left* (London: Verso, 2003), 2–3.

36. Buck-Morss, *Thinking Past Terror,* 10–12.

37. Buck-Morss, *Thinking Past Terror,* 15, 27, 42, 65, 106.

38. Michael Mann, *Incoherent Empire* (London: Verso, 2003), 159–60, 162–63, 185–86, 190. In addition to focusing on the defeat of international terrorism, Mann argues that the US "should denounce terrorism and state terrorism equally, and accompany this with its best conciliation services, backed by material incentives for those willing to compromise" (189).

39. Carol K. Winkler, *In the Name of Terrorism: Presidents on Political Violence in the Post-World War II Era* (Albany: State University of New York Press, 2006), 189, 191, 194–97, 212.

40. Winkler, *In the Name of Terrorism,* 198, 206–07. On the symbolism of striking the World Trade Towers and the Pentagon, see Stephen John Hartnett and Laura Ann Stengrim, *Globalization and Empire: The U.S. Invasion of Iraq, Free Markets, and the Twilight of Democracy* (Tuscaloosa: The University of Alabama Press, 2006), 7.

41. Winkler, *In the Name of Terrorism,* 190.

42. Terry Eagleton, *Holy Terror* (Oxford: Oxford University Press, 2005), 131, 134.

43. Hartnett and Stengrim, *Globalization and Empire*, 1.

44. Hartnett and Stengrim, *Globalization and Empire*, 15–16.

45. Hartnett and Stengrim, *Globalization and Empire*, 137–38, 118, 95–96, 11.

46. Quoted in Lewis Lapham, *The Theater of War In Which the Republic Becomes an Empire* (London: The New Press, 2002), 231.

47. Lapham, *Theater of War*, 231.

48. Danielle S. Allen, *Talking to Strangers: Anxieties of Citizenship since Brown v. Board of Education* (Chicago: The University of Chicago Press, 2004), xiii, xx–xxii.

49. Sheldon S. Wolin, *Politics and Vision: Continuity and Innovation in Western Political Thought*, Expanded Edition (Princeton, NJ: Princeton University Press, 2004), 592, 594, 605, 593.

50. Wolin, *Politics and Vision*, 592–93.

51. Wolin, *Politics and Vision*, 598, 603; see also 597, 601, 604.

52. Wolin, *Politics and Vision*, 605.

53. Allen, *Talking to Strangers*, 119, 129.

54. Allen, *Talking to Strangers*, 138.

55. Allen, *Talking to Strangers*, 140, 165; see also 127, 171.

56. Allen, *Talking to Strangers*, 142–44, 149.

57. Aristotle, *Rhetoric*, trans. W. Rhys Roberts (New York: The Modern Library, 1954), 92–93, 95–98 (Book II, Chapters 2–3); Allen, *Talking to Strangers*, 150.

58. Aristotle, 103–06 (Book II, Chapter 5).

59. Aristotle, 114 (Book II, Chapter 8); see also 100–03, 107–15 (Book II, Chapters 4, 6–8).

60. Allen, *Talking to Strangers*, 152–53, 157–58.

61. Ervand Abrahamian, "Empire Strikes Back: Iran in U.S. Sights," in Bruce Cumings, Ervand Abrahamian, and Moshe Ma'oz, *Inventing the Axis of Evil: The Truth about North Korea, Iran, and Syria* (New York: The New Press, 2004), 93–94.

62. Abrahamian, "Empire Strikes Back," 95, 105, 107; see also 96, 106.

63. Abrahamian, "Empire Strikes Back," 137, 143; see also138–39.

64. Abrahamian, "Empire Strikes Back," 108–09; see also 110–14.

65. Abrahamian, "Empire Strikes Back," 133–34; see also 116–20, 124, 126–27, 135, 141.

66. Abrahamian, "Empire Strikes Back," 147, 101; see also 98, 100.

67. Abrahamian, "Empire Strikes Back," 145; see also 140–41, 144.

68. Cady, *Warism*, 92, 77; see also 78, 81, 84–85, 87.

69. Cady, *Warism*, 84.

70. Howard Zinn, *Artists in Times of War* (New York: Seven Stories Press, 2003), 7–8, 11, 14, 17; see also 19.

71. Zinn, *Artists*, 22–23, 34; see also 31–33.

72. Zinn, *Artists*, 25–26.

73. Joseph Heller, *Catch-22* (1961; New York: Simon & Schuster, 1996).

74. Zinn, *Artists*, 28; see also 26. Kurt Vonnegut, *Slaughterhouse-Five or the Children's Crusade: A Duty-Dance with Death* (1969; New York: Dell, 1999).

75. Erich Maria Remarque, *All Quiet on the Western Front*, trans. A. W. Wheen (1929, New York: Fawcett Columbine, 1996); John Dos Passos, *Three Soldiers* (1921; Mineola, NY: Dover Publications, Inc., 2004); Pat Barker, *Regeneration* (1991; New

York: Penguin Books, 1993); Nick Arvin, *Articles of War* (New York: Doubleday, 2005); Charles Frazier, *Cold Mountain* (New York: Vintage Books, 1997); John Updike, *Terrorist* (New York: Alfred A. Knopf, 2006).

76. Francisco Goya, *The Disasters of War* (1863; New York: Dover Publications, 1967).

77. The People for Peace Project, *We Want Peace on Earth: A Guide for the Peace on Earth Movement*, rev. ed (Bloomington, Indiana: Authorhouse, 2003), 9–11; see also vii, 1, 3–4, 12–13, 15, 23–24, 27, 97, 107, 109–13.

78. The People for Peace Project, *Peace on Earth*, 15, 27, 111-12, viii; see also vii, 1.

79. The People for Peace Project, *Peace on Earth*, 15, 37; see also 25, 34–35, 49–54, 67–74, 82–83, 98–99, 102, 104–06, 115–19; Cady, 87–88.

80. The Dalai Lama interviewed by Scott Hunt in Scott A. Hunt, *The Future of Peace: On the Front Lines with the World's Great Peacemakers* (New York: Harper-SanFrancisco, 2002), 83, see also 3.

81. Thomas Merton, *New Seeds of Contemplation* (1961; Boston: Shambhala Publications, 2003), 209, 57, 79.

82. Merton, *New Seeds*, 126, 180, 98.

83. Hunt, *Future of Peace*, 7.

84. Hunt, *Future of Peace*, 28, 35, 39–40, 70.

85. Juana Alicia, "Picture Peace," in *Stop the Next War Now: Effective Responses to Violence and Terrorism*, ed. Medea Benjamin and Jodie Evans (Maui, Hawaii: Inner Ocean Publishing, 2005), 210–12.

86. Juana Alicia, "An Introduction to Juana Alicia," Juana Alicia: About, available online.

87. Liticia Hernandez, "Juana Alicia: A Muralist Takes a Global Look at the Spirit of Women," The National Organizers Alliance Newsletter, Issue 21, June 2004, available online; images of the murals are available on Juana Alicia's web site.

88. "The Great Wall of Los Angeles: A Mural of California History" available online; Amalia Mesa-Bains, "A World Without Walls: The Mural Tradition of Judith F. Baca," available online; Luciano Hernández, "Judith Francisca Baca," April 22, 1998, available online.

89. "The World Wall: A Vision of the Future without Fear," available online; Judith Baca, "Philosophy," available online.

90. Ira Chernus, *American Nonviolence: The History of an Idea* (Maryknoll, New York: Orbis Books 2004), 193, 195, 201. Chernus's chapter 13 is devoted to explicating Thich Nhat Hanh's ideas.

91. Thich Nhat Hanh, "The Miracle of Mindfulness," (1975) trans. Mobi Ho, in Thich Nhat Hanh, *The Wisdom of Thich Nhat Hanh* (New York: One Spirit, 2000), 45.

92. Thich Nhat Hanh, "Being Peace," (1987) ed. Arnold Kotler and trans. Mayumi Odi, in Naht Hahn, *Wisdom*, 155.

93. Nhat Hanh, "Miracle," 15, 27–28.

94. Nhat Hanh, "Being Peace," 161, 224, 230.

95. Nhat Hanh, "The Sun My Heart," (1988) in Nhat Hanh, *Wisdom*, 402.

96. Thich Nhat Hahn, "Touching Peace: Practicing the Art of Mindful Living," (1992), ed. Arnold Kotler and trans. Mayumi Oda, in Nhat Hanh, *Wisdom*, 543, 541, 421–23; see also Nhat Hahn, "Miracle," 45–47.

97. Nhat Hahn, "Being Peace," 229; also see 220, 222, 230.

98. Sumaya Farhat-Naser and Gila Svirsky, "We Refuse to be Enemies," in Benjamin and Evans, *Stop the Next War*, 97.

99. Rabia Roberts, "Pilgrimage for Peace," in Benjamin and Evans, *Stop the Next War*, 105–08.

100. C. J. Herington, "Introduction," in Aeschylus, *Persians*, trans. Janet Lembke and C. J. Herington (New York: Oxford University Press, 1981), 5.

101. Aeschylus, *Persians*, numbers in parentheses correspond to the lines in Lembke and Herington's translation.

102. Shirin Ebadi, "The Pillars of Peace," in Benjamin and Evans, *Stop the Next War*, 98.

103. Ebadi, "Pillars of Peace," 98–99.

104. Shirin Ebadi (with Azadeh Moaveni), *Iran Awakening: A Memoir of Revolution and Hope* (New York: Random House, 2006), 209–10, 213–14.

105. Ebadi, *Iran Awakening*, 214; also see 215.

106. Ali Gheissari and Vali Nasr, *Democracy in Iran: History and the Quest for Liberty* (New York: Oxford University Press, 2006), vi–vii.

107. Gheissari and Nasr, *Democracy in Iran*, 153, 158.

108. Gheissari and Nasr, *Democracy in Iran*, vi.

109. Kenneth M. Pollack, *The Persian Puzzle: The Conflict between Iran and America* (2004; New York: Random House, 2005), 172.

110. Pollack, *Persian Puzzle*, 146.

111. Pollack, *Persian Puzzle*, 181, 128.

112. Pollack, *Persian Puzzle*, 218.

113. Gheissari and Nasr, *Democracy in Iran*, 4, use the term "postfundamentalism" to describe contemporary, post-Khomeini Iran as it struggles with democratic reform.

114. Pollack, *Persian Puzzle*, 381.

115. Pollack, *Persian Puzzle*, 382.

116. Pollack, *Persian Puzzle*, 383, 379, 384, 381.

117. Pollack, *Persian Puzzle*, 389, 392–93.

118. Pollack, *Persian Puzzle*, 400–01, 405–06, 415–16.

119. Bloomington Peace Action Coalition, "Mission Statement," available online.

120. Bloomington Peace Action Coalition, "Core Message," available online.

121. Information on the PC (USA) United Nations Office and the National Council of Churches is available online.

122. The Peace Museum, "Home," available online.

123. The Peace Museum, "About Us: History," available online.

124. The Peace Museum, "Current Exhibits," available online.

125. Nicole Kauffman, "Artist Uses Languages of the World to Make a Universal Call for Peace," *Hoosier Times* (Bloomington, Indiana), July 9, 2006; see BloomingtonArts.info, "Illuminating Peace," available online, and BloomingtonArts.info, "Merridee LaMantia, Visual Artist," available online.

126. "Sample Resolution for the International Day of Peace, September 21," available online.

127. Governor Frank O'Bannon, "State of Indiana Proclamation of Peace Day," May 22, 2003, available online.

6

Making War Difficult

Conscience is an early casualty of war, as Norman Solomon concludes in his critical review of the propaganda techniques that have made war easy in present-day America. War is now nearly automatic. Presidents routinely have their way with the media and citizenry who acquiesce to a regimen of propaganda that manages political perceptions, manufactures a virtual consensus, and sets the national agenda.[1] Propaganda normalizes war, rendering it habitual, seemingly rational, and largely immune to challenge, especially in the beginning before the ugly consequences of the killing fields become too obvious to ignore entirely.

The proper "democratic role of citizens," though, "is not simply to observe and obey the exigencies of war," Solomon insists.[2] Citizenship in a democracy should be an active, conscious, and conscientious role of critical reflection, not a cynical or habitual acceptance of war's ubiquity or its inevitability in any given case. War habits are subject to change by constructive acts of democratic citizenship, or are they? Can a people's conscience be restored enough to make war less easy, less automatic, and more difficult to justify?

RESISTING THE HABIT OF WAR PROPAGANDA

Solomon aims to increase the public's awareness of propaganda techniques as a way of stimulating democratic participation, overcoming the "self-restraint" (or "tacit consent of the governed") that lubricates the machinery of war, and thus lifting the "fog of media war."[3] Yet, his enlightening account of the nation's war habits underscores just how bad those habits are and how deeply engrained in political culture they have become. Even as he challenges the validity of each premise in the propagandist's rationalization of contemporary warfare, Solomon charts a mindset so firmly established and so daunting that it discomfits the most dedicated peacemakers. These hardened public pieties etched deeply into sacred patriotic stone include dictums such as:

204

- America is a fair and noble superpower.
- Our leaders will do everything they can to avoid war.
- This guy [the enemy] is a modern-day Hitler.
- This [war] is about human rights.
- This [war] is not at all about oil or corporate profits.
- They are the aggressors, not us.
- If this war is wrong, Congress will stop it.
- Opposing the war means siding with the enemy.
- The Pentagon fights wars as humanely as possible.
- Our soldiers are heroes, theirs are inhuman.

This is the largely unquestioned logic by which we make people in "faraway places" all around the globe—people who are "not so different from us" in their basic humanity—seem so deserving of our militant fury.[4]

Indeed, militarism has become the mindset of American empire—the mindset, Andrew Bacevich argues, that seduces Americans to support a state of warfare. America has adopted the outlook of a security state, of an empire projecting its power worldwide rather than a republic defending itself from foreign attack. The American people in an age of empire have become persuaded that their "safety and salvation lies with the sword." The citizen army has become a professional "imperial army." America's "global military supremacy" has become central to its "national identity." International problems are seen first and foremost as "military problems," and military means are believed to be the way to reshape the world consistent with American values and the nation's self-professed utopian ends, which are perceived in turn as "universal truths." The very aesthetic of war is changing from an image of ugly, wasteful, and degrading brutality to a new, twenty-first century image of high-tech warfare as a smart, surgical spectacle—a virtual spectator sport. In Bacevich's blunt and considered assessment, contemporary America has fallen prey to militarism—romanticizing soldiers, fostering nostalgia for military ideals, and adopting military power as the measure of national greatness—to "a degree without precedent in US history."[5]

The attitude of militarism that is running rampant in America, Bacevich maintains, is "unlikely to disappear anytime soon" because, even though it is unprecedented in its current intensity, it has deep roots in the nation's past and, consistent with Michael Sherry's observation, has reshaped American politics, foreign policy, economics, social relations, and general culture over the past half-century so much that it permeates all domains of life. The terrorist attacks of 9/11 gave "added impetus to already existing tendencies"; America became more itself rather than something different after 9/11, increasingly adopting a militaristic ethos with broad support and too little dissent from mainstream political leaders and the general public. The present-day "infatuation with military power" is a bipartisan project and the handiwork of multiple and disparate groups of opinion leaders. Moreover, it has developed over the last several decades "in full view and with considerable popular approval." Thus, Bacevich argues, "society at large . . . [cannot] abdicate responsibility for what has come to pass," and what has come to pass is systemic, broad-based, and deeply ingrained in political culture rather than simply the outcome of a particular presidential election, the fault of an individual president, or the scheming of a single set of presidential advisors.[6] A late turning of public opinion in the fall elections of 2006 against a stymied occupation of Iraq, we might conclude, reflects impatience with a particular war, not a basic transformation of the war culture.

The image of an imperial army fighting continuous wars of empire does not inspire confidence that an ingrained system of militarism can be changed, habits of war broken, the conscience of a nation restored, or a culture of peace established. Indeed, political theorists Michael Hardt and Antonio Negri maintain that contemporary imperial warfare is perpetual because it functions to sustain the status-quo network of global power relations. War, they argue, is inevitable in a condition of "Empire" and constant as "an instrument of rule." It is the "general matrix for all relations of power and techniques of domination," a "form of rule" for controlling populations and shaping "all aspects of social life." Imperial war today regulates life in general and legitimizes itself in the process by propagandizing "the constant presence of an enemy and the threat of disorder." The "presence of the enemy," they note, "demonstrates the need for security."[7] The imagined presence of an enemy is crucial to the system and motive of war.

Making evil enemies present by means of dehumanizing propaganda— propaganda that deifies the US as it demonizes the nation's adversaries—is a destructive ritual of redemption by vicarious sacrifice. It produces the heightened perception of threat and intensified sense of national insecurity that motivates and excuses a call to arms. Evil, as in the image of an enemy evil-doer, is the ultimate symbol of bedlam, babble, and disarray—the Biblical monster of chaos. In a condition of empire and imperial warfare, then, the routine rationalization for resorting to violence is to preserve global order against supposedly evil forces of disorder. This "abuse of evil"—this "discourse of good and evil [that] lacks nuance, subtlety, and judicious discrimination"—Richard Bernstein insists is "extremely dangerous in a complex and precarious world" because it stifles thinking instead of prompting us to question and think.[8] For this purpose, war rules.

Yet, resisting the rule of war is possible, according to Hardt and Negri, despite the dominant mindset of militarism in a controlling paradigm of empire that bases politics on coercion and violence. Indeed, resisting war is "the most important task for resistance today." They contend it is reasonable to imagine, under emerging conditions of desire for democracy, peace, and justice, that a multitude of ordinary people might contest militarism through a multiplicity of distributed networks of democratic collaboration. That is, individuals intersecting with one another in multiple ways to create matrices of cooperation and communication—what Hardt and Negri call "singularities" acting in common with deference to their differences and without reduction to a "unity"—may well erode the order of Empire to achieve a "peaceful life in common." The need for peace corresponds with the need for enriched democracy to overcome "the global state of war." To be sure, "the only democracy that makes sense today is one that poses peace as its highest value."[9]

Consistent with Hardt and Negri and for the purpose of working toward a peacebuilding culture, democracy is usefully understood as a practice of collective self-rule constituted by matrices of individuals cooperating and communicating with one another at multiple points of intersection to produce fair and equitable social relations within and against a recalcitrant system of empire, a system of empire that relies on incessant violence and legitimizing images of evildoers to maintain status-quo relations of global power. Democracy is expressed most directly, acutely, and cogently in collaborative acts of resistance to enemy-making discourses. Surely, as a guiding model for contesting the mindset of militarism, the vision of resisting dehumanizing propaganda by cultivating matrices of democratic dissent makes the prospect of building peace and inhibiting war more plausible over the long haul and less daunting in immediate circumstances.

Understood as constructive democratic resistance, dissent evokes the more judicious and relatively sustainable expectation that acts of peacebuilding can be augmented collectively and habits of war attenuated over time. Dissent cultivates democratic relations and coordinated resistance from the ground up by producing humanizing acts of identification, that is, acts of communication and coordination that articulate practical points of intersection without effacing the distinguishing identities, cultures, religions, or nationalities of cooperating parties. Constructing intersecting points—points to be held in common by those who would oppose the war regime—is a bridging action rather than a fusing process. It is not an attempt to eliminate pluralism, diminish defining differences, or achieve a structured unity in which relative merit is determined, for example, by how white or rich or Christian or Western or American a given category of people is perceived to be. Thus, peacebuilding activism and dissent from war can be imagined as a sustained boundary-spanning project of decentralized and overlapping networks of democratic resistance to the habit of dehumanizing propaganda.

Just as society is constituted in habit, habit itself is subject to reproduction and revision, for good or ill, by acts of communication.[10] In negative acts of reproduction, communication habituates society to war through a normalizing regimen of propaganda. War propaganda is ubiquitous and concealed in a perceptual fog of supposed objectivity that reduces much of the common humanity to a mere cipher of evil and inferiority. To be sure, war is "unimaginable without the galvanizing agency of propaganda" to channel popular sentiment by giving it an enemy. In a "Symbolic State" preoccupied with imagery, propaganda is about enemy-making. Thus, Nicholas Jackson O'Shaughnessy concludes, it is a "fulcrum" of history, not some peripheral aspect or epiphenomenon of underlying social formations. As such, it excites a voracious appetite to demonize, to summon up "the imagery of the dehumanised enemy" absent all reference to a common humanity in order to establish a mindset for killing. Creating enemies by expressions of contempt for a scapegoat is the easy way to make war easy.[11]

Yet, the easy habit of enemy-making is susceptible to resistance. It can be inhibited by countervailing expressions of identification and rites of humanization—not easily, quickly, completely, or permanently, but enough to make war less automatic and more accountable to democratic practices. No path to addressing the problem of war is more direct than countering dehumanizing propaganda with humanizing, peacebuilding discourses of identification to coordinate and cooperate with a common humanity across political barriers.

Developing the practice of humanizing discourse is a positive response to war propaganda, a way of constructively addressing harmful motives of fear and arrogance provoked by recurring dramas of national insecurity and redemption via vicarious sacrifice. Although fear is an organic process, an experience of the body, it is prompted and shaped in public discourse. As Joanna Bourke observes, "Shifts in the way people narrate fear alter their subjective experience"—how one speaks of fear changes the "*sensation* of fear." Bourke even postulates that there is a language of fear complete with narrative structures, "including genre, syntax, form, order and vocabulary." Fear is just so "*constituted*," she emphasizes, and is thus substantially a matter of "social *construction*." As such, "it has become the emotion through which public life is administered" under a specter of "the Terrorist," which is an object of fear in the post-9/11 world "equivalent to the plague of earlier times or the Satan of religion." Moreover, other strong emotions in the age of terror such as "anger, disgust, hatred and horror all contain elements of fear," especially fear of the "Terrorist Monster."[12]

The international terrorist monster—otherwise identified as Islam, the Muslim or, even more broadly, the Arab—is a permutation in post-Cold War times of the earlier theme of the "Red Menace of World Communism." The dramatic attack of 9/11 on the twin towers of US corporate power served as a declaration of war that brought Americans together through a shared perception of threat. In Bourke's view, being able to identify the enemy as an outsider brought a kind of relief to the nation, the relief of marking the enemy's clear otherness as that of the foreign Islamic fundamentalist.[13] This permutation in the image of the ubiquitous enemy was made effortless by the historical representation of Arabs as evil villains in popular media. In more than 900 English-language films featuring Arabs over the previous century and prior to 9/11, according to Jack Shaheen, Arabs had been portrayed almost always as "brutal, heartless, uncivilized, religious fanatics and money-mad cultural 'others' bent on terrorizing civilized westerners, especially Christians and Jews."[14]

The habit of channeling fear into demonizing images of an enemy serves the purposes of a broad spectrum of social actors, including powerful economic interest groups as well as "theologians, politicians, the media, physicians and the psychological services," all with a stake in creating and sustaining fear "while promising to eradicate it."[15] The fear of terrorism, Cory Robin concurs, is "orchestrated and manipulated by the powerful," who conjure "fantastic enemies in order to preserve their rule" with assistance not only from collaborators but also from "bystanders who do nothing to protest fear's repressive hold." Political fear is a political tool so deeply embedded in American public culture that it no longer seems aberrant, even as it routinely distorts a real threat of terror through the lens of political opportunism, thus making a mockery of the liberal-democratic principles of freedom and equality.[16]

If Joost Meerloo is correct, this amounts to an unhealthy social psychology of projecting onto the scapegoat characteristics we most despise and wish not to confront in ourselves.[17] Fear can be internally debilitating but also can be channeled outward to become destructive, transforming fright into an impulse to fight. Political fear conjured in ugly metaphors of terror and personified in the scary figure of the Muslim scapegoat promotes militarism and suppresses recognition of contributing factors such as the dark history of imperialism and US support for repressive regimes in the Middle East. The word "terrorist," Bourke notes, was sufficiently "frightening in itself that it deflected attention from the serious consideration of foreign policy and incursions into civil liberties at home."[18]

Yet, even under the tyrannizing influence of discourses of fear, the human imagination can be remarkably resilient. Throughout Bourke's extended account of the cultural history of fear, traumatized people who proved capable of responding constructively to terror did so by seeking answers to the basic question of what makes all of us human.[19] Humanizing ourselves as well as our adversaries reduces the need for a scapegoat and thus for redemption by vicarious sacrifice. Locating a common humanity among adversaries can help to see beyond the narrow lens of victim and victimizer, or at least not to view matters solely in the language of victimization, and thus can encourage us to take a closer look at options other than a resort to deadly force in responding to the problems and deep divisions manifested as terrorism.

Similarly, resisting the dehumanizing habits of war propaganda can help to constrain the corrosive influence of moralistic intolerance and arrogance in the excessive application of America's vast military power. The living legacy of American exceptionalism, as Seymour Lipset observes, is "a double-edged sword." Americans subscribe to a moralistic creed that insists they are opposed to evil in their foreign relations and "on God's side against Satan" in matters of warfare.[20] America is the one essential nation above all others, the beacon and exemplar of standards that no other country can match. As one of the nation's founding myths and, Michael Hirsh notes, the "wellspring" of the current imperialist war against terrorism, exceptionalism stands for remaking the world in America's image.[21]

In this self-indulgent application of the American Creed, according to Lipset, a commitment to the welfare of the wider community is undermined by an emphasis on individualism that promotes "a virulent strain of greedy behavior." Patriotism is based on an ideology of Americanism—rooted in an ideological commitment to a conservative-liberal creed of laissez-faire individualism and liberty—to the extent that anyone who rejects "American" values is deemed un-American. American pride of patriotism is an expression of national exceptionalism founded firmly on the belief that the United States is a country superior to all others.[22]

Yet, paradoxically, a complex of values also exists within this same ideology of moral and material superiority, as Lipset notes, which has fostered "principled opposition to wars."[23] A formative Protestant influence on US political culture has made opposition to war historically no less moralistic than pro-war rhetoric. Both sides in the American Civil War, including the initially nonviolent advocates of abolitionism, tended to view the other as satanic. Whether the cause is to eliminate slavery, make the world safe for democracy, or defeat totalitarianism and terrorism, whether it is a pro-war or an anti-war position, Americans easily default to an uncompromising attitude of moral superiority to which they expect their enemies to surrender unconditionally. "Moralism" on either side of the issue of war, in Lipset's words, "is as American as apple pie."[24]

Arrogant, moralistic utopianism of this kind, whether one is crusading for war or for peace, routinely reduces to dehumanizing habits of discourse that perpetuate the cycle of victimization and sustain an attitude of warism. Perhaps Joseph Heller's Captain Yossarian, who was determined in the end to escape insane orders mixed with disingenuous patriotic admonitions to fly ever more bombing missions over civilian targets, expressed as well as any seriously comic character the violence inherent to chronic, self-perpetuating rituals of blame and counter-blame. While "going absent without official leave," Yossarian thought to himself that "someone had to do something sometime. Every victim was a culprit, every culprit a victim, and somebody had to stand up sometime to try to break the lousy chain of inherited habit that was imperiling them all."[25]

CULTIVATING AN ATTITUDE OF RECONCILIATION

Indeed, the pragmatic and prudent aim of a democratizing practice of dissent from war—a practice that would articulate compensatory points of identification between parties in conflict in order to cultivate a custom of reconciliation—is to break the chain of interchangeable culprits and victims, resist the pull of war propaganda without resorting to reciprocal habits of recrimination, overcome the dehumanizing consequences of fear, and moderate the arrogance of self-righteous indulgence, which is the dark side of American exceptionalism. Although the American creed of exceptionalism establishes unreachable, utopian ideals that set in motion the cycle of pride, guilt, and redemption via the sacrifice of scapegoats, it is also the case that demonizing, fear-inducing discourses of victimization can produce a backlash of pride and guilt. The ritual of guilt and redemption by scapegoat is not simply a linear chain of cause and effect but instead one of reciprocal, back and forth influence. Conjuring images of satanic enemies can stimulate fear, just as falling inevitably short of unrealistic expectations can generate guilt, both of which prompt a collective desire to sacrifice the scapegoat. Likewise, articulating humanizing points of identification to offset war propaganda's enemy-making stereotypes can promote an alternative, constructive mode of redemption by reducing guilt, hate, and fear instead of exciting such anxieties and then offloading them onto the back of a scapegoat.

Redemption by reconciliation, rather than by rituals of victimization, is therefore the standard by which to measure peacebuilding dissent from war. Cultivating a social attitude of reconciliation is perhaps the single most important and immediately compelling task for war dissenters to undertake if they aim to bolster the conscience of the nation. Might the republic that has lost its way and embraced the militarist attitude of an imperial colossus be redeemed more realistically by increased identification with, rather than total alienation from and attempted domination over, a recalcitrant world of adversaries and rivals? What better test of the productive possibilities of dissent exists than resisting the overwrought and tyrannizing image of Islamic terrorism that justifies an ill-defined and unlimited state of imperial warfare? Is it possible to imagine the humanity of such an enemy? Can Americans even conceive of a discourse of reconciliation with the Islamic World?

Especially when the ugly consequences of the killing fields in Iraq become too unsightly to ignore, the fighting too interminable to experience as sheer spectacle, the specter of another military and moral quagmire too palpable to rationalize with political clichés, and the presence of a viable exit strategy too faint to detect, one might expect the question of reconciliation with Islam to command some consideration, both as a moral alternative to the dehumanizing mentality of militarism and as a feasible option to the futility of wars of empire. One might hope for a custom of forethought someday to prevent such an unwise resort to arms as the invasion and occupation of Iraq, but the development of a predisposition to conscience and a sensible constraint of rising consciousness may depend on our ability to learn from mistakes when they happen and to make reasonable corrections along the way so that we might navigate a middle course between the Scylla of Pyrrhic victory and the Charybdis of ignoble defeat. Peacebuilding seeks a way past the polarity of victory and defeat.

Accordingly, for those who would seek the way of reconciliation, Fawaz Gerges' exploration of Muslim militancy is suggestive of plausible correctives to the stock image of a crazed Islamic monster. Gerges brings to his study a perspective informed by the experience of being raised a Christian among Muslims in Lebanon, the vocation of an ABC and NPR news analyst, and the acumen of a professor of Middle Eastern Studies. His purpose in *Journey of the Jihadist* is to dispel the myth that Islam embraces a "culture of death" and to discount "the simplistic notion that all Muslims and all Arabs speak with one voice—a voice baying for bloodshed in the name of religion."[26]

Gerges confronts this widespread stereotype with a "determination to present the human dimensions and motivations of the jihadist movement" and thereby challenges the tendency in the West to demonize Muslims by misrepresenting them as the "New Barbarians" who threaten Western civilization. Contrary to the stereotype of the Islamic barbarian, he argues, "Muslim piety does not incubate radicals and terrorists," and thus religious fervor should not be conflated with militancy. Gerges' bold claim is that neither mainstream Muslims nor jihadists are beasts or barbarians; there is no Islamic cult of death; Islam and Islamists, in the concluding words of Egyptian jihadist Kamal el-Said Habib, are "full of humanity."[27]

To uncover this hidden store of humanity, Gerges disassembles the muddled notion of Islam that engenders "Islamophobia" in the West. As he observes:

> The Western media still perpetuate the myth that the [9/11] attacks were
> widely embraced by the ummah [the worldwide Islamic community], that

the nineteen suicide bombers reflected the amorality of Muslim political culture as a whole. Suicide bombings and beheadings sustain this myth and rekindle deep Islamophobic tendencies.

Muslims are "misrepresented and misunderstood" in this way. They are perceived indiscriminately in the US as "carriers of a plague of nihilism" despite the fact, he maintains, that there is "a wide spectrum of Muslim voices," even among Islamist political activists.[28]

The foundation of Muslim political community in the Middle East consists of a mainstream electorate that has turned increasingly to religion for spiritual sustenance as it has become disaffected with the relentless Westernization of Arab society and the insidious corruption and oppression of secular rulers—dictators whose power is the modern legacy of earlier British and French colonialism. Disaffected Muslim voters as a whole are neither radical nor fundamentalist Islamists. Their political support goes more and more to moderate Islamists, who have used religion as a tool of political mobilization with the aim of establishing Islamic governments consistent with Quranic law (sharia).[29]

Islamists in overwhelming numbers—perhaps 95 percent or more—are nonviolent. They are the mainstream of religious political activists who "accept the rules of the political game, embrace democratic principles, and oppose violence." They want moderate, not radical governance, but a form of democratic governance that reflects their community's own identity, traditions, and values—not a replica of Western democracy. Militant Islamists and jihadists, on the contrary, have been willing "to use all means at their disposal, including terrorism, to overthrow the existing secular order and replace it with a theocratic one." Mainstream Muslims in the Middle East—including pious middle-class Muslims, everyday citizens, and most religious political activists—are opposed to militancy and "repelled by the indiscriminate terrorist methods." Thus, there is "little love lost" between the moderate majority of "pious Muslims" and the small militant vanguard of radical Islamist-jihadist "soldiers of God."[30]

Gerges focuses his study on the small minority of militant Islamists and jihadists—the hardcore—rather than the considerable majority of nonviolent Islamists or the moderate mainstream of the Muslim electorate, which is neither fundamentalist nor inclined to violence. Drawing on interviews with scores of radicals about their attitudes toward government and the use of violence at home and abroad, Gerges probes jihadist religious rhetoric to comprehend its shifting political aims and to discern an emerging belief among even radicals that a moral society must evolve from the bottom up rather than be imposed from the top down by revolutionary means. This is the human dimension of Islam's most radical voice that Gerges is determined to impart to his readers. This emerging belief, he argues, is what we must come to understand about "the moral and spiritual mission that drives today's jihadists" if we are not to "remain forever baffled at the 'irrationality' of their speech and the 'insanity' of their actions."[31]

Kamal, a key Egyptian figure in the startup of the jihadist movement, is taken by Gerges as a barometer of the fluctuating mindset among militant Islamists. His views were evolving even throughout the years of his several interviews with Gerges. He no longer thought Israel should be destroyed. He acknowledged the mistakes he and his generation of jihadists had made and recognized that their violent methods had repelled the Egyptian public. Constructing an authoritarian Islamic state in Egypt or elsewhere would have been a "terribly naïve" mistake, he opined, "that did not appreciate the complexities of society and the requirements of social and political change." The lesson he would draw from his generation of jihadists is that they had "relied too much on muscle and not enough on political persuasion and mobilization." He was no longer enamored of armed resistance to pro-Western secular rulers, even as he retained the goal of establishing an Islamic state, hopefully by nonviolent political means. Moreover, he now recognized that there were different currents of opinion within the US, not just a monolithic commitment to dominating the Middle East, and he expressed a desire "to meet America halfway."[32]

The drift of Kamal's thinking was consistent with that of other militant Islamists. Thus, Osama bin Laden had miscalculated when he thought that the 9/11 attack on the US would attract local jihadists into the fold of global jihad. Abau al-Walid al-Masri, a senior Al Qaeda member who broke with bin Laden after September 11, thought the attack on the US was a calamity for the jihadist cause. His criticism, Gerges reports, was "echoed by others, including the Egyptian al-Jama'a al-Islamiya," who had led more than ten times the number of fighters than the total of Al Qaeda's membership at its peak but now believed there was no necessary clash of cultures between Islam and the West. Engagement, mutual respect, and peaceful coexistence were the reasonable alternatives to war with the US. Instead of more mayhem, the US should adopt a just foreign policy in the Middle East, and Muslim states should become more democratic. These were the views of "the founding fathers of a major wing of the jihadist movement," Gerges reports, as well as the majority of other Islamist leaders who "condemned Al Qaeda's internationalization of jihad." Indeed, "the general realignment within the jihadist family [had] turned decidedly against the global jihad."[33]

The US invasion and occupation of Iraq confounded this emerging realignment of opinion within Islamist circles, however. The American incursion was widely perceived as a new crusade, an occupation of Islam with the goal of restructuring Muslim society. It was a war on Islam's most sacred values—indeed, its very identity. The occupation of a Muslim country revealed the war on terror to be a war on Islam, observed a distraught, reradicalized Kamal. Islamists, he concluded, were left with "no choice but to defend ourselves and our faith." The war on Iraq transformed Al Qaeda into a decentralized umbrella network of jihadist forces loosely linked together in a common struggle against the American "crusaders" and "imperialists." The broad perception of an American global war on Islam, symbolized by the occupation of Iraq, had given undue prominence to terror tactics and to what would otherwise have remained, even among radical Islamists, a marginalized Al Qaeda. Thus, the evolution of radical Islamist and jihadist opinion toward dialogue with the West, which was occurring before the invasion of Iraq, suffered a serious setback that, Kamal believed, could only be reversed by the American people reclaiming "their values of tolerance and respect for the rule of law," bringing an end to "the new crusade against Muslims," and acknowledging "the common ties that bind us and our shared humanity."[34]

Not everyone, including every expert on the Middle East, chooses to affirm signs of a shared humanity or to give credence to a quest for reconciliation. Fouad Ajami, also a professor of Middle East Studies who was born in Lebanon and served as consultant and contributor to major US media, including CBS and *U.S. News & World Report*, has written appreciatively of the US war in Iraq, calling it a "legitimate" response to "a deep American frustration" with an entrenched and dominant "culture of terrorism" in Arab lands. The war, he believed, was a noble, if chastened attempt to subdue the "malignancies" of the Arab world, a much needed but unappreciated "stranger's gift" to a benighted Middle East. Although there was no proof of Iraq's involvement in 9/11 or of operational links between Saddam Hussein's regime and Al Qaeda, Ajami avers, no satisfaction could be had simply by "decapitating the Taliban regime" in the minor outpost of Afghanistan, not after the American psyche had been shattered by nineteen young Islamist men. "Iraq offered a way, geographically and psychologically, into the Arab world," a "more appropriate battleground" where there were "targets aplenty" for the war on terror. Since there were no weapons of mass destruction to be found in Iraq, the war rationale morphed into "a campaign for the wider reform of the Arab world," a determination to "root out Arab malignancies," specifically Islamist radicalism. "Pax Americana" would be imposed by the architects of the "American imperium" on an Arab world that could not contain its terrorism. The US would bestow democracy and prosperity to "wean" the region from "the false temptations of Arab radicalism," the specter of theocracy, and the reign of Islamist violence. No apologies were needed for America's motives or its "foreign presence" in an Arab land and culture that "had turned its back on political reason."[35]

Thus, we might conclude from Ajami's narrative that the American war in Iraq was a war of choice and an act of redemption by vicarious sacrifice, that is, a choice to seek redemption by sacrificing an evil dictator and bestowing on his blighted land the gift of liberty and democracy in order to reaffirm America's exceptional virtue. Yet, Ajami argued, the brutal, sectarian Arab world was not ready to receive the foreigner's gift of even "a modicum of liberty." The fall of Baghdad became a symbol of invasion, which equated Americans with the Mongols of 1258. The US was perceived as an occupier, not a liberator, who coveted Iraq's oil and defiled Islam. "Despotism, sectarianism, antimodernism, willful refusal to name things for what they are," Ajami insisted, were "the malignancies of Arab politics." These dysfunctional core beliefs and "atavistic loyalties" nourished a dense "thicket" of Arab "victimology and wrath" that was beyond American penetration or influence. American willpower was confounded by the law of Arab gravity.[36]

The animus of dark "sectarian attachments" was the real story behind the ruse of pan-Arabism, according to Ajami. In Iraq, the jihadist insurgency was the convenient tool of deposed Sunni Arabs who would deny Iraqi Shiites a theocratic state and Kurds federal autonomy. This "heavy legacy of sectarianism" translated into a reflexive anti-Americanism. The defense of Islam was mere cover for the return of minority Sunni rule in Iraq. No American concessions to the idea of pan-Arabism could diminish the sectarian malignancy haunting Middle Eastern political culture.[37]

Whereas a sense of futility pervades Ajami's analysis of Arab animus and recalcitrance confronting America's war of redemption and its imperial presence in Iraq, a possibility of reconciliation is suggested by Gerges' investigation of evolving attitudes among Islamic radicals. Ajami defaults to a dehumanizing image of chronic sectarian malignancy that is unlikely to change in the foreseeable future, even under the pressure of military force. Gerges sketches the humanizing theme of an emerging, moderating commitment to nonviolence among purposeful, hardcore Islamists, a development stymied by the American occupation of Iraq. Defense of the Islamic homeland took priority over participating in the political process or meeting US and Arab secular authority halfway. Even the weakened appeal of global jihad rebounded from its setback in Afghanistan, reinventing itself in a more decentralized and virulent form after the US invasion of Iraq. Thus, it would seem that America's determination to remake and reform the Middle East by force of arms and according to its own design required a demonizing image of Islamist global terrorists in order to avoid facing up to the possibilities of reconciliation and the implications of militarism in the service of empire.

Indeed, cultivating a peacebuilding attitude of reconciliation to resist the seductive call to arms requires coming to terms with imperial America, both by acknowledging the existence of empire and by holding imperialism accountable to the conscience of a nation that is politically and culturally self-identified as Christian. Yet, as historian Niall Ferguson demonstrates, the US suffers from a long-term condition of "imperial denial." It "has always been, functionally if not self-consciously, an empire"—an unspoken empire precisely because most Americans are so uneasy about acknowledging or analyzing their country's imperial eminence. No wonder Americans were reluctant to "grasp that occupying and trying to transform Iraq . . . was a quintessentially imperial undertaking." The time for denial has passed, Ferguson suggests, and now the best therapy may be "to determine the precise nature of this empire."[38]

The crux of the problem, in Ferguson's view, is that Americans "lack the imperial cast of mind" needed to run the empire they have acquired. The world needs the American empire, he believes, to maintain international order, deal with global threats such as epidemics and terrorism, depose tyrants, halt local wars, and minister to economic woes in countries incapable of self-correction. This is the proper and necessary work of a "liberal empire," in his view. No other country has military power and economic influence with sufficient reach to fulfill this role. America has proved it has the "guts" to declare a global war on terrorism, but does it have the "grit" to finish what it has started in Afghanistan and Iraq? That is Ferguson's ultimate worry about America's "attention deficit" and his view of the requirements of imperial peacekeeping.[39]

By this account, war is the price of empire. Indeed, historians Fred Anderson and Andrew Cayton argue that Americans have defined themselves throughout their history by fighting imperial wars.[40] If militarism is the reality of empire and empire is the reality of America's global standing and role, must Americans sacrifice and/or rationalize away their collective Christian conscience, broadly speaking, or can they hold empire accountable to an ethic of nonviolence and an attitude of reconciliation? Can Christianity be saved from "reckless militarism" and empire, as Jack Nelson-Pallmeyer asks, especially when "the reality of violence at the heart of the US Empire is buried beneath rhetorical avalanches with religious overtones that cover imperial ambitions"? Can religion help to make war strange and difficult to support rather than normal and easy? Just as religion is made by many to contribute to fear, hatred, and violence, can it be made by others to serve the ends of peacebuilding in a nation where four-fifths of adults consider themselves to be Christians, or must America abandon empire for the sake of peace and Christian principles?[41]

Certainly, as Nelson-Pallmeyer underscores, the biblical tradition of nonviolence and reconciliation has been routinely marginalized to make Christianity into empire's "willing servant":

All Christianity had to do to become a servant of the U.S. Empire was to stress certain biblical themes over others and to interpret and apply them on behalf of imperial objectives. The Bible offers a rich and deep reservoir of diverse and incompatible ideas about God and faith from which to choose. Useful themes adaptable to U.S. Empire include the idea of a particular people being chosen by God; the notion that God works through an exceptional nation to accomplish divine purposes; *the association of salvation with defeat of enemies*; the definition of divine and human power as superior violence; the belief that historical prominence is a sign of God's blessing; and the use of sharp dichotomies such as good versus evil to define the nature of the cosmos, earthly life, and spiritual struggle. [Emphasis added.]

This is the prevailing view that legitimizes violence as an instrument of national security and divine mission. It is the view, in particular, that redemption is achieved by sacrificing evil enemies. The alternative to a vision of atonement by vicarious sacrifice is, of course, the Christian teaching of reconciliation with one's enemies in order to break the spiral of violence one modest step at a time, much like planting tiny mustard seeds of dissent from war to grow and multiply like weeds in the imperial garden of warfare.[42]

Tolstoy insists that "only humility stops everything that builds obstacles in the way of peace for all."[43] The rule of war cannot be overthrown in one great heroic thrust. Americans cannot suddenly escape from empire by retreating to the lost republic, which is the path to peace and Christianity's ultimate salvation envisioned by Nelson-Pallmeyer. Instead, the nation's Christian-centric conscience must be tested within the context of empire as a foundation of resistance to war, specifically as an alternative to the "myth of redemptive violence."[44] This myth is primal and thus basic to the nation's sense of reality. It is a recurring story of good and evil in which an evildoer's savagery necessitates the righteous, redemptive violence of a pious people. It is a dehumanizing narrative that "has provided the rationale for every war in the political history of the United States" and that has deluded the nation into thinking that violence is the solution to the problem of evil.[45] It is a myth that makes war easy by making ourselves hard to recognize in the image of our enemies.

Yet, humility and reconciliation with one's enemies, John Roth rightly insists, is the very heart of Christian faith expressed in the Hebrew Bible and the New Testament. People of Christian faith are called "to listen with care and empathy and to preserve the dignity of others" in an attempt to achieve "a deeper understanding of the worldview" of a stranger and adversary.[46] Identifying with another, including an enemy, enough to grasp the stranger's perspective, needs, and aspirations, instead of engaging in self-righteous judgment of evildoers, is an act of understanding that requires sustained resistance to stereotypes.[47]

There is much more that can be said about the implications of a country's Judeo-Christian ethos, writ broadly within the larger political culture. Perhaps it is enough for present purposes, and to avoid splitting theological hairs, to acknowledge the tension that necessarily exists between adhering to such an ethos and fighting wars of empire. Clearly, this tension has been reduced at great cost by rationalizing "just wars," and it can be increased by upholding an absolute principle of pacifism.[48] Yet, the tension persists in some degree, and determining the morality or immorality of any given war should never be a simple matter of choosing between good and evil. "Responsible decisions," Duane Cady confirms, "involve the investment of time and energy to understand sources of conflict."[49] War propaganda, to the contrary, urges society to endorse war with a minimum of reflection. Operating on simplistic stereotypes is irresponsible decision-making, and endorsing a resort to arms, with all its horrific consequences, is always a moral compromise at best and thus always a defeat, in some serious measure, of the conscience of the nation, unless we just succumb completely to warism.

Accordingly, the tactics of democratic dissent from wars of empire, in order to transcend the narrow framework of good versus evil to which the political culture so readily defaults and thus makes war so easy to choose, must contribute variously, consistently, and persistently to a strategy of humanizing the parties in conflict. Taking this path to reconciliation is an ethical act of responsible citizenship. Moreover, it is a feasible act of political communication by everyday citizens in the degree to which they adhere to the democratic idiom of consubstantial rivalry, which involves dissenting (at a sharp but oblique angle) from dehumanizing stereotypes through a double gesture of nonconforming solidarity—a double gesture that balances the sharp edge of criticism with a reassuring embrace of society's redeeming values. This is an act of citizenship that can be expressed constructively in small and large ways by contesting language that demonizes rather than participating in rituals of reciprocal recrimination, by fostering the humanizing language of political friendship, by endorsing a positive, for-peace perspective, and by apprehending the adversary's perspective. These are personal, mindful, and social acts of conscience and reconciliation that are amplified as they reverberate throughout the larger peacebuilding community. Together, they can weave an intricate web of constructive human relationships against the negative pull of enemy-making propaganda and the deadly myth of redemptive violence.

Dissent, in a state of empire and for the purpose of making war appropriately difficult by humanizing adversaries, is a quintessentially democratic practice. It would hold imperialism accountable to an American ideal of collective self-rule and thus balance the protection of liberty with the pursuit of equality. Empire does not naturally incline to a robust practice of democracy.

Indeed, the prevailing formulation of American empire purports to spread democracy by force of arms as a formula for achieving perpetual and universal peace.[50] The White House's *National Security Strategy of the United States of America* of 2002 removed any doubt that the American colossus could strike preventatively anywhere it perceived danger or the possibility of danger, with or without the benefit of allies or the approval of international organizations. It would allow no nation or combination of nations to challenge its military superiority or to hold it legally accountable for its weapons of choice.[51] Can a truly democratic people accede to the militaristic vision of empire that has been advanced so blatantly by executive authority? Wouldn't it be in America's best interest, asks Robert Bellah, to constrain the imperial principle of rule by force with the democratic value of consent by the governed?[52]

What might it mean to democratize US political culture by fostering dissent under the prevailing condition of empire? To make peacebuilding dissent from war an everyday act of the many, not just the heroic act of the few or of one great leader?[53] To make it a conscientious act of resistance to war culture, the outcome of which cannot be fully anticipated or strictly rendered in causal terms? To make it a perennial act of reconciliation that transcends national borders? To make it a democratic act of collective conscience, guided by a humanizing strategy of communication as an alternative or corrective to redemptive violence?

It would mean, at a minimum, adopting a global perspective more conducive to a dialogue of cultures.[54] A "reglobalization" of Christianity, Michael Budde observes, would serve as an obstacle to militarism in the service of narrow national ambition because "nationalism, especially when armed and on the march, ought [to] be seen as a sectarian heresy in conflict with the universality of the Christian gospel."[55] American Christians, Stephen Chapman adds, need to embrace "a nonmessianic vision of nationhood that stresses openness instead of jingoistic defensiveness, cooperation instead of isolationism, generosity instead of retribution, responsibility instead of privilege, and modesty instead of imperial ambition—a robust vision of nationhood nevertheless haunted by the ultimate insignificance of all nations before God."[56] Assuming a global perspective is necessary to escape the trap of cultural stereotypes enough to listen to what one's adversaries are saying.[57] In the case of the Middle East, as Wes Avram suggests, thinking globally of Muslims as our neighbors entails "understanding more about the internal dynamics of Muslim life and thought."[58] Moreover, he argues, it raises the question of whether "we should treat Islam with more respect," of whether Palestinians deserve self-determination, of whether the US should do less harm in the name of free trade, of whether there is some legitimacy in the view from the ground that American militarism is more the creator of terror than terror's remedy, and so on.[59] If, from a global perspective and with a Christian ethic, the US were to "forgo the fear of 'rewarding' terror," might it not reduce the appeal of radical calls to violence by global jihadists?[60]

National self-righteousness, Wendell Barry observes, is a sign of weakness rather than of strength and a mistaken attitude of perpetual warfare, of "war to end war," rather than a true commitment to "peaceableness." Peace is an active, not a passive, state of being, which resists caricaturing adversaries and seeks to understand them better.[61] Even if the US were to declare victory in Iraq and call an end to the war on terror, as James Fallows recommended during the hot summer of 2006 and contrary to President Bush's decision to send a "surge" of more troops to Iraq in the winter of 2007, the dehumanizing mentality of militarism must also change in order to transcend the "standing state of war" that "encourages a state of fear" and a tendency to "overreact" above a commitment to diplomacy, reconciliation, and keeping danger in perspective.[62] Enemy-making as a vehicle of violent salvation is a deadly ritual from which the nation must learn collectively to dissent if it is to make any war, not just the war on terror, honestly accountable to the Christian ethos of peacemaking by reconciliation.

NOTES

1. Norman Solomon, *War Made Easy: How Presidents and Pundits Keep Spinning Us to Death* (Hoboken, New Jersey: John Wiley & Sons, 2005), 1, 8–9, 24–26, 236–37.

2. Solomon, *War Made Easy*, 1.

3. Solomon, *War Made Easy*, 26, 236.

4. Solomon, *War Made Easy*, v, 231.

5. Andrew J. Bacevich, *The New American Militarism: How Americans Are Seduced by War* (New York: Oxford University Press, 2005), 208, 218, 1–2; see also 20.

6. Bacevich, *New American Militarism*, 4–6; see also 13–14, 18–25. Michael S. Sherry, *In the Shadow of War: The United States since the 1930s* (New Haven, Connecticut: Yale University Press, 1995), x; see also 4.

7. Michael Hardt and Antonio Negri, *Multitude: War and Democracy in the Age of Empire* (New York: The Penguin Press, 2004), xiii, 13, 30–32.

8. Richard J. Bernstein, *The Abuse of Evil: The Corruption of Politics and Religion since 9/11* (Cambridge, UK: Polity, 2005), 10–11.

9. Hardt and Negri, *Multitude*, 63–64, xi; see also xviii, 67, 334, 347, 349, 354–56, 311.

10. Hardt and Negri, *Multitude*, 197.

11. Nicholas Jackson O'Shaughnessy, *Politics and Propaganda: Weapons of Mass Seduction* (Ann Arbor: The University of Michigan Press, 2004), 242, 9, 129; see also 35, 134, 243–44.

12. Joanna Bourke, *Fear: A Cultural History* (Emeryville, California: Shoemaker & Hoard, 2005), 8, 287, x, 364; see also 288–90.

13. Bourke, *Fear*, 365, 372–73.

14. Jack G. Shaheen, *Reel Bad Arabs: How Hollywood Vilifies a People* (New York, 2001), 7. Quoted in Bourke, 374.

15. Bourke, *Fear*, 385–86.

16. Corey Robin, *Fear: The History of a Political Idea* (Oxford: Oxford University Press, 2004), 25, 162–63, 16, 251–52; see also 199–25.

17. Joost Abraham Mauritis Meerloo, *Aftermath of Peace: Psychological Essays* (New York: International Universities Press, 1946), 94–95; quoted in Bourke, 383.

18. Bourke, *Fear*, 371, 373.

19. See Bourke, *Fear*, 380, 389.

20. Seymour Martin Lipset, *American Exceptionalism: A Double-Edged Sword* (New York: W. W. Norton & Company, 1996), 19–20; see also 65–67.

21. Michael Hirsh, *At War with Ourselves: Why America Is Squandering Its Chance to Build a Better World* (Oxford: Oxford University Press, 2003), 70–71.

22. Lipset, *American Exceptionalism*, 268, 31, 51.

23. Lipset, *American Exceptionalism*, 268.

24. Lipset, *American Exceptionalism*, 176; see also 20, 65.

25. Joseph Heller, *Catch-22* (New York: Simon & Schuster, 1994), 405–06.

26. Fawaz A. Gerges, *Journey of the Jihadist: Inside Muslim Militancy* (Orlando, Florida: Harcourt, Inc., 2006), 5, 18.

27. Gerges, *Journey*, 30, 91–92, 272.

28. Gerges, *Journey*, 5, 18.

29. Gerges, *Journey*, 10–11; see also 18.

30. Gerges, *Journey*, 12–13, 91; see also 54.

31. Gerges, *Journey*, 144; see also 13–14, 17, 54.

32. Gerges, *Journey*, 56, 169; see also 49, 59, 168.

33. Gerges, *Journey*, 213, 220, 224; see also 202–03, 209–15, 218–19.

34. Gerges, *Journey*, 244, 271; see also 236–39, 251–54, 256, 267–70.

35. Fouad Ajami, *The Foreigner's Gift: The Americans, the Arabs, and the Iraqis in Iraq* (New York: Free Press, 2006), xi–xii, xiv, 52, 55, 67, 107–08; see also 56, 61, 137–138.

36. Ajami, *Foreigner's Gift*, 108, 165, 159; see also 77, 85–86, 141; see also 343.

37. Ajami, *Foreigner's Gift*, 179, 231, 174; see also 173, 176, 189, 247, 256–57, 293.

38. Neall Ferguson, *Colossus: The Rise and Fall of the American Empire* (New York: Penguin Books, 2004), "Preface to the Paperback Edition," vii–viii, xvi, 7.

39. Ferguson, *Colossus*, 29, 301, 293.

40. Fred Anderson and Andrew Cayton, *The Dominion of War: Empire and Liberty in North America, 1500–2000* (New York: Viking, 2005).

41. Jack Nelson-Pallmeyer, *Saving Christianity from Empire* (New York: Continuum, 2005), 7, 11–12, 105.

42. Nelson-Pallmeyer, *Saving Christianity*, 108, 129, 133; see 145–51.

43. Leo Tolstoy, *Wise Thoughts for Every Day: On God, Love, Spirit, and Living a Good Life*, trans. Peter Sekirin (New York: Arcade Publishing, 2005), 230.

44. On the "myth of redemptive violence," see Walter Wink, *The Powers That Be: Theology for a New Millennium* (New York: Doubleday, 1988, 42–62; and John D.

Roth, *Choosing Against War: A Christian View* (Intercourse, Pennsylvania: Good Books, 1989), 54–60.

45. Roth, *Choosing Against War*, 56.

46. Roth, *Choosing Against War*, 117; see 64, 108.

47. Lisa Sowle Cahill, *Love Your Enemies: Discipleship, Pacifism, and Just War Theory* (Minneapolis: Fortress Press, 1994), 31–32, 35, 37–38.

48. The just-war doctrine, which originated as an attempt to conform Christian pacifist beliefs to fighting in Roman imperial wars, has been an instrument throughout Western history for rationalizing and legitimizing warfare. Two prominent figures writing in this tradition are Jean Bethke Elshtain, *Just War Against Terror: The Burden of American Power in a Violent World* (New York: Basic Books, 2003) and Michael Walzer, *Just and Unjust Wars*, 3rd ed. (New York: Basic Books, 2000). See also Jean Bethke Elshtain, ed. *Just War Theory* (New York: New York University Press, 1992), and Michael Walzer, *Arguing about War* (New Haven: Yale University Press, 2004). For a recent discussion of "just war" that argues for its compatibility with the teachings of Christianity, without endorsing militarism, per se, see J. Daryl Charles, *Between Pacifism and Jihad: Just War and Christian Tradition* (Downers Grove, Illinois: InterVarsity Press, 2005). See also Peter S. Temes, *The Just War: An American Reflection on the Morality of War in Our Time* (Chicago: Ivan R. Dee, 2003). For an efficient discussion of the continuum of pacifist thought, see Duane L. Cady, *From Warism to Pacifism: A Moral Continuum* (Philadelphia: Temple University Press, 1989), especially 57–75.

49. Cady, *Warism*, 75.

50. For a critique of the democratic peace theorem, see Robert L. Ivie, *Democracy and America's War on Terror* (Tuscaloosa: University of Alabama Press, 2005), 92–122.

51. For a concise interpretation along these lines of *The National Security Strategy of the United States of America*, see Robert N. Bellah, "The New American Empire: The Likely Consequences of the 'Bush Doctrine,'" in *Anxious about Empire: Theological Essays on the New Global Realities*, ed. Wes Avram (Grand Rapids, Michigan: Brazos Press, 2004), 21–26; and, also in *Anxious about Empire*, see the perceptive critique by Wes Avram, "On Getting Past the Preamble: One Reading of the *Strategy*," 27–41. A copy of *The National Security Strategy of the United States of America* is reprinted in an appendix, 187–215.

52. Bellah, "New American Empire," 26.

53. For a discussion of popular dissent as a multifaceted, decentralized, and discursive act of resistance by the many that cannot be reduced to strictly causal terms, see Roland Bleiker, *Popular Dissent, Human Agency and Global Politics* (Cambridge: Cambridge University Press, 2000).

54. David L. Johnston, "Loving Neighbors in a Globalized World: U.S. Christians, Muslims, and the Mideast," in Avram, *Anxious about Empire*, 63, 71.

55. Michael L. Budde, "Selling America, Restricting the Church," in Avram, *Anxious about Empire*, 81.

56. Stephen B. Chapman, "Imperial Exegesis: When Caesar Interprets Scripture," in Avram, *Anxious about Empire*, 100.

57. Johnston, "Loving Neighbors in a Globalized World," 60–61.

58. Avram, "Introduction," in *Anxious about Empire*, 13.

59. Avram, "On Getting Past the Preamble," 37; see also Johnston, "Loving Neighbors," 63.

60. Avram, "Introduction," 12; see also Johnston, "Loving Neighbors," 63–67, 71.

61. Wendell Berry, "Thoughts in the Presence of Fear," in Avram, *Anxious about Empire*, 45–46.

62. James Fallows, "Declaring Victory," *The Atlantic* 298 (September 2006): 71–73.

Selected Bibliography

Aeschylus. *Persians.* Trans. Janet Lembke and C. J. Herington. New York: Oxford University Press, 1981.

Ajami, Fouad. *The Foreigner's Gift: The Americans, the Arabs, and the Iraqis in Iraq.* New York: Free Press, 2006.

Allen, Danielle S. *Talking to Strangers: Anxieties of Citizenship since Brown v. Board of Education.* Chicago: The University of Chicago Press, 2004.

Alterman, Eric and Mark Green. *The Book on Bush: How George W. (Mis)leads America.* New York: Viking, 2004.

Anderson, Fred and Andrew Cayton. *The Dominion of War: Empire and Liberty in North America, 1500–2000.* New York: Viking, 2005.

Anonymous [Michael Scheuer]. *Imperial Hubris: Why the West is Losing the War on Terror.* Washington, D.C.: Brassey's, Inc., 2004.

Aristotle. *Rhetoric.* Trans. W. Rhys Roberts. New York: The Modern Library, 1954.

Armstrong, Karen. *A Short History of Myth.* New York: Cannongate, 2005.

Auer, J. Jeffery, ed. *Antislavery and Disunion, 1858–1861: Studies in the Rhetoric of Compromise and Conflict.* New York: Harper and Row, 1963.

Aune, James Arnt. "The Argument from Evil in the Rhetoric of Reaction." *Rhetoric and Public Affairs* 6 (2003): 518–22.

Avram, Wes, ed. *Anxious About Empire: Theological Essays on the New Global Realities.* Grand Rapids, Michigan: Brazos Press, 2004.

Bacevich, Andrew J. *American Empire: The Realities and Consequences of U.S. Diplomacy.* Cambridge, Massachusetts: Harvard University Press, 2002.

_____. *The New American Militarism: How Americans Are Seduced by War.* New York: Oxford University Press, 2005.

Bagdikian, Ben H. *The New Media Monopoly.* Rev. ed. Boston: Beacon Press, 2004.

Barber, Benjamin. *Strong Democracy: Participatory Politics for a New Age.* Berkeley: University of California Press, 1984.

Beer, Francis A. *Meanings of War and Peace.* College Station: Texas A&M University, 2001.

Bell, Catherine. *Ritual Perspectives and Dimensions.* New York: Oxford University Press, 1997.

_____. *Ritual Theory, Ritual Practice.* New York: Oxford University Press, 1992.

Benjamin, Medea and Jodie Evans, eds. *Stop the Next War Now: Effective Responses to Violence and Terrorism.* Maui, Hawaii: Inner Ocean Publishing, 2005.

Bernstein, Richard J. *The Abuse of Evil: The Corruption of Politics and Religion since 9/11.* Cambridge, UK: Polity, 2005.

Biesecker, Barbara A. "Remembering World War II: The Rhetoric and Politics of National Commemoration at the Turn of the 21st Century." *Quarterly Journal of Speech* 88 (2002): 393–409.

Blair, Carole, Marsha S. Jeppeson, and Enrico Pucci, Jr. "Public Memorializing in Post-modernity: The Vietnam Veterans Memorial as Prototype." *Quarterly Journal of Speech* 77 (1991): 263–88.

Bleiker, Roland. *Popular Dissent, Human Agency and Global Politics.* Cambridge: Cambridge University Press, 2000.

Boggs, Carl, ed., *Masters of War: Militarism and Blowback in the Era of American Empire.* New York: Routledge, 2003.

Bormann, Ernest G. *The Force of Fantasy: Restoring the American Dream.* Carbondale: Southern Illinois University Press, 1985.

Bostdorff, Denise M. "George W. Bush's Post-September 11 Rhetoric of Covenant Renewal: Upholding the Faith of the Greatest Generation." *Quarterly Journal of Speech* 89 (2003): 293–319.

Boulding, Elise. *Cultures of Peace: The Hidden Side of History.* Syracuse, New York: Syracuse University Press, 2000.

Bourke, Joanna. *Fear: A Cultural History.* Emeryville, California: Shoemaker & Hoard, 2005.

Boyd, Gregory A. *The Myth of a Christian Nation: How the Quest for Political Power is Destroying the Church.* Grand Rapids, Michigan: Zondervan, 2005.

Brown, Seyom. *The Causes and Prevention of War.* New York: St. Martin's Press, 1987.

Brigance, W. Norwood. "The Backwash of War." *Vital Speeches of the Day* 12 (December 1, 1945): 105–08.

Buck-Morss, Susan. *Thinking Past Terror: Islamism and Critical Theory on the Left.* London: Verso, 2003.

Burke, Kenneth. *Attitudes toward History.* 3rd ed. Berkeley: University of California Press, 1984.

_____. *A Grammar of Motives.* 1945; Berkeley: University of California Press, 1969.

_____. *The Philosophy of Literary Form.* 3rd ed. Berkeley: University of California Press, 1973.

_____. *A Rhetoric of Motives.* 1950; Berkeley: University of California Press, 1969.

_____. *The Rhetoric of Religion: Studies in Logology.* 1961; Berkeley: University of California Press, 1970.

Butterworth, Michael L. "'Ritual in the 'Church of Baseball': Suppressing the Discourse of Democracy after 9/11." *Communication and Critical/Cultural Studies* 2 (2005): 107–129.

Cady, Duane L. *From Warism to Pacifism: A Moral Continuum.* Philadelphia: Temple University Press, 1989.

Cahill, Lisa Sowle. *Love Your Enemies: Discipleship, Pacifism, and Just War Theory.* Minneapolis: Fortress Press, 1994.

Campbell, David. *Writing Security: United States Foreign Policy and the Politics of Identity.* Rev. ed. Minneapolis: University of Minnesota Press, 1998.

Campbell, John Angus. "Evil as the Allure of Perfection." *Rhetoric & Public Affairs* 6 (2003): 523–30.

Carter, C. Allen. *Kenneth Burke and the Scapegoat Process.* Norman: University of Oklahoma Press, 1996.

Certeau, Michel de. *The Capture of Speech and Other Political Writings*. Ed. Luce Giard and Trans. Tom Conley. Minneapolis: University of Minnesota Press, 1997.
_____. *The Practice of Everyday Life*, Trans. Steven Rendall. Berkeley: University of California Press, 1984.
_____. "The Weakness of Believing: From the Body to Writing, a Christian Transit," in *The Certeau Reader*. Ed. Graham Ward. Oxford: Blackwell, 2000.
Chang, Nancy. *Silencing Political Dissent*. New York: Seven Stories Press, 2002.
Charles, J. Daryl. *Between Pacifism and Jihad: Just War and Christian Tradition*. Downers Grove, Illinois: InterVarsity Press, 2005.
Chatfield, Charles, ed. *Peace Movements in America*. New York: Schocken Books, 1973.
Chatfield, Charles and Ruzanna Ilukhina, eds. *Peace/Mir: An Anthology of Historic Alternatives to War*. Syracuse, New York: Syracuse University Press, 1994.
Chernus, Ira. *American Nonviolence: The History of an Idea*. Maryknoll, New York: Orbis Books, 2004.
Coffin, Levi. *Reminiscences of Levi Coffin, The Reputed President of the Underground Railroad*. 2nd ed. Cincinnati, Ohio: Robert Clarke and Company, 1880.
Cumings, Bruce, Ervand Abrahamian, and Moshe Ma'oz. *Inventing the Axis of Evil: The Truth about North Korea, Iran, and Syria*. New York: The New Press, 2004.
Curti, Merle. *Peace or War: The American Struggle, 1636–1936*. New York: W. W. Norton and Company, 1936.
Dahl, Robert A. *How Democratic Is the American Constitution?* New Haven: Yale University Press, 2001.
Darsey, James. *The Prophetic Tradition and Radical Rhetoric in America*. New York: New York University Press, 1997.
DeBenedetti, Charles. *The Peace Reform in American History*. Bloomington: Indiana University Press, 1980.
De Luca, Tom and John Buell. *Liars! Cheaters! Evildoers! Demonization and the End of Civil Debate in American Politics*. New York: New York University Press, 2005.
Dolan, Frederick M. and Thomas L. Dumm, eds. *Rhetorical Republic: Governing Representations in American Politics*. Amherst: The University of Massachusetts Press, 1993.
Donk, Vim van de, Brian D. Loader, Paul G. Nixon, and Dieter Rucht, eds. *Cyberprotest: New Media, Citizens and Social Movements*. London: Routledge, 2004.
Douglass, Frederick. *My Bondage and My Freedom*. 1855; New York: Barnes and Noble Classics, 2005.
_____. *Narrative of the Life of Frederick Douglass, An American Slave*. 1845; New York: Barnes and Noble Classics, 2003.
Doty, William G. *Mythography: The Study of Myths and Rituals*, 2nd ed. Tuscaloosa: The University of Alabama Press, 2000.
Dower, John W. *War Without Mercy: Race and Power in the Pacific War*. New York: Pantheon Books, 1986.
Doxtader, Erik. "Reconciliation—A Rhetorical Concept/ion." *Quarterly Journal of Speech* 89 (2003): 267–92.
Eagleton, Terry. *Holy Terror*. Oxford: Oxford University Press, 2005.
Ebadi, Shirin (with Azadeh Moaveni). *Iran Awakening: A Memoir of Revolution and Hope*. New York: Random House, 2006.
Elshtain, Jean Bethke. *Just War Against Terror: The Burden of American Power in a Violent World*. New York: Basic Books, 2003.

_____. Ed. *Just War Theory*. New York: New York University Press, 1992.

Farrell, Thomas B. *Norms of Rhetorical Culture*. New Haven: Yale University Press, 1993.

Ferguson, Neall. *Colossus: The Rise and Fall of the American Empire*. New York: Penguin Books, 2004.

Foote, Shelby. *The Civil War, A Narrative: Fort Sumter to Perryville*. New York: Vintage Books, 1958.

_____. *The Civil War, A Narrative: Fredericksburg to Meridian*. New York: Vintage Books, 1963.

Fussell, Paul. *Wartime: Understanding and Behavior in the Second World War*. New York: Oxford University Press, 1989.

Garrison, Jim. *America as Empire: Global Leader or Rogue Power?* San Francisco, California: Berrett-Koehler Publishers, 2004.

Gerges, Fawaz A. *Journey of the Jihadist: Inside Muslim Militancy*. Orlando, Florida: Harcourt, Inc., 2006.

Gheissari, Ali and Vali Nasr. *Democracy in Iran: History and the Quest for Liberty*. New York: Oxford University Press, 2006.

Girard, René. *The Scapegoat*. Trans. Yvonne Freccero. Baltimore, Maryland: The Johns Hopkins University Press, 1986.

Giroux, Henry A. *Fugitive Cultures: Race, Violence, and Youth*. New York: Routledge, 1996.

Goya, Francisco. *The Disasters of War, 1863*. New York: Dover Publications, 1967.

Grossman, Lawrence K. *The Electronic Republic: Reshaping Democracy in the Information Age*. New York: Viking, 1995.

Gregg, Gary L. *The Presidential Republic: Executive Representation and Deliberative Democracy*. Lanham, Maryland: Rowman and Littlefield Publishers, 1997.

Hackett, Robert A. and Yuezhi Zhao, eds. *Democratizing Global Media: One World, Many Struggles*. Lanham, Maryland: Rowman and Littlefield Publishers, 2005.

Hanson, Russell L. *The Democratic Imagination in America: Conversations with Our Past*. Princeton, New Jersey: Princeton University Press, 1985.

Hardt, Michael and Antonio Negri. *Multitude: War and Democracy in the Age of Empire*. New York: The Penguin Press, 2004.

Hartnett, Stephen John. *Democratic Dissent and the Cultural Fictions of Antebellum America*. Urbana: University of Illinois Press, 2002.

Hartnett, Stephen John and Laura Ann Stengrim. *Globalization and Empire: The U.S. Invasion of Iraq, Free Markets, and the Twilight of Democracy*. Tuscaloosa: University of Alabama Press, 2006.

Hatch, John B. "The Hope of Reconciliation: Continuing the Conversation." *Rhetoric & Public Affairs* 9 (2006): 259–78.

Hatzenbuehler, Ronald L. and Robert L. Ivie. *Congress Declares War: Rhetoric, Leadership, and Partisanship in the Early Republic*. Kent, Ohio: Kent State University Press, 1983.

Hauser, Gerard A. and Amy Grim, eds. *Rhetorical Democracy: Discursive Practices of Civic Engagement*. Mahway, New Jersey: Lawrence Erlbaum Associates, 2004.

Hedges, Chris. *War Is a Force That Gives Us Meaning*. New York: Anchor Books, 2003.

Heller, Joseph. *Catch-22*, 1961; New York: Simon & Schuster, 1996.

Hillman, James. *The Terrible Love of War*. New York: The Penguin Press, 2004.

Hirsh, Michael. *At War with Ourselves: Why America Is Squandering Its Chance to Build a Better World*. Oxford: Oxford University Press, 2003.

Hunt, Scott A. *The Future of Peace: On the Front Lines with the World's Great Peacemakers*. New York: Harper San Francisco, 2004.

Hunter, James Davison. *Culture Wars: The Struggle to Define America*. New York: Basic Books, 1991.

Hyde, Michael J. "The Rhetor as Hero and the Pursuit of Truth: The Case of 9/11." *Rhetoric & Public Affairs* 8 (2005): 1–30.

Ignatieff, Michael. *The Lesser Evil: Political Ethics in an Age of Terror*. Princeton, New Jersey: Princeton University Press, 2004.

Ingebretsen, Edward. *At Stake: Monsters and the Rhetoric of Fear in Public Culture*. Chicago: University of Chicago Press, 2003.

Ivie, Robert L. *Democracy and America's War on Terror*. Tuscaloosa: University of Alabama Press, 2005.

_____. "Fire, Flood, and Red Fever: Motivating Metaphors of Global Emergency in the Truman Doctrine Speech." *Presidential Studies Quarterly* 29 (1999): 570–91.

_____. "Rhetorical Deliberation and Democratic Politics in the Here and Now." *Rhetoric & Public Affairs* 5 (2002): 277–85.

Jensen, Robert. *Writing Dissent: Taking Radical Ideas from the Margins to the Mainstream*. New York: Peter Lang, 2001.

Johnson, Chalmers. *Blowback: The Costs and Consequences of American Empire*. New York: Henry Holt and Co., 2000.

_____. *The Sorrows of Empire: Militarism, Secrecy, and the End of the Republic*. New York: Metropolitan Books, 2004.

Joseph, Paul. *Peace Politics: The United States Between the Old and New World Orders*. Philadelphia: Temple University Press, 1993.

Judis, John B. *The Folly of Empire: What George W. Bush Could Learn from Theodore Roosevelt and Woodrow Wilson*. New York: Scribner, 2004.

Kamalipour, Yahya R. and Nancy Snow, eds. *War, Media, and Propaganda: A Global Perspective*. Lanham, Maryland: Rowman and Littlefield Publishers, 2004.

Kant, Immanuel. "To Perpetual Peace: A Philosophical Sketch." In *Immanuel Kant: Perpetual Peace and Other Essays on Politics, History, and Morals*. Ed. and trans. Ted Humphrey, 107–43. Indianapolis, Indiana: Hackett Publishing Company, 1983.

Keen, Sam. *Faces of the Enemy: Reflections on the Hostile Imagination*. San Francisco, California: Harper and Row, 1986.

Keillor, Garrison. *Homegrown Democrat: A Few Plain Thoughts from the Heart of America*. New York: Viking, 2004.

Kellner, Douglas. *From 9/11 to Terror War: The Dangers of the Bush Legacy*. Lanham, Maryland: Rowman and Littlefield Publishers, 2003.

_____. "The Media and the Crisis of Democracy in the Age of Bush-2." *Communication and Critical/Cultural Studies* 1 (2004): 29–58.

Laclau, Ernesto and Chantal Mouffe. *Hegemony and Socialist Strategy: Towards a Radical Democratic Politics*. 2nd ed. London: Verso, 2001.

Lakoff, George. *Don't Think of an Elephant!* White River Junction, Vermont: Chelsea Green Publishing, 2004.

_____. *Moral Politics: How Liberals and Conservatives Think*. 2nd ed. Chicago: The University of Chicago Press, 2002.

Lampe, Gregory P. *Frederick Douglass: Freedom's Voice, 1818–1845*. East Lansing: Michigan State University Press, 1998.

Lapham, Lewis. *The Theater of War In Which the Republic Becomes an Empire*. London: The New Press, 2002.

Lederach, John Paul. "Cultivating Peace: A Practitioner's View of Deadly Conflict and Negotiation." In *Contemporary Peacemaking: Conflict, Violence and Peace Processes*. Ed. John Darby and Roger MacGinty, 30–37. New York: Palgrave Macmillan, 2003.

_____. *The Moral Imagination: The Art and Soul of Building Peace*. New York: Oxford University Press, 2005.

Leone, Richard C. and Greg Anrig, Jr., eds. *The War on Our Freedoms: Civil Liberties in an Age of Terrorism*. New York: Public Affairs, 2003.

Lifton, Robert J. and Greg Mitchell. *Hiroshima in America: A Half Century of Denial*. New York: Avon Books, 1995.

Lipset, Seymour Martin. *American Exceptionalism: A Double-Edged Sword*. New York: W. W. Norton & Company, 1996.

Lucaites, John Louis. "The Irony of 'Equality' in Black Abolitionist Discourse: The Case of Frederick Douglass's 'What to the Slave is the Fourth of July?'" In *Rhetoric and Political Culture in Nineteenth-Century America*. Ed. Thomas W. Benson, 47–69. East Lansing: Michigan State University Press, 1997.

MacBride, Sean, et al. *Many Voices, One World: Towards a New, More Just, and More Efficient World Information and Communication Order, 1980*. Lanham, Maryland: Rowman and Littlefield Publishers, 2004.

McCaughey, Martha and Micael D. Ayers. *Cyberactivism: Online Activism in Theory and Practice*. New York: Routledge, 2003.

McChesney, Robert W. *The Problem of the Media: U.S. Communication Politics in the 21st Century*. New York: Monthly Review Press, 2004.

McGowan, John. *Democracy's Children: Intellectuals and the Rise of Cultural Politics*. Ithaca, New York: Cornell University Press, 2002.

Madison, James H. *The Indiana Way: A State History*. Bloomington: Indiana University Press, 1986.

Mann, Michael. *Incoherent Empire*. London: Verso, 2003.

Medhurst, Martin J., ed. *Eisenhower's War of Words: Rhetoric and Leadership*. East Lansing: Michigan State University Press, 1994.

Merskin, Debra. "The Construction of Arabs as Enemies: Post-September 11 Discourse of George W. Bush." *Mass Communication and Society* 7 (2004): 157–75.

Merton, Thomas. *New Seeds of Contemplation*. 1961; Boston: Shambhala Publications Inc., 2003.

Mouffe, Chantal, ed. *Deconstruction and Pragmatism*. London: Routledge, 1996.

_____. *The Democratic Paradox*. London: Verso, 2000.

_____. *The Return of the Political*. London: Verso, 1993.

Murphy, John M. "'Our Mission and Our Moment': George W. Bush and September 11th." *Rhetoric & Public Affairs* 6 (2003): 607–32.

Nelson-Pallmeyer, Jack. *Saving Christianity from Empire*. New York: Continuum, 2005.

Newhouse, Jack. *Imperial America: The Bush Assault on the World Order*. New York: Alfred A. Knopf, 2003.

Noon, David Hoogland. "Operation Enduring Analogy: World War II, The War on Terror, and the Uses of Historical Memory." *Rhetoric & Public Affairs* 7 (2004): 339–66.

O'Leary, Cecilia Elizabeth. *To Die For: The Paradox of American Patriotism*. Princeton, New Jersey: Princeton University Press, 1999.

O'Shaughnessy, Nicholas Jackson. *Politics and Propaganda: Weapons of Mass Seduction*. Ann Arbor: The University of Michigan Press, 2004.

Page, Robert. *Dying to Win: The Strategic Logic of Suicide Terrorism*. New York: Random House, 2005.

Peckham, Howard H. *Indiana: A History*. Urbana: University of Illinois Press, 1978.

Pick, Daniel. *War Machine: The Rationalisation of Slaughter in the Modern Age*. New Haven: Yale University Press, 1993.

Pollack, Kenneth M. *The Persian Puzzle: The Conflict between Iran and America*. New York: Random House, 2004.

Prestowitz, Clyde. *Rogue Nation: American Unilateralism and the Failure of Good Intentions*. New York: Basic Books, 2003.

Randall, J. G. and David Donald. *The Civil War and Reconstruction*. 2nd ed. Boston: D. C. Heath and Company, 1961.

Rappaport, Roy A. *Ecology, Meaning and Religion*. Richmond, California: North Atlantic Books, 1979.

Reed, T. V. *The Art of Protest: Culture and Activism from the Civil Rights Movement to the Streets of Seattle*. Minneapolis: University of Minnesota Press, 2005.

Ritter, Kurt W. and James R. Andrews. *The American Ideology: Reflections on the Revolution in American Rhetoric*. Falls Church, Virginia: Speech Communication Association, 1978.

Roach, Colleen, ed. *Communication and Culture in War and Peace*. Newbury Park, California: Sage Publications, 1993.

Robin, Corey. *Fear: The History of a Political Idea*. Oxford: Oxford University Press, 2004.

Roth, John D. *Choosing Against War: A Christian View*. Intercourse, Pennsylvania: Good Books, 1989.

Rothenbuhler, Eric W. *Ritual Communication: From Everyday Conversation to Mediated Ceremony*. Thousand Oaks, California: Sage, 1998.

Rueckert, William H. *Encounters with Kenneth Burke*. Urbana: University of Illinois Press, 1994.

Schell, Jonathan. *The Unconquerable World: Power, Nonviolence, and the Will of the People*. New York: Henry Holt and Company, 2003.

Scherer, Randy. *The Antiwar Movement*. Farmington Hills, Michigan: Greenhaven Press, 2004.

Schirch, Lisa. *Ritual and Symbol in Peacebuilding*. Bloomfield, Connecticut: Kumarian Press, 2005.

Scranton, Phil, ed. *Beyond September 11: An Anthology of Dissent*. London: Pluto Press, 2002.

Segal, Robert A. *Myth: A Very Short Introduction*. Oxford: Oxford University Press, 2004.

_____. *Theorizing About Myth*. Amherst: University of Massachusetts Press, 1999.

Sherry, Michael S. *In the Shadow of War: The United States Since the 1930s*. New Haven: Yale University Press, 1995.

Shiffrin, Steven. *Dissent, Injustice, and the Meanings of America*. Princeton, New Jersey: Princeton University Press, 1999.

_____. *The First Amendment, Democracy, and Romance*. Cambridge, Massachusetts: Harvard University Press, 1990.

Simon, Jeffrey D. *The Terrorist Trap: America's Experience with Terrorism*. 2nd ed. Bloomington: Indiana University Press, 2001.

Skinner, Quentin. *Reason and Rhetoric in the Philosophy of Hobbes*. New York: Cambridge University Press, 1996.

Solomon, Norman. *War Made Easy: How Presidents and Pundits Keep Spinning Us to Death*. Hoboken, New Jersey: John Wiley & Sons, 2005.

Soyinka, Wole. *Climate of Fear: The Quest for Dignity in a Dehumanized World*. New York: Random House, 2005.

Spielvogel, Christian. "'You Know Where I Stand': Moral Framing of the War on Terrorism and the Iraq War in the 2004 Presidential Campaign." *Rhetoric & Public Affairs* 8 (2005): 549–69.

Stone, Geoffrey R. *Perilous Times: Free Speech in Wartime, From the Sedition Act of 1798 to the War on Terrorism*. New York: W. W. Norton & Company, 2004.

Sunstein, Cass. *Why Societies Need Dissent*. Cambridge, Massachusetts: Harvard University Press, 2003.

Temes, Peter S. *The Just War: An American Reflection on the Morality of War in Our Time*. Chicago: Ivan R. Dee, 2003.

Tolstoy, Leo. *The Kingdom of God is Within You*. Trans. Constance Garnett. 1893; New York: Barnes and Noble Books, 2005.

_____. *Wise Thoughts for Every Day: On God, Love, Spirit, and Living a Good Life*. Trans. Peter Sekirin, New York: Arcade Publishing, 2005.

Torfing, Jacob. *New Theories of Discourse: Laclau, Mouffe and Žižek*. Oxford: Blackwell, 1999.

Vidal, Gore. *Imperial America: Reflections on the United States of America*. New York: Nation Books, 2004.

Vonnegut, Kurt. *Slaughterhouse-Five or the Children's Crusade: A Duty-Dance with Death*. 1969; New York: Dell, 1999.

Wallis, Jim. *God's Politics: Why the Right Gets It Wrong and the Left Doesn't Get It*. New York: Harper San Francisco, 2005.

Walzer, Michael. *Arguing about War*. New Haven: Yale University Press, 2004.

_____. *Interpretation and Social Criticism*. Cambridge, Massachusetts: Harvard University Press, 1987.

_____. *Just and Unjust Wars*. 3rd ed. New York: Basic Books, 2000.

Wills, Garry. *Lincoln at Gettysburg: The Words that Remade America*. New York: Simon & Schuster, 1992.

Wink, Walter. *The Powers That Be: Theology for a New Millennium*. New York: Doubleday, 1988.

Winkler, Carol K. *In the Name of Terrorism: Presidents on Political Violence in the Post-World War II Era*. Albany: State University of New York Press, 2006.

Wolin, Sheldon S. *Politics and Vision: Continuity and Innovation in Western Political Thought*. Expanded Edition. Princeton, New Jersey: Princeton University Press, 2004.

Zarefsky, David. *Lincoln, Douglas, and Slavery: In the Crucible of Public Debate*. Chicago: University of Chicago Press, 1990.

Zinn, Howard. *Artists in Times of War*. New York: Seven Stories Press, 2003.

Index

About the Author

Robert L. Ivie is professor of rhetoric and public culture in the Department of Communication and Culture at Indiana University. He also serves as a member of the faculties of the American Studies, Cultural Studies, and Myth Studies programs at Indiana University. His teaching and writing focus on the critique of US war culture and the study of democratic dissent and peacebuilding communication. He has served as editor of several journals of communication scholarship, including *Communication and Critical/Cultural Studies* and the *Quarterly Journal of Speech*. His previous books include *Democracy and America's War on Terror; Cold War Rhetoric: Strategy, Metaphor, and Ideology* with Martin Medhurst, Philip Wander, and Robert Scott; and *Congress Declares War: Rhetoric, Leadership, and Partisanship in the Early Republic* with Ronald Hatzenbuehler.

Also from Kumarian Press . . .

Peacebuilding and Conflict Resolution:

Nation-Building Unraveled? Aid, Peace and Justice in Afghanistan
Edited by Antonio Donini, Norah Niland and Karin Wermester

War's Offensive on Women: The Humanitarian Challenge in Bosnia, Kosovo and Afghanistan
Julie Mertus

Ritual and Symbol in Peacebuilding
Lisa Schirch

Reducing Poverty, Building Peace
Coralie Bryant and Christina Kappaz

New and Forthcoming:

Born of War: Protecting Children of Sexual Violence Survivors in Conflict Zones
Edited by R. Charli Carpenter

Complex Political Victims
Erica Bouris

Zones of Peace
Edited by Landon Hancock and Christopher Mitchell

Visit Kumarian Press at **www.kpbooks.com** or call
toll-free 800.289.2664 for a complete catalog.

green
press
INITIATIVE

Kumarian Press, Inc. is committed to preserving ancient forests
and natural resources. We elected to print *Dissent From War* on
30% post consumer recycled paper, processed chlorine free. As a
result, for this printing, we have saved:

   6 Trees (40' tall and 6-8" diameter)
  2,361 Gallons of Waste Water
   950 Kilowatt Hours of Electricity
   260 Pounds of Solid Waste
   511 Pounds of Greenhouse Gases

Kumarian Press, Inc. made this paper choice because our printer,
Thomson-Shore, Inc., is a member of Green Press Initiative, a
nonprofit program dedicated to supporting authors, publishers,
and suppliers in their efforts to reduce their use of fiber obtained
from endangered forests.

For more information, visit www.greenpressinitiative.org

*Kumarian Press, located in Bloomfield, Connecticut, is
a forward-looking, scholarly press that promotes active
international engagement and an awareness of global
connectedness.*